The Open Economy and the Environment

To
Ingi, Aiki and Rhea
and
Sreeni and Tanya
for understanding, support and love

The Open Economy and the Environment

Development, Trade and Resources in Asia

Ian Coxhead

University of Wisconsin-Madison

Sisira Jayasuriya

University of Melbourne

Edward Elgar
Cheltenham, UK • Northampton, MA, USA

Published by
Edward Elgar Publishing Limited
The Lypiatts
15 Lansdown Road
Cheltenham
Glos GL50 2JA
UK

Edward Elgar Publishing, Inc.
William Pratt House
9 Dewey Court
Northampton
Massachusetts 01060
USA

Reprinted 2016

A catalogue record for this book is available from the British Library

Library of Congress Cataloguing in Publication Data
Coxhead, Ian, 1957–
    The open economy and the environment : development, trade and resources in Asia / by Ian Coxhead, Sisira Jayasuriya.
        p. cm.
    Includes bibliographical references and index.
    1. Economic development–Environmental aspects–Asia. 2. Asia–Foreign economic relations. I. Jayasuriya, S. K. II. Title.

HC415.E5.C69 2003
338.95'07–dc21   2002032052

ISBN 978 1 84064 434 0

Printed and bound in Great Britain by
Marston Book Services Limited, Didcot

Contents

Figures

Tables

Acknowledgements

This book is the culmination of a decade-long accumulation of insights from many sources, and we owe thanks to many who contributed ideas, support and timely criticism.

We have drawn on collaborative work undertaken with Jay Bandara, Tony Chisholm, Agnes Rola, Jerry Shively, Peter Warr and many other colleagues in Australia, the Philippines, Sri Lanka, Thailand and the USA. Sections of the text were read and commented upon by Prema-chandra Athukorala, Raghbendra Jha and Peter Warr, as well as by seminar participants at the Australian National University. We are also grateful to colleagues and students at the University of Wisconsin-Madison, University of Melbourne and La Trobe University (Melbourne) for discussions and comments, and to Gladys Buenavista, Marie Fenton, Padma Lal, Ken Menz and Liz Telford, who facilitated this effort in diverse ways. A month in an idyllic cottage overlooking the Mississippi greatly enhanced the pleasure of working on this manuscript, for which we are grateful to Carolyn and David Scott of McGregor Manor, McGregor, Iowa. We also thank Toni Rose Domingo and Tanya Silva (Manila) and Colin Thomson and Arriya Mungsunti (Canberra) for research assistance, Tanya Jayasuriya for helping check references and grammar, and Sreeni Jayasuriya for drawing the graphs and figures. Any remaining errors are entirely our responsibility.

We are grateful to Beth Thomson for editorial assistance, and to the editorial staff at Elgar – especially Nep Athwal and Alison Stone – for their dedication with seeing the project through to completion.

Funding for the research and writing has come from the Australian Centre for International Agricultural Research, the United States Agency for International Development through the SANREM CRSP, and the Graduate School of the University of Wisconsin-Madison.

1. Development–environment interactions

1.1 INTRODUCTION

The World Commission on Environment and Development (WCED) was formed in 1983 by the United Nations to examine 'the critical environment and development issues and to formulate realistic proposals for dealing with them'. The inquiry – and its 1987 report, *Our Common Future* – did much to raise international public awareness of the environmental consequences of economic growth. It was the catalyst for a surge in research on growth and the environment, and its 'call for action' motivated major initiatives in national and international policy, including the 1992 Earth Summit held in Rio de Janeiro.

The WCED characterized the world of the late twentieth century as experiencing dramatic rates of population increase, economic growth and industrialization accompanied by 'a sharp increase in economic interdependence among nations'. It noted that 'the industries most heavily reliant on environmental resources and most heavily polluting are growing most rapidly in the developing world, where there is both more urgency for growth and less capacity to minimize damaging side effects' (WCED 1987: 5). It highlighted what it described as the 'dissolving of boundaries' between compartments within which areas of human activity – energy, agriculture and trade – and areas of concern – environmental, economic, and social – were traditionally kept separate. And it emphasized the particular environmental challenges posed, for developing countries, by their dependence on the international economic relationships of trade, aid and investment:

> Agriculture, forestry, energy production, and mining generate at least half the gross national product of many developing countries and account for even larger shares of livelihoods and employment. Exports of natural resources remain a large factor in their economies . . . Most of these countries face enormous economic pressure, both international and domestic, to overexploit their environmental resource base. (WCED 1987: 6)

The years since *Our Common Future* have seen tremendous advances in understanding of the interdependence of economic and environmental phenomena. However, developing economies still face daunting challenges in managing their environmental resources while achieving growth and poverty alleviation. While the WCED's 'boundaries' may have dissolved in practice, it is all too clear that they live on in the policies of developing country governments, donor agencies and environmental activists.[1] In particular, economic development policies and environmental policies all too often remain functionally separate, in spite of rhetorical commitments to vague notions of 'sustainable development'. In the era of globalization – trade liberalization, international flows of capital and labour, and the growing influence of international institutions such as the World Trade Organization – to maintain this separation is to undermine both long-term economic growth and environmental quality.

In this book we examine aspects of the interdependence between economy and environment in natural resource-dependent developing economies. We ask what their dependence on trade means for their use of environmental and natural resource assets. Our goal is to contribute to economic and environmental policy formation in developing economies. This is achieved by developing theoretical models which reflect key developing- economy characteristics. We use these models to understand how globalization and domestic policies affect resource allocation, payments to capital and labour, income and welfare, and incentives to deplete critical natural resource endowments such as forests and agricultural land. We present empirical applications using economy-wide models of several representative developing economies.

On this very broad canvas, we specifically focus on the conditions of developing countries in the humid tropical zones of South and Southeast Asia. These economies, most of which are relatively 'open' by developing country standards, have experienced very rapid economic growth in recent decades (Figure 1.1), and have undergone major changes in the structure of production (Figures 1.2 and 1.3). The experience of this group of countries foreshadows the likely path of many more developing economies in Africa and Latin America, as they too confront the challenges of integration within the global economy.

1.2   THE SCOPE OF THE PROBLEM

Natural Resource Depletion and Degradation

Sustained rates of economic growth, such as those shown in Figure 1.1, are associated with changes in the structure of production and consumption, and these inevitably entail changes in the use of natural and environmental resources. Since the 1990s much effort has been devoted to documenting,

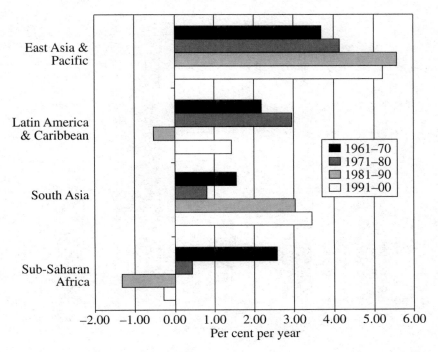

Source: World Bank, *World Development Indicators, 2001*

Figure 1.1 GDP growth rates, developing regions, 1965–2000

measuring and valuing environmental trends in developing countries. Although subject to problems of definition and measurement errors, the data nevertheless indicate clearly that growth rates of energy demand, industrial emissions, and the depletion and degradation of many forms of environmental and natural resources exceed growth rates of gross domestic product (GDP) in most developing countries. Even in the countries with the brightest record of success it seems that rapid growth has come at considerable environmental cost. This places a question mark over the long-term sustainability of conventional economic development strategies.

Industrialization and urbanization are key features of economic growth, and industrial emissions and urban pollution are typically the most readily visible forms of environmental damage. In the fastest-growing economies, increases in the intensity of industrial emissions have exceeded industrial output growth (Figure 1.4). During the years of peak industrial expansion in developing Asian economies, the difference between growth rates of

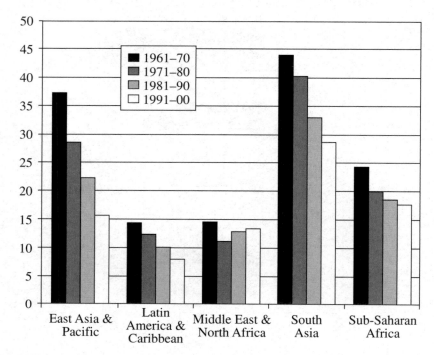

Source: World Bank, *World Development Indicators, 2001*

Figure 1.2   GDP share of agriculture, developing regions, 1965–2000

GDP and emissions increased almost exponentially (Brandon and Ramankutty 1992).

The strikingly high growth rates of emissions are indicators of the importance of industrial expansion to overall growth in most developing economies. Industrial expansion has also been highly concentrated in and around urban areas; urban pollution thus consists both of industrial effluents (emissions into air and water, as well as solid waste), and of post-consumer effluents (vehicle emissions, sewage and solid waste). In most countries, recent urban population growth rates far exceed national averages (Table 1.1). As a consequence both of the spatial concentration of industry and of the growing size and density of urban populations, air and water pollution problems are most acute in cities. Table 1.2, showing mid-1990s levels of three major air pollutants, exemplifies the nature of urban pollution problems in major cities of developing Asian economies.

Problems of air and water pollution and of solid waste disposal are per-

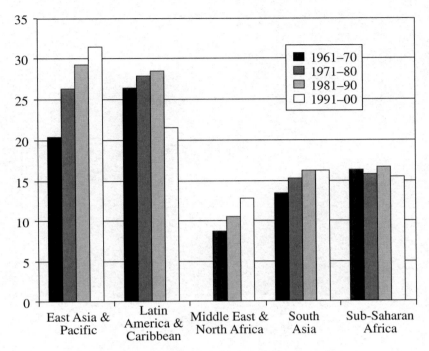

Source: World Bank, *World Development Indicators, 2001*

Figure 1.3 GDP share of manufacturing, developing regions, 1965–2000

vasive and severe in nearly all population centres of the developing world. However, these are typically not the most significant forms of environmental damage. In most developing countries, much larger numbers of people are affected by natural resource depletion, specifically deforestation, soil degradation and loss of watershed functions. Estimated values of these damages typically exceed estimates of the aggregate costs of urban and industrial pollution.[2]

Deforestation[3] and the conversion of land to agricultural production are major phenomenons in most developing countries. According to data from the Food and Agriculture Organization of the United Nations (FAO), between 1980 and 1995 the world lost some 180 million hectares of forest, of which the bulk was in the developing world. During 1990–2000, global forest cover declined at an annual rate of about 0.2 per cent (Table 1.3). Among developing countries, the average rate was 0.3 per cent; however, this average masks substantial variation. East and South Asian developing

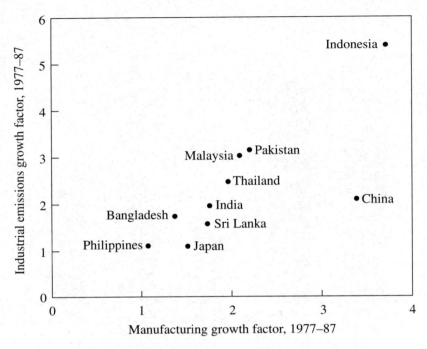

Source: World Bank (1992) and *World Development Report, various years*

Figure 1.4   *Growth of industrial output and industrial emissions intensity,
Asian economies*

countries lost forest cover at average rates of 0.2 per cent and 0.1 per cent
respectively, although country-specific rates varied much more widely
(Table 1.4).

Compared with the 1980s, the official data suggest some deceleration in
global deforestation rates during the 1990s, which the FAO attributes to a
lower rate of deforestation in the Amazon and reforestation in parts of Asia.
However, the total extent of global deforestation is not known with accu-
racy, and estimates vary considerably. This is due partially to problems with
measurement, but also because of differences in definitions. In particular,
the FAO data for deforestation in 1990–2000 report a *net* change in which
the loss of natural forest is in many countries compensated (and in some
cases completely offset) by an increase in plantation forestry. Calculations
of changes in *natural* forest cover – that is, net of area established to plantations – indicate much higher rates of natural forest loss. In tropical Asia
this rate is estimated at –1.9 per cent per year, more than double the tropical

Table 1.1 Population and urbanization in Asia and developing regions

Country	Total population ('000)		Urban population (%)		Annual growth rate			
					1980–2000		1990–2000	
	1980	2000	1980	2000	Total	Urban	Total	Urban
China	1,004,168	1,282,437	20.0	32.5	1.23	3.71	1.00	2.59
South Asia	886,004	1,331,684	22.4	28.6	2.06	3.31	1.92	3.21
Bangladesh	85,438	137,439	14.4	24.5	2.41	5.15	2.25	4.74
Bhutan	1,318	2,085	3.9	7.1	2.32	5.51	2.09	5.53
India	688,856	1,008,937	23.1	28.4	1.93	3.00	1.79	2.89
Nepal	14,559	23,043	6.5	11.9	2.32	5.42	2.42	5.36
Pakistan	81,230	141,256	28.1	37.0	2.81	4.24	2.55	4.10
Sri Lanka	14,603	18,924	21.6	23.6	1.30	1.75	1.06	2.10
Southeast Asia	354,683	517,038	23.8	36.6	1.90	4.12	1.71	3.86
Cambodia	6,613	13,104	12.4	15.9	3.48	4.79	3.13	5.57
Indonesia	150,341	212,092	22.2	40.9	1.74	4.90	1.52	4.52
Lao PDR	3,205	5,279	13.4	23.5	2.53	5.45	2.48	5.20
Malaysia	13,763	22,218	42.0	57.4	2.42	4.03	2.22	3.68
Myanmar	33,706	47,749	24.0	27.7	1.76	2.49	1.66	2.85
Philippines	48,035	75,653	37.5	58.6	2.30	4.61	2.17	4.06
Thailand	46,015	62,806	17.0	21.6	1.57	2.78	1.38	2.84
Vietnam	53,005	78,137	19.2	19.7	1.96	2.09	1.69	1.69
All developing countries	3,258,633	4,742,170	2.1	3.7	1.89	4.83	1.72	1.89
Africa	466,871	793,626	27.4	37.9	2.69	4.36	2.51	4.22
East Southeast Asia	414,854	593,662	28.8	41.6	1.81	3.70	1.62	3.36
Latin America & Caribbean	361,332	518,809	64.9	75.3	1.83	2.59	1.65	2.26
North Africa & Near East	215,453	361,509	43.7	58.2	2.62	4.10	2.37	3.44
South Asia	886,162	1,331,975	22.4	28.6	2.06	3.31	1.92	3.21

Source: World Bank, *World Development Indicators 2001*, Washington, DC: World Bank

Table 1.2   Air pollution indicators in major Asian cities, 1995

Country	City	Population ('000)	Total suspended particulates (TSP) (μ/m^3)	Sulphur dioxide (SOX) (μ/m^3)	Nitrogen dioxide (NOX) (μ/m^3)
China	Beijing	11,299	377	90	122
	Chongqing	—	320	340	70
	Guangzhu	—	295	57	36
	Shanghai	13,584	246	53	73
	Shenyang	—	374	99	73
	Tianjin	9,415	306	82	50
	Wuhan	—	211	40	43
India	Bombay	15,138	240	—	—
	Calcutta	11,923	375	49	34
	Delhi	9,948	415	24	41
	Hyderabad	—	152	12	12
	Mumbai	—	240	33	39
Indonesia	Jakarta	8,621	271	—	—
Japan	Osaka	10,609	43	19	63
	Tokyo	26,959	49	18	68
	Yokohama	3,178	—	100	13
Korea, Rep.	Pusan	4,082	94	60	51
	Seol	11,609	84	44	60
	Taegu	2,432	72	81	62
Malaysia	K. Lumpur	1,238	85	24	—
Philippines	Manila	9,286	200	33	—
Singapore	Singapore	2,848	—	20	30
Thailand	Bangkok	6,547	223	11	23

Notes:
WHO guidelines for acceptable levels of pollutants are: TSP<90 μ/m^3; SOX<50 μ/m^3; NOX<50 μ/m^3.
— = data not available.

Source: As Table 1.1.

country average (Table 1.5). The data on plantation forest area are less reliable than those on aggregate forest cover, so these calculations must be treated with caution.[4] Nevertheless, the picture that emerges for developing Asia is one of high rates of removal of natural forest cover, and its partial replacement in some countries by industrial tree crops.

Freshwater resource depletion is an equally serious problem. About three-quarters of the world's available fresh water is used for agriculture

Table 1.3   *Average annual deforestation rates, developing countries,*
              1990–2000

	Area ('000 km²) 2000	% of total area 2000	Annual deforestation rate, 1990–2000	
			km²	%
World	38,609	29.7	90,399	0.2
Low income	8,840	26.8	71,466	0.8
Middle income	21,791	32.9	26,930	0.1
LDC (low + middle income)	30,630	30.9	98,396	0.3
High income	7,979	26.1	−7,997	−0.3
East Asia & Pacific	4,341	27.2	7,048	0.2
Europe & Central Asia	9,464	39.7	−8,143	−0.1
Latin America & Caribbean	9,440	47.1	45,878	0.5
Middle East & North Africa	168	1.5	−239	−0.1
South Asia	782	16.3	889	0.1
Sub-Saharan Africa	6,436	27.3	52,693	−0.1

Source: FAO data reported in World Bank, *World Development Indicators 2001*,
Washington, DC: World Bank

(more in most developing countries; see Table 1.6). Agricultural growth and the spread of irrigation both contribute to rapid increases in withdrawals. Globally, continued population growth will ensure that the agriculture-driven increases in water demand will continue for the foreseeable future.[5] While agricultural growth will continue to dominate total water demand because of its high initial share, water demand by industry will grow much more quickly. Therefore, the magnitude of the likely increase in freshwater demand both for production and for direct consumption is clearly very large; the situation is all the more serious when it is noted that most of this added demand will occur in developing countries, where water resources are already under stress.

At an aggregate level, water stress or shortages[6] do not appear to pose serious problems for most Asian countries. However, there is a pronounced declining trend in per capita water availability (Alexandratos 1995); moreover, the aggregate data indicate average supply per inhabitant per year and should thus be seen as providing extreme lower-bound measures of water stress or shortage. True availability is contingent on time, place, quality and cost, and all Asian developing countries have regions and/or times of year in which water for specific uses is very scarce.

The trend in water demand also places the trends in soil resources in

Table 1.4 *Forest cover and deforestation, Asian developing countries*

Country	Forest area ('000 km²)			Forest area (% total area)	Average annual deforestation (km²)		Average change (% per year)	
	1980ᵃ	1990ᵇ	2000ᵇ	2000ᶜ	1980–90	1990–2000	1980–90ᵃ	1990–2000ᵇ
China	126,398	133,756	145,417	163,480	17.50	−735.80	−1806.30	0.60	1.20
South Asia								
Bangladesh	1,258	1,054	1,169	1,334	10.20	20.40	−16.50	−1.80	1.30
Bhutan	2,975	2,803	3,016	3,016	n.s.	17.20	n.s.	−0.60	n.s.
India	58,259	64,969	63,732	64,113	21.60	−671.00	−38.10	1.10	0.10
Nepal	5,580	5,096	4,683	3,900	27.30	48.40	78.30	−0.90	−1.80
Pakistan	2,749	2,023	2,755	2,361	3.20	72.60	39.40	−3.10	−1.50
Sri Lanka	2,094	1,897	2,288	1,940	30.00	19.70	34.80	−1.00	−1.60
Southeast Asia								
Cambodia	13,484	10,649	9,896	9,335	52.90	283.50	56.10	−2.40	−0.60
Indonesia	124,476	115,213	118,110	104,986	58.00	926.30	1312.40	−0.80	−1.20
Lao PDR	14,470	13,177	13,088	12,561	54.40	129.30	52.70	−0.90	−0.40
Malaysia	21,564	17,472	21,661	19,292	58.70	409.20	236.90	−2.10	−1.20
Myanmar	32,901	29,088	39,588	34,419	52.30	381.30	516.90	−1.20	−1.40
Philippines	11,194	8,078	6,676	5,789	19.40	311.60	88.70	−3.30	−1.40
Thailand	18,123	13,277	15,886	14,762	28.90	484.60	112.40	−3.10	−0.70
Vietnam	10,663	9,793	9,303	9,819	30.20	87.00	−51.60	−0.90	0.50

Note: n.s. = not significant, indicates a very small value.

Sources:
ᵃ WRI (2000)
ᵇ FAO (2000) (measurement method different from source ᵃ above; see Mathews 2001
ᶜ World Bank, *World Development Indicators 2001*, Washington, DC: World Bank.

Table 1.5   WRI estimates of changes in natural forest and plantation cover

Region	1990 ('000 ha)		2000 ('000 ha)		Average annual change of natural forest	
	Nat. forest	Plantation	Nat. forest	Plantation	'000 ha	%
Africa	697,882	4,415	641,828	8,038	−5,589	−0.8
Oceania	36,201	149	34,869	263	−133	−0.4
S. America	903,199	7,279	863,739	10,455	−3,946	−0.4
Asia	495,340	56,117	431,422	115,873	−6,392	−1.3
Tropical	289,820	22,486	233,448	54,624	−5,637	−1.9
Temperate	5,520	33,631	197,974	61,249	−755	−0.4

Source: Matthews (2001)

perspective. Worldwide, about 25 billion tons of productive topsoil is being lost from fields every year – with most of the losses again occurring in developing countries. Of course, some soil is merely transported to other agricultural locations, but a large fraction is deposited in streams, lakes and coastal waters where it is not only lost to agriculture but becomes a source of pollution. Accurate data on soil quality and propensity for erosion or, more broadly, land degradation are difficult to obtain except at a very fine scale, but indicative data from the FAO suggest that agricultural land degradation in developing countries is a serious and pervasive problem (Table 1.7). Soils in most humid tropical countries, while typically relatively deep and rich in nutrients, are also vulnerable to erosion under certain combinations of slope and soil type. The soils of Southeast Asian countries are particularly susceptible (FAO 2000).[7] Nor is the land degradation problem restricted to sloping or upland areas. Lowland and irrigated land, on which the bulk of agricultural production takes place, face degradation from two main sources: on-site fertility decline attributable to overcropping, and the deleterious effects of upstream erosion. Studies based on times-series data suggest that, in spite of varietal improvements and 'best practices' management, rice yields from intensively farmed irrigated land in Asia are no longer rising, and may even be falling (Cassman and Pingali 1995)[8]. Other studies have established apparent causal linkages between the removal of forest cover in upper-watershed areas and the decline of irrigation systems and crop yields in lowlands downstream (Pingali 1997).

Trends in the functioning of watersheds reflect the joint effects of deforestation, water withdrawals and land degradation. Forest conversion

Table 1.6 Freshwater withdrawals and availability, Asian developing countries

Country	Year	Annual withdrawals (million m³)	Withdrawals by sector (% share)			Annual per capita withdrawal (m³), 1996	Renewable water availability ('000 m³ per inhab.), 1996
			Agriculture	Domestic	Industry		
China	1993	525,489	77	5	18	424	2.2
South Asia							
Bangladesh	1990	14,636	86	12	2	122	10
Bhutan	1987	20	54	36	10	11	52
India	1990	500,000	82	5	3	529	2
Nepal	1994	28,953	99	1	0	1,315	10
Pakistan	1991	155,600	97	2	2	1,277	3
Sri Lanka	1990	9,770	96	2	2	540	3
Southeast Asia							
Cambodia	1987	520	94	5	1	51	46
Indonesia	1990	74,346	93	6	1	371	14
Lao PDR	1987	990	82	8	10	196	66
Malaysia	1995	12,733	77	10	13	619	28
Myanmar	1987	3,960	90	7	3	86	23
Philippines	1995	55,422	88	8	4	780	7
Thailand	1990	33,132	91	5	4	564	7
Vietnam	1990	54,330	86	4	10	723	12

Source: FAO: AQUASTAT database

Table 1.7   Human-induced land degradation rates, Asian developing countries

Country	Total land area (1000 km²)	Severity of human-induced land degradation (% of total area)				
		None	Light	Moderate	Severe	V. severe
China	9,550	28	8	30	25	10
South Asia	4,716	33	3	15	38	13
Bangladesh	144	5	0	68	27	0
Bhutan	47	2	67	24	0	7
India	3,517	37	1	4	43	16
Nepal	141	23	29	30	27	0
Pakistan	802	25	2	49	22	2
Sri Lanka	65	0	17	29	22	32
Southeast Asia	4,485	1	17	33	32	13
Cambodia	181	13	2	36	27	22
Indonesia	1,916	1	36	26	32	6
Lao PDR	237	0	16	83	0	1
Malaysia	333	0	0	17	83	0
Myanmar	677	1	0	63	35	1
Philippines	299	3	0	76	3	3
Thailand	513	0	2	20	28	50
Vietnam	329	0	0	21	29	49
World	134,907	34	18	20	20	6
Asia and Pacific	28,989	28	12	32	22	7
North Africa & Near East	12,379	30	18	17	30	5
South & Central America	20,498	23	27	23	22	5
Sub-Saharan Africa	23,754	33	24	16	15	12

Source: FAO (2000)

for agriculture contributes to diminished watershed function through loss of water storage capacity in trees and soils. It also contributes a large fraction of atmospheric carbon releases from natural resource-rich developing countries (Table 1.8). Time-series data show that the removal of forest cover and the conversion of sloping uplands to agriculture are processes strongly associated with diminished stream flow as well as increased amplitude of seasonal fluctuations (see, for example, Deutsch *et al.* 2001). Soil and other pollutants displaced by tillage contribute to total suspended sediment (TSS) loadings and chemical pollution. Soil loss from fields, particularly those cultivated to short-term crops, is a key component of declining agricultural productivity in uplands, requiring compensatory expenditure on fertilizer, and/or the construction of physical structures such as bunds and hedgerows, to maintain soil quality. Finally, TSS delivery raises sedimentation in dams and canals, accelerates wear on turbines and other

Table 1.8   CO$_2$ emissions by sectoral source, selected developing countries, 1991 ('000 tonnes)

Country	From industrial processes	From land use change	% from land use change
Bangladesh	15,444	6,800	30
Indonesia	170,466	330,000	70
Malaysia	61,196	110,000	65
Philippines	44,587	110,000	71
Thailand	100,896	91,000	47
Vietnam	20,573	33,000	62

Source: Estimates reported in World Resources Institute, *World Resources 1994–95*, Washington, D.C.: WRI

hydroelectric power generation equipment, and contributes to eutrophication of lakes, higher health costs for downstream human and animal populations, and turbidity and related damage in coastal and estuarine areas.[9]

Valuation of Losses

Estimating the economic costs of deforestation and land degradation is difficult, for several reasons. First, the costs of deforestation take many forms, of which land degradation through soil erosion is just one.[10] Second, natural resources provide a variety of benefits, only some of which are traded in markets. Forest outputs that have market values, at least in principle, include timber as well as non-timber products such as fruit, nuts, forage, animal fodder and amenities. But information on the many non-marketed benefits of forests, including carbon sequestration, local climatic influences, biodiversity and aesthetic existence values, is not widely available, is highly location-specific, and is subject to considerable measurement error. Hence it is difficult to generalize about the costs of deforestation or the degradation of soil and water resources without reference to specific circumstances.

Biodiversity, genetic reserves and global climate influences obviously have international value in addition to their local or national significance, and their loss is intrinsically difficult to cost. They are typically not marketed, and the development of such markets is inhibited by complications arising from property rights issues at every level. Furthermore, there are no simple relationships between these losses and changes in deforestation, or other forms of natural resource depletion. While it is a widely held view that this is a source of potentially very large losses, there is no consensus on the issue[11] and, not surprisingly, there are no generally accepted global estimates.[12] Similarly, the valuation of the impact of deforestation on local climate change as well as its contributions to global warming is fraught with difficulty.[13] In all these cases, however, there is a growing acceptance that the aggregate costs are potentially so large that remedial steps are urgently needed.

On the methodological front, valuing environmental and natural resource changes has required innovations to compensate for the fact that depreciation in the conventional System of National Accounts (SNA) – which measures a country's GDP, for example – includes only man-made capital, not natural or environmental 'capital'. As a result, SNA-based measures of net national product and net domestic investment have been argued to overstate true measures of the extent to which environmental or natural resource assets are depleted in the production of income. Since the early 1990s it has become increasingly common to augment the SNA with 'satellite accounts' which include valuations of environmental and natural resource changes. In developing countries, these exercises typically result in estimates of 'adjusted' net domestic product (ANDP) that are substantially lower than measured net domestic product (NDP). A pioneering study for Indonesia calculated that, allowing for changes in forests, soils and hydrocarbon stocks, ANDP growth in the 1970s and 1980s was closer to 4 per cent per annum than the 7 per cent indicated by the SNA, and that the 'adjusted' ratio of net investment to GDP was about one-third less than the estimated 26 per cent average for the same period (WRI 1989). A study of Costa Rica found that natural resource depreciation, primarily deforestation and soil erosion, caused a 25–30 per cent reduction in potential economic growth during the period 1970–89 (TSC/WRI 1991). A detailed review of evidence for Malaysia indicated that financial returns from deforestation (the conversion of land to agriculture) were profitable, but that 'important non-timber values were sacrificed when forests were converted' (Vincent, Rozali and Associates 1997: 142). This study found many non-timber values (including erosion control and protection of water systems) to be rather small, but the cost of reduced biodiversity and loss of amenity values to be quite large. Other accounting studies in developing countries indicate proportionally much larger losses: 1–4 per cent of GDP in Indonesia and the Philippines (World Bank 1989, 1990); 0.75–1.0 per cent in Sri Lanka (Somaratne 1998); 9 per cent in Burkina Faso; and as high as 17 per cent in Nigeria (Barbier and Bishop 1995). These estimates, although imprecise, are nevertheless too large to ignore. In poor and wealthy countries alike, governments are absorbing the magnitude of estimates like these and are beginning to grapple with the question of an appropriate policy response.

1.3   POVERTY, GROWTH AND THE 'ENVIRONMENTAL RESOURCE BASE'[14]

The majority of the population in the developing world live in rural areas, and depend directly or indirectly on the exploitation of natural resources, especially soil, water, forests, animals and fisheries, for their livelihoods. Households in poor, resource-dependent economies face a dilemma. On one hand, they need to exploit depletable resources or degradable environmental assets – often the only directly productive capital to which they have access – but, on the other hand, they also need to conserve the productive capacity of these assets in order to sustain livelihoods over the long term. Poverty, the lack of alternative opportunities, competition for resources, and uncorrected environmental externalities can drive these agents to act in ways that not only undermine the longer-term health of the natural resource base but also generate social costs at the local, national or even global scale.

Poverty is both a cause and an effect of natural resource depletion and environmental degradation. Initial poverty is a function of poor endowments of 'capital' (in its broadest sense, including environmental assets), and its alleviation depends on increases in the capital stock. Low rates of investment in reproducible forms of capital result in low growth rates of per capita income growth and non-agricultural employment creation. In combination with rapid population increase, slow growth implies declining labour productivity throughout an economy. Low accumulation rates of physical capital are typically also accompanied by underinvestment in education, or human capital. Together, both kinds of investment shortfall contribute to a low-level poverty trap into which many developing countries, most notably (although by no means exclusively) in Sub-Saharan Africa, have fallen.

Populations caught in this trap increasingly turn to the natural resource base as a source of productive factors with which unskilled labour may be combined to produce either subsistence goods or cash income. The search naturally concentrates on factors over which property rights are not well established, as they can be obtained or used at low cost. Open-access land at the agricultural frontier – at the forest margin, in much of the humid tropics – provides the easiest (and sometimes the only) opportunity for such purposes. Thus poverty, combined with relatively unfettered access to forests and cultivable land near the frontier of settlement, drives migration and land conversion in 'upland' (frontier) areas. By this means, once-stable forest, bush-fallow or pastoral systems are progressively converted to more intensive uses, and in particular to the production of food. Land colonization for food production thus entails two types of environmental damage:

removal of the original forest cover, and the use of the land for food crops which, unlike perennials, are typically associated with high rates of nutrient uptake and high erosion potential (David 1988; Repetto 1989). The open-access nature of resources at the frontier, together with the fact that part of the environmental damage caused by their use is exported as an externality, virtually guarantees that they will be exploited beyond a socially optimal rate.

Therefore, in economies that have experienced little economic progress, persistent poverty and the geographic expansion of impoverished agriculture are both symptomatic of a broader development failure. This failure is related to low rates of reproducible capital formation coupled with the availability of open-access resources and uncorrected environmental externalities.

If persistent poverty poses a direct threat to environmental resources, what is the effect of growth? As individuals get richer, they value more highly natural capital and environmental services, both as economically productive factors and as sources of aesthetic satisfaction. At the community level, higher valuations are associated with increased propensity to conserve these resources, for example through the adoption of laws or conventions that constrain environmentally damaging activities. In addition to this preference shift, it is an intrinsic feature of sustained economic growth that the importance of agriculture declines, whether measured by its proportional contribution to national income, the ratio of farm employment to total employment, or food expenditures as a share of total consumption. Economic growth thus diminishes – relatively if not absolutely – the degree to which incomes depend directly on environmental services and natural capital.

Observation of these preference shifts and structural changes has led economists to posit a non-linear relationship between per capita income and the quality of the environment, in which economic growth initially causes rapid environmental degradation but later leads to rising expenditures on abatement and conservation. This inductive reasoning has been summarized as the 'environmental Kuznets' curve' or EKC (Grossman and Krueger 1993), an inverse-U curve relating measures of environmental quality to per capita income (Figure 1.5). The EKC reflects the observation that as per capita incomes increase, the intensity of emissions per unit of income first rises, then later declines.

There is some empirical justification for expecting that, over time, the population of a poor country undergoing growth will face ever-higher incentives to conserve natural and environmental resources (we return to this point in Chapter 2). However, poverty and the actions of subsistence-oriented poor farmers in fragile ecological regions are by no means the only

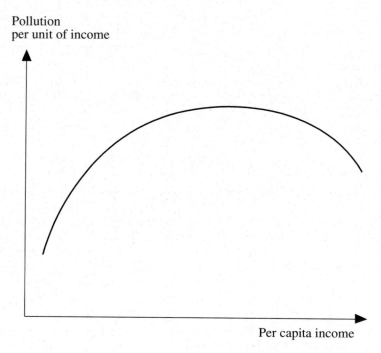

Figure 1.5   The environmental Kuznets' curve (EKC)

(or even the main) factors driving environmental and natural resource degradation. Wealthier or more commercially oriented farmers, logging companies, large plantation and agribusiness ventures, and governments themselves also contribute to unsustainable and undesirable levels of natural resource exploitation. Thus in many developing countries, the decisions that drive forest and land use changes in remote areas may be determined as much in the board rooms of the capital city as by poor farmers in upland areas. Yet neither a shift in the balance of decision making from the poor to the rich, nor the fact that many countries have moved well beyond low-income status, have demonstrably reduced many types of resource depletion and environmental degradation in developing countries; frequently the outcome is the opposite. Simply alleviating poverty is not a sufficient condition for a switch to more sustainable patterns in the use of natural resources and environmental services.

Although resource use incentives in economies that have escaped the low-level poverty trap differ from those in countries that have not, outcomes – including the colonization of land at agriculture's extensive margin

– are often quite similar. Rapid growth, opening to trade or the expansion of trade, and associated changes in the structure of production and consumption help to create new markets or markets for new goods. As a result, farmers, migrants and others along the agricultural frontier are encouraged to move to new commercial crops, intensive livestock operations or commercial forestry. In contrast with market development, institutions governing property rights are relatively slow to evolve. Consequently, occupying open-access land continues to be an option, at least for a time, in rapidly commercializing economies. As an example, the expansion of temperate-climate vegetable production in cool highland areas of the tropics (a phenomenon associated with deforestation and the rapid depletion of soil resources, as well as with the introduction of pesticide and fertilizer residues in upland water systems) is the result not of a poverty-driven 'push' to the frontier but of the 'pull' of attractive economic and climatic conditions for the production of highly profitable crops (Hefner 1990; Lewis 1992; Coxhead *et al.* 2002).

When the growth of incentives for resource-depleting activities outpaces the development of formal property rights institutions, privately optimal land use decisions are unlikely to match social preferences. Divergences arise not only because of open access to resources such as forests, but also when the 'free' disposal of pollutants is possible. Producers at the frontier seldom have to bear the full social costs of their actions, since in addition to many direct and indirect subsidies for natural resource exploitation, there is virtually no accounting for off-site damages associated with upland agricultural development.

The existence of environmental externalities indicates market failure, but does not mean that incentives faced by environmental and natural resource decision makers are not influenced by what happens in both local and distant markets. All but the most remote areas of developing countries are linked to broader economies through migration, commodity flows, media outlets and other means. It follows that the prices of land, labour and goods produced or consumed in frontier areas are rarely determined strictly (or at all) in local markets. To understand resource use incentives at the frontier, it is essential first to understand the nature of market and institutional ties linking such regions to the national, and in some cases international, economy.

1.4 TRADE–ENVIRONMENT LINKAGES AND THE ROLE OF POLICY

The 'globalization' of the developing economies, a process that began in earnest around 1980, is strongly associated with higher rates of economic growth. Globalization, at least in its narrowly economic interpretation, means greater openness to trade and factor flows across national borders. This occurs as the result mainly of policy changes adopted by developing country governments. These changes include reductions in the level and dispersion of import tariffs and other protective instruments, and the relaxation of restrictions on cross-border capital flows.[15] Globalization increases the relative importance of both trade and international capital in an economy, with the consequence that international markets have correspondingly greater influence over domestic prices and resource allocation decisions. Since the 1960s, the ratio of exports to GDP in developing economies has doubled, from an average of 12 per cent to 25 per cent, with the largest rise occurring in the years after 1980 (World Bank 2001b). Dependence on foreign capital has also increased, in some countries at an even faster rate (World Bank 2001b).[16]

While the past two decades have seen a fairly general trend towards more open policies, both the initial restrictiveness of trade policy regimes and the degree of liberalization have varied greatly (Martin 2001). The correlation between trade and growth is overwhelmingly positive, even if economic theorists are still divided on the direction of causality. Developing countries that have relaxed restrictions on international trade and capital flows have incontrovertibly grown much faster than countries that have not (Levine and Renelt 1992; Dollar 1992; World Bank 2001b).

On the basis of this correlation, it is tempting to posit an additional relationship between international trade and environmental damage.[17] A strong form of this conjecture, the 'pollution haven hypothesis', asserts a causal relationship by arguing that poor economies, which place a lower value on pollution damages and environmental amenities than wealthy economies precisely because they are poorer, will 'optimally' adopt policies that attract dirty production processes and resource-intensive industries (for an examination of this hypothesis, see Copeland and Taylor 1994).[18] A counterpart argument, that poor countries adopting policies aimed at environmental protection would thereby reduce their international competitiveness, follows from the pollution haven idea.

There can be no doubt that trade (and thus, by extension, the liberalization of trade policies) does indeed contribute to increases in some forms of environmental damage. This occurs both directly, because trade alters incentives to engage in certain kinds of economic activity, and indirectly, because trade may increase factor accumulation and thus the economic growth rate (Levine and Renelt 1992).[19] However, this type of 'globalization' also *discourages* some activities, including some that may be polluting or natural resource depleting. Consider the huge shifts in the composition of developing country exports brought about by increases in physical and human capital stocks, along with more liberal trade policies. The average share of agriculture in total exports of all developing countries fell from 50 per cent in 1965 to 10 per cent in 1998; the share of manufactures rose over the same period from 15 per cent to more than 80 per cent (Martin 2001). Production in both sectors causes environmental damage, but their specific contributions obviously differ. It cannot be asserted *a priori* that trade or trade policy reform is unambiguously bad for the environment. Finer definitions of 'environment' as well as more careful studies of trade are needed.

The inherent complexity of the trade–environment relationship requires in-depth investigation before policies that aim to balance growth and environmental protection can be designed.[20] In order to have value to researchers and to policy makers, empirical investigation of the environmental effects of trade, trade policies and other aspects of development strategy must be firmly grounded in rigorous theory, establishing what has been called 'the grammar of policy arguments' (Frank Hahn, cited in Sandmo 2000). In this book we strive to present both the 'grammar' – the theoretical foundations – as well as empirical evidence for trade–environment relationships in relatively resource-dependent market economies, as are found in many parts of developing Asia.

1.5   METHODOLOGICAL APPROACHES

Private decisions about the use and management of natural resources generate income for those controlling the resources, but may also confer externalities on others – locally, nationally and, in some cases (such as actions that affect the production of greenhouse gases), globally. Factors that influence natural resource decisions originate at all three levels: in global markets and international agreements on trade or environment; in the broader national economy; and in local factor and product markets and institutional conditions. Resource-use decisions made locally and driven (typically) by strictly private concerns are usually intimately linked to broader sets of economic, institutional and policy conditions. Abundant evidence indicates that this holds true for all but the most remote areas, in spite of weaknesses in physical infrastructure and communications systems and in the institutions that underpin market-based transactions.

The ties that link international trade and other 'macroeconomic' phenomena to private decisions on the use of environmental and natural resources raise a methodological challenge. Households and firms at the 'margin' of cultivation have location-specific resource endowments, and their decisions are constrained in the ways described above. Ideally, the analysis of resource-use decision making should strive faithfully to reflect these special conditions of specific areas *vis-à-vis* other regions or sectors of the economy. At the same time, there is clearly an overriding need to take account of the economy-wide (or general equilibrium) relationships that serve as conduits for the transmission of price and policy signals from the national and international economy to households and firms. The need for a detailed micro-theoretic basis for analysis cannot easily be met simultaneously for all levels of the economy: individual households and firms as well as larger regional, sectoral or national units.

The household or firm-level microeconomics underpinning local use of environmental assets in the developing world has been, and remains, the subject of a great deal of analytical attention (see, especially, Barbier 1998; Shively 1998; and earlier literature as surveyed in Anderson and Thampapillai 1990). Economists and other social scientists have examined the motives and consequences of resource-use decisions made by farmers, loggers, fishers and others whose actions have a direct impact on a stock of natural resource wealth. Environmental concerns and questions about economic welfare are only two among many motivations for such studies, and the range of findings is equally broad.

Another rapidly growing body of literature is concerned with 'global' environment and trade issues and the mechanisms that link them. Research addresses the international ramifications of greenhouse gas production, biodiversity reduction, species extinction and other environmental concerns that transcend national boundaries, as well as the protocols and treaties by which the international community attempts to regulate the actions of individual states. Most studies in this field take aggregate national economies or even groups of nations as their observational units.

Without seeking to diminish the importance of research at the scale either of the firm or of supra-national units, the primary domain of the research presented in this book is the national economy and its component sectors and geographical regions. This is a scale that we feel has been neglected, in a relative sense, in discussions of environment–economy relationships.[21] Global markets and local institutions notwithstanding, national-level drivers are arguably the dominant influences over resource-use decisions, such as those affecting the depletion of forest or fisheries stocks or the use of agricultural land. Among these drivers, national markets (themselves the filters for global markets), economic policies, and the legislative and regulatory settings controlled by national governments and their agencies are clearly of primary importance. It is also the case that outcomes depend critically on how spatial/geographical characteristics within national economies interact with these drivers.

The effects of changes in national markets and policies are transmitted throughout the domestic economy through induced adjustments in markets for goods and services, labour and other factors of production. Some such adjustments are region-specific, for instance when primary factors such as forests or agricultural land are geographically immobile. When autonomous or policy-driven changes occur in markets that are large in relation to national aggregates – exports and imports, household income and expenditure, government budgets and so on – they have the potential to induce responses in all regions and sectors. Thus (as we shall argue in later chapters) industrialization policies, for example, may affect the use of agricultural and forest resources through their effects on the national markets for labour and/or for foreign exchange. A practical implication is that economic policies may sometimes cause 'surprises' in the use of environmental and natural resources; in effect, every economic policy that causes a change in the use or valuation of natural resources is a *de facto* environmental policy. Conversely, region-specific price and other market changes as well as environmental externalities can also have effects at the level of the national economy. Our goal is to identify and examine these mechanisms in the setting of a small, open developing economy. This requires a general equilibrium approach.

1.6   GOALS AND CONTRIBUTION OF THIS BOOK

In this book we explore the foregoing issues within an explicitly open economy framework, one that takes account of the role of international trade and of the major structural and institutional features of national economies. Our starting point is the need to analyse resource and environmental issues within a framework that recognizes the dependence of resource-use decisions in a given location or sector on conditions in other sectors and regions, and in global markets.

Our broad objective is to contribute to the development of economy-wide policies that promote better natural resource-use patterns and lower pollution levels, recognizing the importance of other major policy goals such as rapid economic growth, poverty alleviation and macroeconomic stability. Hence, our analytical work is directed at understanding the impact of policies not only on environmental variables, but on all major variables related to economic development. Economic growth, poverty alleviation and distributional equity (including spatial equity) cannot be ignored in practical policy formulation and implementation. In all economies, but most certainly in developing economies where the fostering of social and national cohesion is a prerequisite for political stability and sustained economic growth, optimal policies must establish a politically sustainable balance among economic, social and environmental goals. Often these involve trade-offs; at times they may be mutually reinforcing, and win–win situations may emerge. But experience indicates clearly that environmental policy formulated in isolation cannot succeed: to achieve multiple policy goals, it is necessary to deploy multiple policy instruments. Our research leads us to stress repeatedly the need both to examine the broader consequences of policies, and to employ mutually consistent policy packages to achieve economic development goals. This is a thread that runs throughout our analytical approach and policy discussions.

Ours is by necessity a 'macro' view of development, growth and environmental degradation. Much of our theoretical analysis takes place at a level of abstraction at which it is unavoidable that complex firm-level and household-level decision making, as well as sector-specific dynamics, are treated in a highly simplified fashion. Our approach focuses on underlying economic forces, and as such has the obvious disadvantage that the socio-cultural, political and other factors that shape power relationships in societies are not well captured. Nevertheless, this approach has the advantage that it helps identify rigorously the broadest economic opportunities facing all economic agents involved in the production or consumption of environmental services. We recognize that the final distributional outcomes reflect (and at times strongly modify) pre-existing patterns of economic and political power, and that what we are grappling with is an evolving, dynamic process unfolding over time. Our chosen approach is in no way intended to underplay the value or importance of more 'micro' approaches, or the valuable insights that emerge from studies that approach these issues from a different disciplinary viewpoint. On the contrary, our analysis should be treated as complementary to them.

With this broad framework in mind, we emphasize in particular that the solutions to natural resource degradation issues in the developing world, are not only to be found in strategies that directly address incentives or behaviour at the land frontier or in the uplands where the predominant environmental and natural resource problems are physically located. Such 'direct' policies and strategies are necessary, but cannot be complete if spatial or economy-wide phenomena are influential in local markets and institutions. An effective environmental strategy requires in addition economy-wide analysis and complementary policies in all sectors. This also helps to delineate the scope of our work: we aim to highlight and analyse the impact of developments – anywhere in the economy, or flowing from international or policy initiatives – that can have potentially large effects on resource and environmental degradation through economy-wide market linkages.

The specific contributions of this book cover analytical model development, empirical analysis and policy. The first contribution is to specify a 'core' analytical general equilibrium framework for the analysis of land use and environment issues in developing countries, one that encompasses the most important country-specific characteristics as special cases. We extend the two-sector framework of an economy producing a 'clean good' and a 'dirty good' used by Antweiler *et al.* (2001) to decompose the levels of industrial emissions arising from changes in the relative size of industries due to trade liberalization ('composition effect'), economic growth ('scale effect') and techniques of production ('technique effect'). The extended model also captures the *welfare effects* of broader changes associated with globalization: changes in technology, trade and investment policy, relative factor endowments and consumer preferences. Then we move on to specify the core model, which has three important features: it has a spatial dimension, with the economy comprising two distinct 'regions'; it explicitly recognizes that property rights in remote regions at the land frontier are often absent or weakly enforced; and, in contrast with many 'small economy' models, it permits domestic food prices to vary in response to changes in domestic food supply and demand. We explore the properties of this model and its variants in order to understand and illustrate the influence of specific structural features and parameters on environmental outcomes, with particular emphasis on the 'composition effect' in the agricultural and forest sectors. Our analytical results demonstrate the dangers of sweeping generalizations about the environmental outcomes of broad phenomena such as globalization, and of specific policy changes such as trade or investment liberalization, and also help to identify the critical factors that determine the direction of change.

The second contribution is to provide illustrative empirical examples, drawn primarily from case studies of the Philippines, Thailand and Sri Lanka. In each case we apply our framework to the analysis of resource degradation issues in the context of economic growth and policy changes. We also explore our theoretical arguments through richer, more fully specified applied general equilibrium (AGE) models. The AGE models both simplify (in some respects) and expand (in other respects) our core model to focus on specific issues. Insights from the theoretical model help to illuminate the economic forces at work in the more complex models.

The third contribution is to analyse the impact of some policy shifts and related developments whose impacts on deforestation and land degradation have been contentious, in Asia and elsewhere in the developing world. These include key elements of the policy reform package associated with globalization, national food security policies, and the effects of public investments and interventions in agriculture. One issue we analyse is the shift from import-substituting industrialization (ISI) to export-oriented industrialization (EOI), a major ongoing policy reform in most developing countries. Many environmentalists hold this policy shift responsible for increased environmental stress. However, our analysis suggests that freer trade and greater integration with the global economy may in some circumstances have a pro-environment effect, at least in terms of deforestation and land degradation.[22] We also shed light on the political economy factors causing trade liberalization in agriculture to be far slower than in manufacturing industries in many developing economies, demonstrating the significantly different distributional effects of manufacturing and agricultural trade liberalization.

A second issue that we analyse is the impact of public investments aimed at agricultural productivity growth. This has both historical and current policy interest, with particular relevance for national and international allocation of agricultural research funds. It has been argued that the Green Revolution in the lowlands of tropical Asia channelled research resources away from upland agricultural improvements, further impoverishing already -poor upland farmers, and aggravating environmental degradation. On the basis of our analysis we arrive at an almost diametrically opposed conclusion: the Green Revolution in the lowlands, by contributing to a dramatic reduction in national food prices, sharply reduced incentives for deforestation and land degradation in the uplands. Indeed, the analysis suggests that the extent of land degradation in many parts of Asia would be far worse than at present if not for the indirect, but salutary, impact of the Green Revolution.

1.7   OVERVIEW OF CHAPTERS

In Chapter 2 we review analytical approaches to the study of growth, trade and the environment, including some prominent economy-wide theoretical models. Most such models have been developed for a generic 'wealthy country' case. Hence, our discussion considers the amendments or extensions needed to analyse issues relevant to developing economies. In the light of our review, we extend the two-sector ('clean goods–dirty goods') model to a growth context influenced by policy reforms, to analyse not only physical levels of pollution but also their welfare effects, highlighting some of the potential income–environment tradeoffs.

In Chapter 3, we examine growth and environmental change in developing Asian economies, with special emphasis on the use of natural resources – specifically forests and land – in the course of economic growth.

In Chapter 4, we further tighten the analytical focus, developing a model of deforestation and the degradation (or conservation) of upland agricultural land in a stylized model of an open developing economy that recognizes important institutional and geographical features. The analysis considers the effects of factor endowment growth, terms of trade and domestic price changes, technical progress and economic policies, and includes a number of extensions, including the case of inter-regional environmental externalities.

In Chapters 5–8 we present analytical case studies of three developing Asian economies, the Philippines, Sri Lanka, and Thailand, including simulation results obtained using AGE models of these economies. Chapter 5 provides an overview of the AGE modelling approach, and Chapters 6–8 report the results of experiments in which we ask what effects policy shocks, such as trade policy reform, might have on factor and product prices, the sectoral structure of production, the allocation of resources among sectors, and the implied environmental costs or benefits.

The study concludes in Chapter 9 with some overarching methodological and policy lessons and an agenda for further research.

NOTES

1. Policy makers' perceptions of the nature of environmental and economic policy interactions typically depend on their functions. In a recent survey conducted in Asian developing countries, only 40 per cent of environmental policy makers agreed that market-based environmental policy instruments could have fiscal benefits, as opposed to 83 per cent of economic policy makers (reported in ADB 1997). Similarly, exploration of the linkages between environment and development is also relatively recent in the economics profession. It has been noted (Dasgupta and Maler 1995) that the first two volumes of North-Holland's authoritative *Handbook of Development Economics* (Chenery and Srinivasan 1988) contained no non-trivial reference to environment in their 1770 pages. Likewise, the counterpart volumes of the *Handbook of Natural Resource and Energy Economics* (Kneese and Sweeney 1985) contained no references to economic development or developing countries. These lacunae persisted in standard texts in both fields until well into the 1990s.
2. For a synthesis of evidence on this point, see Jha and Whalley (1999).
3. By deforestation we mean the conversion of forested land to some other use, usually some form of agriculture, that involves full or partial removal of existing tree cover. Deforestation is sometimes defined more narrowly to refer to any kind of significant change to the existing flora in 'virgin' forests (or, at least, forests that have not been disturbed by human activities for a relatively long period of time). We prefer a definition incorporating the implication that forest land, once cleared, is seldom abandoned but more typically converted to another economic use.
4. See FAO (2001b, para. 25, p. 5), and Matthews (2001: 9 fn 5).
5. World population is projected to increase by a third between 1995 and 2020, with an average of about 73 million people being added every year. Almost all of this increase (97.5 per cent) is expected to be in the developing countries, with over a billion more being added in Asia (UN 1999). The increase in water demand to meet the expected growth in food and other agricultural production will clearly be very large.
6. *Water stress* is defined as 600–1,000 inhabitants per million cubic metres of water availability per year. *Severe shortage* is defined as more than 1,000 inhabitants per million cubic metres (Dasgupta and Mäler 1995).

7. The FAO definition of erosion hazard uses information about slopes and soil types. Land classified as having a severe erosion hazard is defined by 'predominantly very steep slopes (>30%) interspersed with areas of steep slope (8–30%) in conjunction with an abrupt textural contrast in the soil profile' (FAO 2000: 12). The study places the Philippines, Malaysia, Cambodia, Laos, Myanmar, Vietnam, and Thailand among the top-ranking 15 countries by this measure.

8. According to the International Rice Research Institute: 'The irrigated area devoted to rice is declining and yields are stagnating. Evidence is mounting that flooded rice soils are not resilient to intensification pressures, and that the productivity made possible by current technology may not be sustainable.' (*Rice Facts*, http://www.irri.org/Facts.htm, accessed 15 March 2002.)

9. We know of no data source covering the complete range of variables listed here. However, a recent Philippines study using time-series data based on subwatershed measures of stream flow and water quality provides graphic evidence of the relationship between agricultural expansion, population density increase and loss of watershed function (Deutsch *et al.* 2001). Related studies for other countries are mentioned in Chapters 6–8.

10. For a useful overview, see World Bank, *World Development Report 1992*.

11. For example, Hyde *et al.* (1996), who refer to evidence that 'these values are not large in any aggregate sense' (p. 235).

12. See Metrik and Weitzman (1998) and references cited therein for a review of some of the measurement issues. Simpson *et al.* (1996) estimated the value of biodiversity in a number of tropical locations for private pharmaceutical research, and concluded it to be quite small. But the methodology and approach, as well as the assumptions, are not universally accepted. See also Garrod and Willis (1999: ch. 9) for a survey of literature and methodological issues.

13. For a brief review, see Chomitz and Kumari (1998).

14. This term was coined by Dasgupta and Mäler (1995).

15. For a minority of developing countries, however, the primary constraint to greater openness comes from geographic or geopolitical forces, such as landlockedness or the effects of war.

16. For trade and investment shares and trends in Asian developing countries, see Tables 3.2 and 3.3.

17. This view persists in populist critiques of globalization, and was widely articulated in worldwide protests against globalization during 1999–2001.

18. A variant of the pollution haven hypothesis received wide publicity in the early 1990s following the rather casual suggestion in 1992 by World Bank economist Larry Summers that since rich country consumers valued the environment more highly than their counterparts in poor countries, both groups could gain by the exporting of rich country waste to poor countries.

19. A third channel links taxes and the environment through the public sector budget and the efficiency of the tax system. Tax reforms which reduce the efficiency of the tax system (that is, which increase the overall level of distortions in the system) may require increases in other taxes to maintain revenues for the provision of public goods; the resulting alterations in relative prices may have environmental effects through changes in intermediate or final demands for goods. See Goulder (1995).

20. Much the same may be said of other policy-driven changes in development strategy besides trade policy, and in the conditions of resource allocation and production in the developing economies.

21. This is not to deny that there is a substantial body of literature which addresses issues at the level of the national economy; but, as we discuss later in some detail, the policy relevance of much of this literature suffers significantly from limitations imposed by the nature of the underlying analytical models and their premises.

22. In this, we confirm, in a formal analytical framework, conjectures made by economists such as Panayotou (1993).

2. Analytical approaches to the trade–environment relationship

2.1 INTRODUCTION

An economy making the move from autarky to international trade faces new prices based on valuations established in the world market rather than in the domestic economy alone. Engaging in trade thus results, in the typical case, in alterations in the allocation of resources to production and in the pattern of consumption. Trade also raises real income, and this may in turn induce further changes in the structure of production or consumption. Other changes, in policies, endowments, or technologies, may likewise contribute to the transformation of economic structure.

Nearly all production processes – and many forms of consumption – generate environmental damage, whether this takes the form of emissions into air and water or the depletion or degradation of natural resources. Thus virtually any pattern of economic change generated by a shift from autarky to trade – or, more generally, by some change in a country's exposure to international markets – may be expected to have environmental consequences. By their nature, many forms of environmental damage cannot easily be measured, let alone assigned monetary valuations; conventional measures of national income certainly do a very poor job of capturing them (WRI 1989). Therefore, a complete assessment of the welfare effects of trade must strive to include the consequences of its impacts on the environment along with its effects on utility derived from the consumption of marketed goods and services. In practice, however, measurement and valuation problems make it difficult to aggregate the utility derived from consumption of marketed goods together with that from non-marketed environmental services.

Most theoretical and empirical studies of trade and the environment measure its impact either on environmental variables, or on welfare as measured by the consumption of marketed goods and services. In this chapter we first review studies of the former kind (section 2.2). We then consider some formal models of the welfare effects of trade and trade policies and their interactions with environmental policy (section 2.3). Finally, we evaluate both branches of the literature in light of the specific focus of this study, the impacts of trade and associated policies on natural resource use and economic welfare in developing countries (section 2.4). Whereas the fundamental insights of the analytical literature provide direction, the modelling and analysis of economy–environment interactions in developing economies necessitate some substantial amendments to, and augmentation of, these largely generic models. Our initial discussion of these necessary extensions lays the groundwork for more detailed analyses in Chapters 3 and 4. A brief conclusion in section 2.5 brings the chapter to a close.

2.2   THE ENVIRONMENTAL EFFECTS OF GROWTH AND TRADE

Much of the literature on trade and the environment is motivated by, and deals mainly with, air and water pollution ('emissions') as by-products of production and consumption. Since the path-breaking study of the environmental implications of trade liberalization between Mexico and the US by Grossman and Kreuger (1993), it is now conventional to decompose the effects of trade on these emissions into three components known as *scale*, *composition* and *technique* effects.

The *scale effect* refers to the association between the size of an economy and the provision of environmental services, where 'size' is defined as the value of GDP at base-period world prices (Antweiler *et al.* 2001). If engaging in trade (or, in an open economy, reducing impediments to trade) allows an economy to produce more output, this will lead, *ceteris paribus*, to more pollution and more demands on the natural resource base. At first glance, it may appear that the scale effect – arising as it does from economic growth and increasing per capita incomes – will be the dominant determinant of long-run environmental outcomes. But such outcomes are also strongly influenced by initial conditions, and the aggregate rate of economic growth does not provide a complete predictor of environmental trends.

The *composition effect* refers to the environmental impact of changes in the structure of production and consumption. This effect has several sources, of which the main one associated with trade is the influence of international markets on relative prices. For given factor endowments and production technology in an economy with well-functioning markets, resources are allocated to production in different sectors so as to equalize their value marginal product in all uses. This marginal condition determines the structure of domestic production. A change in relative prices, by altering value marginal products, induces a reallocation of resources among sectors. If sectors differ in their propensity to pollute or to use natural resources, it follows that emissions and/or natural resource depletion will also change.[1]

Clearly, the environmental impacts of the composition effect can be either harmful or benign. The two-factor, two-good Heckscher–Ohlin model of trade predicts that opening up to trade leads an economy to expand its production of the good making intensive use of the relatively abundant factor, and to reduce production of the other good. It follows that when a country with comparative advantage in a 'dirty' good (that is, one that produces a relatively large quantity of pollution as a by-product) opens to trade, the quantity of pollution it produces will increase. Conversely, the same move by a country with comparative advantage in a 'clean' industry will see a reduction in pollution.[2] This principle applies in weaker form to higher-dimensional models (Ethier 1982), although unambiguous predictions of the composition effect of trade are harder to obtain.

Structural changes driving the composition effect can also be caused by growth in factor endowments. These operate through the same basic mechanism as for relative price changes; unequal rates of endowment growth alter the marginal productivity of resources used in production, and this triggers intersectoral resource movements until equilibrium is restored. When relative prices remain constant, endowment growth causes the composition of output to change in ways predicted (for a two-factor, two-sector economy) by the Rybczinski theorem. This theorem implies that when an economy experiences unequal rates of factor endowment growth, its production structure will alter, given constant commodity prices, such that the output of the good that is relatively intensive in the factor whose endowment is growing more rapidly will increase relative to that of the other good. In a typical example, if the net capital investment rate exceeds the rate of growth of the labour force, the GDP share of the labour-intensive sector will decline over time, as capital growth raises the output of the capital-intensive sector.

The predictive power of the Rybczinski theorem diminishes in higher-dimensional models, and the theorem has little to say about other real-world complexities, including the emergence and disappearance of industries in the course of economic growth. A variety of multi-sectoral trade-theoretic models have been presented showing systematically how, as factor endowments change, some industries that were initially below break-even point may come into existence while others may disappear (Leamer 1987; Deardorff 1999). Of course, similar structural change effects may also occur due to changes in technology and/or consumer demand.

The composition effect may also be generated by structural changes due to the interaction of price changes and factor endowment growth. These interactions will be observed in an economy with some endogenous product prices, or one in which factor supplies are responsive to price. The nature and the significance of these effects depend on structural parameters, such as the elasticity of factor supply with respect to price, and can, therefore, be expected to vary across economies. As the elaboration of this point forms an important part of the models we develop in subsequent chapters, further discussion is reserved until then.

Finally, the demand for environmental services associated with any given output level also depends on techniques of production and consumption. Changes in these – the *technique effect* – may be stimulated by relative price changes that cause shifts in the input mix, or by the introduction of new technologies that alter the ratio of emissions to output.[3] The technique effect reflects these supply-side changes and their underlying causes, among which it is conventional to include changes in government policies limiting permissible emissions or intensities, on the grounds that demand for such policies reflects income-elastic demand for a cleaner environment. Accordingly, the technique effect is normally expected to reduce rates of environmental damage;[4] there may be exceptions, however, such as 'smoke-stack chasing' competition, in which governments relax environmental standards in order to attract employment-creating investment.

For a small economy producing internationally traded goods (tradables), the decomposition of the total environmental effect of growth and/or policy reforms can be shown geometrically. Consider first the case of trade policy reform, with no change in factor endowments – the case analysed by Antweiler *et al.* (2001). Figure 2.1, which we adapt from their paper, depicts an economy producing 'clean' and 'dirty' goods, with comparative advantage in the latter. Combinations of the two goods that may be produced with full use of the resources with which the economy is endowed are shown by the production possibilities frontier (PPF). In the initial equilibrium associated with relative price p^T, the mix of goods indicated by point A is produced. The quantity of pollution (z) emitted is determined by the volume of dirty good output as well as by the technique, or emission intensity, of its production, and is shown in the lower quadrant of the figure. Thus $z = \phi^i(\theta)x$, where x is the quantity of the dirty good produced, and $\phi^i(\theta)$ is the technique used, conditional on a range of influences θ that includes policies, investment, preferences and so on.

Suppose that some impediment to trade causes the domestic price ratio p^T to diverge from the free trade ratio p^W; at the distorted prices, the dirty good is cheaper than it would be at world prices. Trade liberalization raises the relative price of the dirty good, and (due to the elimination of the trade distortion) raises total income. This increase in real income, shown in the figure in terms of the dirty good, is measured by the distance $Y^W - Y^T$. Trade

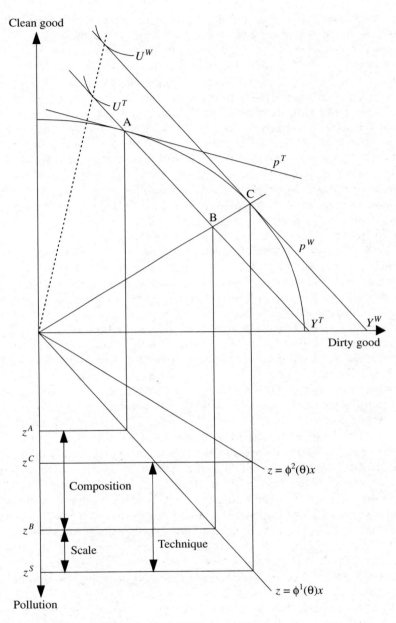

Source: Adapted from Antweiler *et al.* (2001)

Figure 2.1   Trade, pollution and welfare in a small open economy

liberalization also induces a reallocation of resources that increases production of the dirty good and reduces that of the clean good.

We can now measure the total pollution effect and its components. The price change causes a shift along the PPF from A to C. This shift can be broken down into two parts. The composition effect is the shift from A to B, capturing the change in the product mix measured at base-period prices. The scale effect – the increase in total output, holding the output mix constant – is shown by the distance from B to C. Each component of the shift from A to C is associated with a change in the production of pollution, z. The total impact of the relative price change on pollution is the sum of composition, scale and technique effects; the latter is shown in the lower quadrant by the rotation of the line $0z$, where a flatter slope indicates lower pollution intensity. As drawn in the figure, the scale and composition effects both contribute to increased pollution. The technique effect partially offsets these, and pollution rises from z^A to z^C.

Now consider the case of factor endowment growth in an economy which (for simplicity) trades at world prices. This is the case shown in Figure 2.2, which depicts an asymmetric outward shift in the PPF in the direction of the dirty good. This asymmetry could be due to disproportionately rapid growth of factors used intensively in the dirty goods sector, or to technological progress biased towards production of dirty goods. Production takes place initially at C, and growth, at constant world prices, results in a new equilibrium production point at E. As in the previous case, the environmental effect of this shift can be decomposed into scale and composition effects. The composition effect, once again measured at constant initial income in terms of world prices, is shown by the move from C to D, and results in an increase in pollution of $z^D–z^C$. The scale effect (the move from D to E) results in a further increase in pollution of $z^I–z^D$. Because of the assumed nature of the growth, both composition and scale effects increase pollution. The technique effect will offset these to some extent; as shown, it reduces pollution by the amount $z^I–z^E$. The net increase in pollution is therefore the amount $z^E–z^C$. Of course, if the shift in the production possibilities frontier were biased towards the clean good, the composition effect would have reduced pollution rather than increasing it.

In practice, the signs of the composition and the technique effects and their magnitudes in relation to the scale effect depend on the initial conditions of individual economies, and the nature of growth paths and policy reforms. Growth and policy reforms often occur simultaneously, and the net environmental effects can be deduced by combining the insights from both previous figures. The so-called 'environmental Kuznets' curve' (EKC) shown in Figure 1.4 is a conjecture based on the idea that the scale, technique and composition effects evolve in a particular way, with the net effect

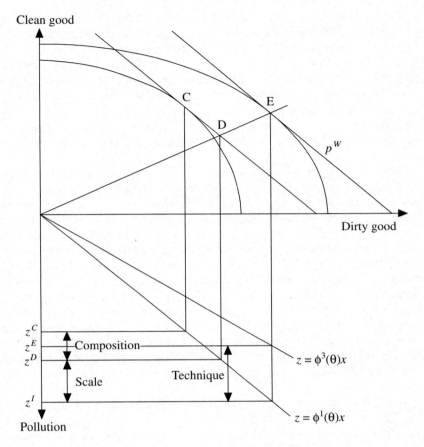

*Figure 2.2   Factor endowment growth and pollution in a small open
              economy*

that the pollution intensity of production increases in the earliest stages of
growth and subsequently declines. We can now analyse this construct in
more detail.

Consider an economy whose initial structure is mainly agrarian.
Economic growth, caused by factor endowment growth and/or increases in
the efficiency of factor use, is accompanied by structural change in the form
of a shift in the composition of GDP from agriculture to industry. For the
purpose of this example we may assume agriculture to be a relatively clean
industry and industry to be a relatively dirty one. The EKC hypothesis conjectures that the scale and composition effects, both tending to increase

overall emissions, are the dominant environmental features of early growth in such initially poor countries. With sustained per capita income growth, however, the composition effect may eventually reverse itself as the growth rate of the manufacturing sector diminishes and that of the income-elastic (and relatively clean) services sector increases, and/or as technique effects driven by investments in new technologies and motivated by changing consumer preferences cause emissions intensity at the margin to decline. The net effect will be that emissions per unit of income generated display an inverse-U-shaped relationship with per capita income, as was illustrated in Figure 1.4.

The EKC hypothesis, like Kuznets' original conjecture on the relationship between income distribution and growth, is fundamentally inductive and, as such, is less easily refuted by theorizing than through empirical tests.[5] A growing number of econometric tests, most using pooled annual cross-country data with single measures of air or water pollution indicators as dependent variables, provide some limited support for this hypothesis (Grossman and Krueger 1993 and 1995; Selden and Song 1994; World Bank 1992). Lacking robust microeconomic foundations, such findings naturally remain vulnerable to criticisms based on data quality, econometric methods and the interpretation of quantitative findings (Stern *et al.* 1996; Jha and Whalley 1999). These qualifications notwithstanding, it seems quite likely that long-run economic growth is associated with declining intensity of emissions (and, in a few cases, absolute falls in pollution output) of the most commonly measured indicators of air and water pollution.

If economic growth eventually results in declining emissions intensity (as the EKC hypothesis predicts), then policy reforms or other changes that raise real incomes may ultimately have beneficial environmental impacts through technique and composition effects. Among policy reforms, trade liberalization is one that economic theory identifies as exerting a powerful influence over structural change in output as well as real income growth. However, the 'net' composition effect of a package of trade policy reforms is likely to conflate expansion by some dirty industries with contractions by others. Given that empirical 'tests' of the EKC usually use aggregate data, therefore, the environmental effects of reform-induced relative price changes are less likely to be observed in practice than are the scale and technique effects associated with real income growth.

Recent econometric studies in which scale, composition and technique effects are separately identified have concluded that trade liberalization tends to reduce pollution, and that, in the long run, environment-conserving technique effects overwhelm the environment-degrading effects of scale and composition effects. Dean (1999: 21), for example, claims that 'trade liberalization may have significant beneficial effects on the environment via its effect on aggregate income', and Antweiler *et al.* (2001) conclude that 'freer trade may be good for the environment'. These empirical conclusions contrast strikingly with the widely held view that expanded trade will almost certainly increase aggregate pollution.

It is important to note, however, that the more credible empirical tests of the EKC make use of cross-country data and cover only specific measures of air and water pollution, primarily the by-products of industrial production and energy generation. In contrast, the smaller number of published studies using as dependent variables measures of natural resource depletion – specifically, deforestation – provide no statistically robust support for the EKC hypothesis (Cropper and Griffiths 1994; Shafik and Bandyopadhyay 1992). For example, Cropper and Griffiths applied a fixed-effects model controlling for factors such as population growth and rural population density (used as a proxy for natural resource dependence) to pooled cross-country data from developing economies. For Africa and Latin America, their econometric predictions of an inverse-U for deforestation barely meet minimum criteria for statistical significance, and the predicted EKC 'turning points' for these groups of economies fall far into the upper tail of the distribution of per capita incomes.[6] Cropper and Griffiths' estimates for Asian countries show no relationship at all between income growth and deforestation, and no turning point can be inferred. Another study using developing country data by Shafik (1994: 761) concludes that '*per capita* income appears to have very little bearing on the rate of deforestation'. These divergent results (relative, that is, to findings for industrial pollutants) may reflect data quality and measurement problems, or they may be indicative of heterogeneity in underlying economy–environment relationships; good positive cases can be made for both (Jha and Whalley 1999). What *cannot* be said is that there is empirical evidence for an EKC in the conservation of tropical forests.

2.3   TRADE POLICY, ENVIRONMENTAL POLICY AND ECONOMIC WELFARE

In the literature just reviewed, the analysis of trade liberalization is motivated largely by the desire to predict the impact of reforms on overall levels of pollution or resource degradation. While there is an underlying concern that increases in global pollution are not desirable, and also that there is a failure at the global level to achieve an optimal level of pollution, the optimality or otherwise of pollution 'production' from the purely national viewpoint is less frequently addressed. Differences among countries in terms of pollution tolerance are typically recognized in this literature, but the question of whether these reflect optimal responses or market failures is frequently ignored in studies that concentrate on the analysis of purely physical measures of environmental outcomes rather than on welfare change at the national level.[7]

In this section we review key elements of the normative theory of trade and environmental policy for a small open economy. Our goal is to expose general equilibrium mechanisms relating trade, environment and policy; for this purpose we maintain, by and large, a deliberately abstract definition of environmental damage. We shall consider more refined definitions (specifically, distinguishing between air and water pollution on one hand and natural resource depletion and degradation on the other) when we turn to more specific instances of trade, growth and environment in section 2.4.

Economic Welfare

At the level of the national economy, issues of the interactions between trade policies and the environment arise in the presence of market failures and uncorrected externalities. These are the sources of distortions that affect economic welfare. Most types of trade policy are similarly the sources of distortions.[8] The key elements of the analysis of such interactions can be introduced, therefore, in a partial equilibrium framework in which we distinguish between social and marginal supply and/or demand schedules.

Consider a small open economy that produces an exportable good.[9] Its production generates pollution that is a cost to society, but producers do not internalize this cost; hence the private cost of production is lower than the social cost. This is the case illustrated in Figure 2.3. The supply curve of the exportable (SS), reflecting the private marginal cost of production, lies below the social marginal cost curve (SS*) by an amount reflecting the pollution damage not internalized by private producers. DD is the domestic demand schedule, and the relevant world price is OP*. Because of a trade policy intervention (for example an export tax), the domestic price, OP, is lower than the world price. Thus there are two distortions, due to the environmental externality and the trade policy. Assume that these are the only sources of distortions,[10] and that their effects are felt only by domestic residents, that is, there are no transboundary spillovers.

If there were no distortions, the socially optimal quantity supplied would be given by the intersection of the social supply curve and the world price, and socially optimal domestic consumption by the intersection of the domestic demand schedule with the same price. Hence optimal production – which would also be Pareto-efficient – would be the quantity P*G; domes-

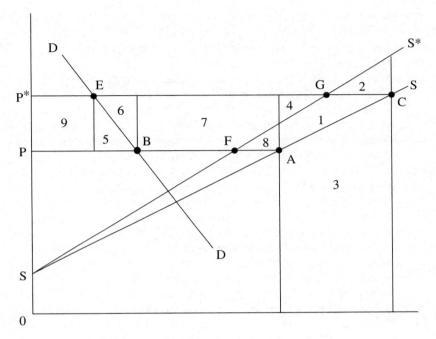

Source: Corden (1997)

Figure 2.3 Economic welfare with production externalities and a trade tax

tic consumption would be P*E, and exports EG. But in the presence of distortions from both policy and environmental sources, producers instead supply PA in total, of which PB is consumed in the domestic market and BA is exported. There is overproduction of the polluting good since, at price P, only PF production is socially optimal. There is also domestic overconsumption, by the horizontal difference between P*E and PB.

If trade is now liberalized, but there is no policy targeting pollution, the domestic price will increase to equal the world price. This will lead to higher production of P*C, lower domestic consumption (P*E), and higher exports, EC. The increased output, valued at the equilibrium world price – that is, in terms of its purchasing power over imports – will be worth the area (1 + 3 + 4). The social cost of producing this will be the increased area under the social marginal cost curve, (1 + 2 + 3). The policy reform will thus yield a net social gain of (4 – 2) due to increased production, but this is not the only gain. Consumers will have lost the area (5 + 9) because the price increased from P to P* (with consumption falling from PB to P*E) but producers will have gained $(5+6+9)$ from additional exports. Therefore, the net gain to society from trade liberalization is $(6+4-2)$. The area 2 is, of course, the cost of pollution – the negative externality – that is not reflected in the private cost of producers. The larger is this divergence between private and social costs, the less society gains from trade liberalization. If the difference is sufficiently large, liberalization may result in a welfare loss.

In this simple model, the imposition of a Pigovian tax – a tax that causes producers to fully internalize pollution costs – will raise private marginal cost to the level of social marginal cost. At every price there will be less production and correspondingly less pollution. In combination with complete trade liberalization, a Pigovian tax will lead to the socially optimal output P^*G thus eliminating the social loss arising from the externality. With area 2 now equal to zero, there is an unambiguous welfare gain from trade liberalization. Pollution will still increase, proportional to the increase in output, but the tax will ensure that each unit of additional pollution increases producer costs by an amount equal to its marginal social cost.

An analogous point could be made by starting with the implementation of environmental taxes, with trade restrictions remaining fixed. While the illustration is of a very specific case, a similar analysis can be developed for more complex cases, and applied to the analysis of instruments other than Pigovian taxes. The point here is that when there is only one externality, only one instrument is required to address it. With many externalities, more than one instrument is needed and, if only a single externality is corrected, a suboptimal welfare outcome may result.

The welfare insight from Figure 2.3 can be given a general equilibrium interpretation for the case of a tariff (with no environmental policy) using Figure 2.1.[11] Suppose once again that the economy has comparative advantage in a dirty good (the exportable) and that a tariff applies to imports of the clean good. In the initial equilibrium, at the tariff-distorted relative price p^T, production takes place at A. Suppose also that in this economy technique effects are relatively minor, so that the expansion of output from the dirty sector will result in more pollution overall (this assumption may be thought of as consistent with a country where per capita incomes are initially low, so it is on the rising section of the EKC). The tariff diverts domestic resources to production of the clean good and thus confers an environmental benefit, at the expense of the usual welfare cost associated with a distorting trade tax.[12] Thus at the tariff-distorted prices, consumers initially obtain income Y^T for the consumption of clean and dirty goods, but must endure pollution at level z^A (we assume utility to be separable between goods and pollution). Removing the tariff induces the altered production mix C as before, and confers the usual increase in the value of output, so consumers now face a higher budget constraint. This occurs, however, at the expense of more pollution (z^C) since, by assumption, the combined composition and scale effects outweigh the technique effect.[13]

If pollution affects utility but its effects do not enter markets and therefore cannot be priced, how can we evaluate whether welfare is increased or reduced by economic growth and policy reforms? Consider the case of trade liberalization shown in Figure 2.1. On one hand, consumers are better off in terms of purchasing power over marketed goods; on the other, they must endure a greater pollution externality. Figure 2.4, derived from this figure, helps answer this question. To focus on the impact of the tariff, assume that it is the only available policy instrument, and that the technique effect associated with trade policy reform is insignificantly small. The figure

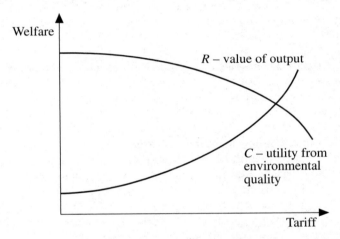

Figure 2.4   *Response of real income (R) and utility from environmental quality (C) to increases in the tariff (t) on imports of the clean good*

shows how the value of output and the utility derived from a clean environment (absence of pollution) will vary as the tariff is altered. The intersections of these curves with the vertical axis show their free-trade values, corresponding to point C in Figure 2.1. When $t = 0$, real income (curve R) is at its maximum; as the tariff increases (corresponding to a move around the PPF in the direction of A in Figure 2.1), the value of output declines at an increasing rate as deadweight costs increase. If consumers were indifferent to pollution, R would be a measure of the welfare associated with each tariff rate, as in the conventional analysis of trade taxes. We assume, however, that consumer welfare increases with less pollution. Suppose that z is produced in direct proportion to the output of the dirty good. As t rises, resources are drawn to production of the clean good. If the PPF is strictly concave, output of the dirty good declines at an accelerating rate; as it does, so too does pollution. As the tariff increases, therefore, utility from a clean environment increases more rapidly. This is shown as curve C.[14] With utility separable in goods and pollution, the vertical sum of R and C is a direct measure of consumer welfare for any specific value of t. This sum will be greatest when the slopes of the two curves are of equal absolute value; hence the optimal tariff can be positive. Optimally protecting the clean industry causes pollution to diminish, and thus confers a net welfare gain. Conversely, were the tariff applied to imports of the dirty good, it would be socially optimal to eliminate it, and indeed to subsidize imports. The use of a trade policy instrument to achieve an environmental goal is not first-best, however; net welfare would be higher with free trade and the imposition of a Pigovian tax on the production of the dirty good, as will be shown more rigorously below.

Figure 2.4 thus clarifies the trade-off between economic and environmental phenomena in terms of consumer welfare. The insights just obtained from consideration of trade liberalization also apply to other aspects of economic growth and 'globalization'. From Figure 2.3, it is clear that some forms of factor endowment growth or technological progress may reduce the utility derived from environmental assets at the same time as they increase the value of output – a 'win–lose' outcome – while others could generate both economic and environmental benefits, or 'win–win' outcomes. A particularly interesting set of cases arises when economies are made more open to foreign investment flows. Suppose the bulk of foreign capital is attracted to the dirty goods sector. The resulting expansion of dirty goods output increases pollution, but due to repatriation of profits by foreign owners of capital, the consumers of the pollution do not capture the full value of additional output. In this context the probability that foreign capital inflows could reduce welfare is greater. Conversely, investment in the clean industry would cause the dirty sector to contract in relative terms, and possibly even absolute terms through Rybczinski effects. In this case the chance of a 'win–win' outcome from foreign capital inflows is high.

Optimal Trade and Environment Policies in General Equilibrium

Although we can, in principle, construct a 'true' welfare measure taking account of pollution, it might be argued that the model as developed thus far still lacks some important elements. In particular, we do not have a systematic explanation for the technique effect. Though it may not make sense to try to model all of the factors contributing to this effect – explaining the adoption of new technologies, for example, is a distinct field of study in itself – a mathematical elaboration of the model can at least embed the socially optimal decision as to the amount of pollution abatement to be financed through the taxation of other activities, such as consumption of goods. This is an important extension, not least because it compels us to deal with the question of interactions among different types of taxes. A growing literature on this subject has indicated that in economies with existing distortions due to tax policies, an environmental tax at the Pigovian rate has the potential to reduce welfare, despite its beneficial environmental effect, if it exacerbates welfare-reducing distortions due to other tax instruments (Bovenberg and de Mooij 1994; Bovenberg and Goulder 1996; Goulder 1995; Fullerton and Metcalf 1997).

To explore these issues in a more rigorous manner, and following Copeland (1994) and Ulph (1999), we consider a model in which the production of goods generates pollution that affects consumer welfare but has no impact on the output of another industry (that is, there are consumption externalities but no production externalities).[15] Imagine a small open economy in which n goods are produced using m factors. Production of each good also generates pollution or an analogous bad. Vectors $\mathbf{p}$, $\mathbf{q}$, $\mathbf{c}$, $\mathbf{y}$ and $\mathbf{z}$, each of length n, denote world and domestic prices, consumption of marketed commodities, domestic supply and pollution respectively. Factor endowments are given by a vector $\mathbf{v}$, with length m. World prices are determined outside the model by the small-country assumption, and domestic prices are related to them by $\mathbf{q} = \mathbf{p} + \mathbf{t}$, where $\mathbf{t}$ is a vector of tariffs or export taxes. Firms are also subject to pollution taxes at rates given by the n-vector $\mathbf{s}$. Choose the first good to be numéraire, so $\mathbf{p} = (1, p_2, ..., p_n)$ and $\mathbf{q} = (1 + t_1, p_2 + t_2, ..., p_n + t_n)$. A representative consumer has a utility function $u(\mathbf{c}, \mathbf{z})$, with $u_c > 0$ and $u_z < 0$; by assumption, this function is strictly quasiconcave in $\mathbf{c}$. Aggregate expenditure is denoted by the conditional expenditure function $e(\mathbf{q}, \mathbf{z}, u) = \min\{\mathbf{q}'\mathbf{c}|u\}$, where a prime denotes the transpose of a vector. The expenditure function is non-decreasing and concave in $\mathbf{q}$, and non-decreasing in $\mathbf{z}$ and u. By Shephard's lemma, partial derivatives of the expenditure function with respect to the ith price give commodity demands by consumers. Thus the vector $\mathbf{c}$ of domestic consumer demands has elements $c_i = \partial e(\mathbf{q}, \mathbf{z}, u)/\partial q_i > 0$.

Aggregate income is given by a revenue or GNP function $g(\mathbf{q}, \mathbf{s}, \mathbf{v}) = \max\{\mathbf{q}'\mathbf{y} - \mathbf{s}'\mathbf{z}|\mathbf{v}\}$. Partial derivatives of this function with respect to prices give domestic output supplies $\mathbf{y}$, a vector with elements $y_i = \partial g(\mathbf{q}, \mathbf{s}, \mathbf{v})/\partial q_i > 0$. Derivatives with respect to environmental taxes give the quantities of pollution emitted, that is, $z_i = -\partial g(\mathbf{q}, \mathbf{s}, \mathbf{v})/\partial s_i > 0$. The revenue function is convex in $(\mathbf{q}, \mathbf{s})$ and concave in $\mathbf{v}$. Net imports, $\mathbf{m}$, are the excess of domestic demands over supplies, or for sector i, $m_i = c_i - y_i$; by definition, $m_i < 0$ if a good is a net export.

Assume that tariff and tax revenues are rebated to consumers in lump-sum form. There is full employment of factors, so that the equilibrium of this economy is reached when expenditures by consumers exactly exhaust their disposable income, the aggregate value of exports exactly equals import demand, and the abatement cost of pollution is just equal at the margin to the social value of damage that it causes. This equilibrium is described by the aggregate budget constraint (2.1), the market-clearing condition for net imports (2.2), and the production of pollution (2.3):

$$e(\mathbf{q}, \mathbf{z}, u) = g(\mathbf{q}, \mathbf{s}, \mathbf{v}) + \mathbf{s}'\mathbf{z} + \mathbf{t}'\mathbf{m} \tag{2.1}$$

$$\mathbf{m} = e_q(\mathbf{q}, \mathbf{z}, u) = g_q(\mathbf{q}, \mathbf{s}, \mathbf{v}) \tag{2.2}$$

$$\mathbf{z} = -\mathbf{g}_s \tag{2.3}$$

These equations can be solved as a system for the three endogenous variables: aggregate welfare, net imports, and the quantity of pollution produced.

The welfare effect of small changes in tariffs and pollution taxes can now be obtained by totally differentiating (2.1), assuming world prices to be fixed so that $d\mathbf{q} = d\mathbf{t}$. This procedure yields:

$$e_u du = -(\mathbf{e}_z - \mathbf{s})'d\mathbf{z} + \mathbf{t}'d\mathbf{m}, \tag{2.4}$$

where e_u is the inverse of the marginal utility of income, so the left-hand side of (2.4) is a money metric of welfare change.

The interpretation of (2.4) is straightforward: the first-best strategy for a social planner is to set environmental taxes equal to marginal damages, that is, $\mathbf{s} = \mathbf{e}_z$, and to pursue free trade, that is, $\mathbf{t} = 0$. Any other policy must be associated with lower welfare: either pollution will not be taxed at the rate that consumers are willing to pay, resulting either in too much pollution or in over-taxation of consumers, or there will be misallocation of resources to production in sectors protected by the tariff, or both. The positive rate of the pollution tax captures one endogenous component of the technique effect, the influence of consumer preferences, expressed through the tax, the practices of polluting firms. The tax provides firms with incentives to switch to cleaner techniques. The first-best result also neatly illustrates the desirability, as measured by consumer welfare, of addressing each type of distortion at its source rather than by indirect means.

In the event that first-best policies are infeasible, however, second-best solutions depend on choosing the appropriate mix of trade and environmental policies; in this setting trade restrictions may serve as instruments of environmental policy. To solve the model in terms of policy instruments, first find the change in pollution by total differentiation of (2.3):

$$\mathrm{d}\mathbf{z} = -(g_{sq}\mathrm{d}\mathbf{t} + g_{ss}\mathrm{d}\mathbf{s}), \tag{2.5}$$

and, from (2.2), find the change in net imports:

$$\mathrm{d}\mathbf{m} = \mathbf{H}_{qq}\mathrm{d}\mathbf{t} + e_{qz}\mathrm{d}\mathbf{z} + e_{qu}\mathrm{d}u - \mathbf{g}_{qs}\mathrm{d}\mathbf{s}, \tag{2.6}$$

where $\mathbf{H}_{qq} = (e_{qq} - g_{qq})$, the matrix of pure substitution effects, is positive semidefinite by the structure of the expenditure and revenue functions. Combining (2.5) and (2.6) in (2.4) yields an expression for welfare change in terms only of changes in the policy instruments $\mathbf{t}$ and $\mathbf{s}$:

$$\gamma e_u \mathrm{d}u = (\delta_z \mathbf{g}_{sq} - \mathbf{t}'\mathbf{H}_{qq})\mathrm{d}\mathbf{t} + (\delta_z \mathbf{g}_{ss} - \mathbf{t}'\mathbf{g}_{qs})\mathrm{d}\mathbf{s}, \tag{2.7}$$

where $\gamma = (1 - \mathbf{t}'\mathbf{m}) > 0$ is the tariff multiplier, and $\delta_z = (e_s' - \mathbf{t}'\mathbf{e}_{qz} - \mathbf{s}')$ captures the excess of pollution costs over environmental tax revenues.

Several fundamental insights emerge from (2.7). The first is that the two distortions in this economy, trade taxes and pollution, may interact. The welfare cost of a tariff has a direct component consisting of distortions in resource allocation and consumer expenditures, as captured in the elements of $\mathbf{H}_{qq}$, and an indirect component through the effects of the trade policy regime on the production of pollution, as captured by $\delta_z \mathbf{g}_{ss}$. In the absence of a pollution tax, the tariff regime generates a pure externality through increases in pollution by industries that expand and reduced emissions by industries that contract; this externality has a first-order welfare effect. Similarly, the welfare change associated with the pollution tax has a direct component (a rise in the tax reduces pollution) and an indirect component through the change in tariff revenues induced by the composition effect of the environmental tax. These are the general equilibrium analogues of the areas described in partial equilibrium in Figure 2.2.

A second insight that follows from the coexistence of the two types of distortion is that no single policy change (such as a tariff reform or pollution tax increase) can be asserted in general to result in improved welfare. The only unambiguously welfare-enhancing reform is one that simultaneously and equiproportionately reduces *all* distortions (see Copeland 1994 for a proof and more detailed discussion). By inspection of (2.7), it can be seen that if the pollution tax is unchanged (so $\mathrm{d}\mathbf{s} = 0$), the direct effect of a rise in tariff rates ($\mathrm{d}\mathbf{t} > 0$) will be welfare-reducing, but the indirect (environmental) effect could produce a rise or a fall in welfare, depending on whether the tariffs confer protection on clean or dirty industries. This follows because when resource constraints are binding, tariffs that increase the output of some industries must also cause that of others to contract. Higher protection for dirty (clean) industries thus means more (less) pollution, due to the composition effect. The case of a tariff for the clean industry was illustrated in Figures 2.3 and 2.4. When environmental policies cannot be set at their Pigovian rates, an *increase* in protection for clean sectors may be socially optimal, as was suggested by Figure 2.4. Conversely, when suboptimal trade policies cannot be altered, there may be a case for setting environmental policies as surrogates.

A fundamental implication of the theory of the second-best in an open economy case is thus that free trade should not be confused with *laissez-faire*, or the absence of a policy. Domestic distortions that create environmental externalities should be addressed with instruments that target them at their source; when this is feasible, free trade is also optimal, as shown in (2.4). This important distinction must be fully appreciated in any analysis of the environmental effects of trade and trade policy reforms.

Further Discussion

A generic model of the kind set out in equations (2.1–2.3) conveys fundamental insights, albeit with the help of strong simplifying assumptions. Relaxing these assumptions inevitably increases complexity and reduces the likelihood of obtaining unambiguous comparative static results. For example, if revenues from trade taxes form a significant part of government income, then a revenue-neutral trade reform may require the imposition of other distortionary taxes, thus offsetting some of the positive welfare effects of trade liberalization. Similarly, the focus on total social (national) welfare disguises the fact that a policy change can be expected to have differential effects on the welfare of groups within the economy when they are defined by their ownership of factors and/or their patterns of consumption.

In the above examples, the reform of trade policy without separate measures targeting polluting activities can lead to a situation in which polluting producers will always gain, even though society as a whole may lose.[16] In simple models, the distributional effects of a particular set of policy reforms in the presence of externalities can be 'read' from their effects on real factor rewards, so long as the pattern of factor ownership by consumers is known. However, the consideration of distributional characteristics becomes non-trivial when a model includes non-traded goods or endogenous factor supply response by distinct groups, together with group-specific marginal propensities to consume or supply such commodities. In these cases, the initial distribution of resources and incomes may condition the ways in which an economy responds to policy reform, and aggregate welfare, environmental outcomes and the distributional effects of policy reforms will be determined simultaneously.[17] More generally still, which policy instruments are deployed and which groups bear the burden of pollution and abatement expenditures are determined in part by property rights, fiscal policy and efficiency considerations, along with other political economy factors. Accordingly, in real-world policy making, an institutional or market failure such as the free disposal of air and water pollution or open access to natural resources could in principle acquire great economic significance. More specialized models presented in Chapter 4 address some of these complicating issues.

The discussion in this section has focused on developing a clear understanding of what it means to make policy in an economy that departs in some way from the assumed structure upon which the fundamental theorems of welfare economics are based. In other respects, however, the model remains highly abstract. This approach is helpful for the purpose of identifying fundamental economic mechanisms, but not for evaluating the interaction of economic and environmental phenomena in country-specific or sector-specific situations. In the next section we begin to narrow the analytical focus, discussing features of developing countries and of the development process that we believe should be incorporated into policy-relevant analytical models. In particular, we begin to focus on features of developing Asian economies that distinguish them both from industrialized economies and, to some extent, from the popular image of developing economies.

2.4 FROM THEORY TO EMPIRICAL MODELS

The above open-economy models all rely on a one-country version of the Heckscher–Ohlin model. This approach, for all its simplicity, provides a powerful tool to guide the *ex ante* analysis of the environmental effects of trade. However, any attempt to generalize or to increase the complexity of the two-good, two-factor model is almost certain to be associated with predictions that are ambiguous in sign and magnitude. Greater complexity requires a corresponding increase in information (whether in the form of restrictions applied to the model, or the provision of numerical values for some parameters) if the answer to any question about the environmental effects of trade is to be anything other than 'it depends'. Moreover, in the presence of pollution externalities, the Heckscher–Ohlin-based model provides no ready means to predict the *welfare* implications of trade or trade policy reform, except in the special case in which all expanding or contracting sectors are 'clean' or 'dirty'. If an economy's opening to trade causes a rise in pollution intensity (as when an expanding sector is relatively pollution-intensive), then its residents gain from higher income but lose from increased pollution.

The recent literature provides several examples of the potential for trade liberalization to reduce welfare when countries have comparative advantage in dirty goods (for example, Brander and Taylor 1997). What all such analyses make clear, however, is that while increased trade may lead to long-run welfare losses, more trade itself is not a *sufficient* condition for losses to occur. It is necessary that trade-based incentives to pollute, or to degrade natural resources, be combined with some other distortion, whether due to policy, missing markets or any other factor that causes a divergence between social and private marginal valuations.[18] This is a point that emerges also from analyses of the 'pollution haven' hypothesis, which asserts that more open trade will result in a migration of 'dirty' industries to poor economies. If engaging in trade or liberalizing trade policy lowers welfare due to increased environmental damages, then the first-best solution is found in the formation of an appropriate environmental policy, rather than in a return to autarky or protection.[19]

The foregoing case illustrates a second important, less widely recognized, pitfall associated with the application of the Heckscher–Ohlin model or its variants together with the rather abstract construct of pollution used so far. Not all forms of pollution and resource degradation are the same, and the differences between them may be sufficiently substantial to generate conflicting predictions about the welfare implications of trade even when the same basic model is employed. The theoretical analyses of trade and the environment reviewed in the preceding sections are motivated primarily by the cases of air or water pollution, that is, emissions assumed to have no long-run impact on an economy's productive capacity. In such treatments, the effects of pollution are fully reversible. However, when the term 'pollution' refers to natural resource depletion instead (and, as established in Chapter 1, this is indisputably the more significant source of environmental problems in most developing countries), irreversibilities may occur. Natural resource depletion and investment are both instances of endogenous changes in factor endowments.

Finally, it is inappropriate to model resource and environmental problems in developing countries as though property rights were well established and markets complete. The basic model in equations (2.1)–(2.3) should be interpreted as a device for establishing optimal policies to be adopted by a notional 'social planner'. In reality – in many wealthy countries as in the developing world – property rights over resources and emissions are not well established, a key characteristic that determines environmental responses to trade and to economic policy.

The importance of different types of property rights regimes can be illustrated by considering the case of a country that exports logs. If trade liberalization increases the domestic price of logs, then with well-established property rights in forests, this will lead to an expansion of forest area. However, if property rights are not well established, then the trade-induced rise in the relative price of logs will lead to more rapid depletion of forests without creating incentives for the replanting and expansion of forest area. So the relationship between trade and forest depletion depends critically on the nature of the property rights regime (Jayasuriya 2001). Analogous stories can be told for other natural resource stocks such as fisheries and even soils.

2.5 CONCLUSIONS

In this chapter, we have reviewed fundamental concepts relating economy and environment in the context of trade. We have presented generic analytical constructs, and some empirical findings from two branches of the literature on trade and the environment: one aiming primarily to measure environmental changes, and the other stressing a broader concept of economic welfare. Finally, we have introduced some elaborations relevant to developing country cases.

Several lessons emerge from the recent literature on trade and the environment. Some reinforce, in an environmental context, insights obtained from the broader literature on trade and trade policy. These include the importance of a general equilibrium approach, the essential ambiguity of welfare outcomes when only a subset of distortions are addressed in an economy characterized by multiple distortions, and the desirability (in a welfare sense) of addressing distortions at their source rather than by the addition of new 'compensating' distortions. Other observations are more specific, especially the analytical decomposition of the environmental effects of economic phenomena – including trade – into scale, composition and technique effects, and their empirical descendant, the inverse-U relationship between per capita incomes and the intensity of demands for environmental services. Many empirical tests using pooled cross-country data find support for the inverse-U hypothesis, with trade (or trade policy) and factor endowment growth rates as dominant influences on environmental change. However, while empirical support for the EKC seems robust for flows such as air and water pollution, no such regularity can be observed in the relationships between growth, trade and the exploitation of natural resources such as forests.

Distilling these findings, three empirical conclusions emerge to guide

further research. One is that among open economies the largest changes in
the demand for environmental services are likely to be found among those
that are growing quickly – and most of all in economies in which relative
factor endowments or production technologies are changing rapidly. In
these economies, scale, technique and above all composition effects are
likely to be larger than average. A second conclusion is that whereas for
major forms of air and water pollution economists might use inverse-U
relationships to predict long-term environmental outcomes with some confidence, long-term trends are much less clear where natural resource depletion rates are concerned. A third conclusion is that the environmental
influence of policy reforms is likely to be greater in economies undergoing
relatively large shifts in policy regimes. Related to this, the policy trade-offs
are likely to be more starkly drawn when environmental externalities
cannot easily be addressed at the source by means of direct policies. All of
these conclusions motivate the study of trade, growth and environment in
the resource-dependent Asian developing countries, using models that
capture the key structural features of their economies and institutions.

NOTES

1. Moreover, the changes may be non-monotonic, as was made clear by the late twentieth-
    century decline of traditional manufacturing and the rise of human capital-intensive
    industries in the US and other wealthy nations.
2. Similarly, when differences in pollution abatement costs form the basis of comparative
    advantage, trade can cause the expansion (or contraction) of the pollution-intensive
    sector (Fredriksson 1999).
3. The introduction of new, typically cleaner, technologies may itself be a direct function
    of the liberalization of trade or investment rules (Grossman and Krueger 1993), as well
    as being indirectly influenced by income-dependent preferences and policies.
4. For example, Anderson and Blackhurst (1992: 19) argue that if appropriate environmen-
    tal policies are in place, then 'trade and trade liberalization benefit the environment
    because the resulting increase in economic growth stimulates the demand for environ-
    mental protection and generates additional income to pay for it'.
5. Andreoni and Levinson (1998) present one of the more rigorous efforts to construct a
    consistent microeconomic theory for the EKC. However, their model depends on
    increasing returns to pollution abatement, and as such is scarcely relevant when the
    environmental problem is one of natural resource depletion or degradation.
6. Mean incomes (in purchasing power-adjusted dollars) in the sample are $718 for Africa
    and $2,039 for Latin America, with standard deviations of $512 and $1,133 respectively.
    The predicted turning points, $4,760 and $5,320, are thus very much higher than the
    upper 99 per cent confidence intervals for the income data ($908 and $2,634 respectively).
7. On the assumption, perhaps, that where transnational or global welfare is concerned, the
    environmental outcome of policy reform in a given country is the relevant indicator of
    welfare change.
8. We use the term 'distortion' for the effects of externalities and market failures as well as
    policy-induced divergences between social and private valuations of goods and services.
    Our usage is therefore broader than that of, for example, Corden (1997: 10), who reserves
    it for divergences due to government policies. Some trade policies may 'correct' domes-

tic distortions rather than create them, as in the case of an optimal trade tax imposed by a country with world market power.

9. This is based on Corden (1997), but see also Anderson (1992). The use of producer and consumer surpluses to measure welfare has well-known limitations but is a convenient tool to illustrate the key points.

10. We focus on policy issues throughout this book, though the famous Coasian analysis of externalities raised the possibility that such externalities may be internalized through direct bargaining among affected parties in certain circumstances, in particular when transactions costs are negligible (Coase 1960). It is assumed here that the class of problems that is being discussed does not lend itself to that kind of solution, because the rather stringent conditions needed for Coasian bargaining are absent. In addition, some have argued that the bargaining solution of the Coase model may not be socially optimal when distributional considerations are taken into account as it ignores the question of whose interests should count in the bargaining process (Bromley 1991).

11. Figure 2.3 can itself also be interpreted in general equilibrium terms by redefining the demand and supply curves (Corden 1997). For example, in a two-sector economy producing both the exportable and an importable, DD can be thought of as a constant-utility demand curve for the exportable relative to the importable, and the supply curve as resulting from movement along the production transformation curve (with constant factor endowments), thus reflecting the marginal cost of producing the exportable in terms of the cost of foregone importable production.

12. The environmental gain associated with the tariff is analogous to the area $(1)+(2)$ in Figure 2.3.

13. If there were no technique effect then tariff removal would result in the new pollution level z^S; the increase from the base level would consist of a composition effect $z^B - z^A$ plus a scale effect $z^S - z^B$.

14. Curve C is shown as increasing at an increasing rate, but its curvature in fact depends on two factors. With convex preferences there is diminishing marginal utility of a clean environment, implying that C increases at a diminishing rate. However, because of convex technology (the PPF is concave to the origin in Figure 2.1), each unit increase in the tariff reduces output of the dirty good by a progressively larger amount. As drawn in the figure, it is the latter effect that dominates.

15. The following analysis makes use of the dual approach to consumer and producer behaviour. Excellent introductions to the standard tools of this analysis – expenditure functions, revenue functions and basic general equilibrium theorems – can be found in Dixit and Norman (1980) and Woodland (1982).

16. In Figure 2.3, for example, part of the producer gain when there is no Pigovian tax is the area $(1)+(4)$. Of this, area 1 is a real cost borne by society, but because producers gain an equivalent amount, it is treated as a transfer within society that has no net welfare effect. Society as a whole, however, loses the additional area (2).

17. We are not aware of published analyses of trade policy and the environment that include endogenous responses conditional on income distribution. For analytical examples from the literature on economic growth, see Murphy *et al.* (1989) and Persson and Tabellini (1994). The applied general equilibrium analysis in Chapter 6 provides an empirical example; see also Warr and Coxhead (1993) and Coxhead and Warr (1995).

18. Nor is trade a *necessary* condition. Another paper by the same authors (Brander and Taylor 1998) reveals that even a closed economy can 'optimally' deplete its resources in such a way as to reduce long-run welfare – or, at the limit, drive the population to extinction.

19. '[M]anipulating a country's trade policies cannot be a meaningful substitute for a direct attack on the source of [environmental] problems. If environmental policies are inappropriate, it is much better to begin working to improve them than to try working around them' (Anderson and Blackhurst 1992: 19).

3.   Growth and the environment in developing Asian economies

3.1   INTRODUCTION

The analysis in Chapter 2 presented a decomposition of the aggregate effects of trade on the environment, and expounded the fundamental methodology for general equilibrium analysis of economic and environmental phenomena in open economies. It was established, among other things, that among countries which are open to international trade, 'shocks' in the form of world price changes or changes in the degree to which a country is open to trade have general equilibrium effects through changes in domestic product and factor prices. It follows that when different sectors of an economy are associated with different types and intensities of pollution or natural resource degradation, the environmental consequences of shocks that have differential sectoral effects can only be traced through general equilibrium mechanisms.

The models that yield these propositions provide general theoretical foundations for both positive and normative economy-wide analyses of environmental problems in open economies. However, they yield insights through a high level of abstraction, and as such have obvious drawbacks for exploring specific issues in a particular kind of economy. While the effects of a shock can in principle be fully identified in the simplest cases, in the presence of both environmental and policy-related distortions it is in general impossible to make firm predictions about the effects of a shock on welfare or the environment. Use of highly abstract models to address questions such as those regarding the relationship between trade, or trade policy reform, and the environment in developing countries can generally only result in a finding that 'it depends'.

In this chapter and in Chapter 4 we move beyond the analysis of environmental issues in very abstract open-economy models towards a more focused analysis using more specialized models which incorporate key features of resource-dependent developing economies. In this chapter, a review of economic and environmental data motivates the construction of several variants of a 'representative' developing economy model. We begin with a discussion of some important features of the countries with which we are concerned, namely economic structure and development strategy (section 3.2), and agricultural development and food policy (section 3.3). We then focus in section 3.4 on some features of the environmentally sensitive upland and forest margin areas of tropical developing countries. In section 3.5 we distil the data into a set of stylized 'representative' economy models. As tools for the analysis of economy–environment interactions, these descriptions take us well beyond the results of the generic models discussed in Chapter 2. The representative economies provide a range of initial conditions from which to evaluate the economic and environmental effects of hypothetical changes in global and domestic economic conditions and policies. These are anticipated briefly in the concluding part of section 3.5, before being addressed formally and in detail in Chapter 4.

3.2 ASIAN DEVELOPMENT STRATEGIES AND OUTCOMES

Until the 1970s, the economies of developing Asian countries were dominated by agriculture and other primary industries. Since then, most countries in the region have grown rapidly by developing country standards. Along with that growth they have experienced a tremendous expansion of industrial activity in general, and of manufacturing in particular. Growth of manufacturing has been rapid both in absolute terms and relative to total GDP, and has been matched by a corresponding decline in the relative importance of agriculture. Table 3.1 reports ten-year averages of the GDP shares of agriculture, industry, manufacturing and services for the major resource-dependent developing Asian economies. The data show uniformly that faster growth is associated with higher rates of change in the structure of production. Countries such as Thailand and the Philippines, with relatively similar initial structure, exhibit marked differences after four decades of growth at dramatically different per capita rates. Others (such as Vietnam and India) with an early history of growth failure are now rapidly converging in structure with countries that have grown more consistently over a longer period.

Within manufacturing sectors, the composition of production and trade has also changed. Processing of primary products – food, fibre and beverages, wood products, and basic metals and minerals – has always been important in the industrial structure of developing Asia. Other types of manufacturing industry have risen to prominence over time, however; most notably labour-intensive industries producing garments, footwear, consumer electronics such as radios, TVs and sound equipment, and semiconductors and other computer components. These industries now account for

Table 3.1   GDP shares of major sectors, developing Asian countries (%)

Country	GDP growth[a]	Years	Agriculture	Industry	*Mfg*	Services
China	6.42	1960–80	35	40	*31*	25
		1981–90	29	44	*36*	27
		1991–00	20	48	*37*	32
Southeast Asia						
Indonesia	3.97	1960–80	42	23	*10*	35
		1981–90	22	37	*16*	40
		1991–00	18	43	*24*	40
Malaysia	4.12	1960–80	29	30	*14*	41
		1981–90	20	39	*21*	41
		1991–00	13	42	*27*	45
Philippines	1.04	1960–80	28	31	*23*	41
		1981–90	24	36	*25*	40
		1991–00	20	32	*23*	48
Thailand	4.34	1960–80	29	25	*17*	46
		1981–90	17	33	*24*	50
		1991–00	11	39	*29*	50
Myanmar	—	1960–80	40	13	*10*	47
		1981–90	52	12	*9*	37
		1991–00	60	10	*7*	30
Vietnam[b]	5.37	1960–80	—	—	—	—
		1981–90	40	29	*26*	32
		1991–00	29	30	*20*	41
South Asia						
Bangladesh	1.35	1960–80	44	14	*11*	42
		1981–90	32	21	*15*	47
		1991–00	26	23	*15*	51
India	2.59	1960–80	43	21	*15*	36
		1981–90	34	26	*17*	40
		1991–00	29	27	*16*	44
Pakistan	2.02	1960–80	37	21	*15*	42
		1981–90	28	23	*16*	49
		1991–00	26	24	*17*	50
Sri Lanka	2.99	1960–80	30	24	*17*	47
		1981–90	27	27	*15*	46
		1991–00	23	26	*16*	50

Notes:
[a] Real per capita income (1995 US$), annual average 1970–2000.
[b] 1991–2000.
— = not available.

Source: World Bank, *World Development Indicators 2001*, Washington, DC: World Bank

the vast majority of manufactured exports by value from developing Asian countries. Heavier industries such as steel, fertilizer and chemicals and transport equipment have experienced mixed fortunes, growing rapidly in some countries at some times and declining in others. The fortunes of these manufacturing sectors reflect shifting comparative advantage as well as the long-term effects of industrialization strategies. Trends in the structure of industrial output and employment have in turn had important influences on labour markets and wages, and these, along with changes in the composition of consumer demand, have in turn affected the growth of agricultural and natural resource industries.

Growth and the transformation of production structure since the 1970s reflect, in part, a period of very high savings and investment rates in most developing Asian economies. In particular, the decade of very rapid growth from the late 1980s (Figure 1.1) was fuelled by investment rates in excess of 30 per cent of GDP, achieved both by mobilization of domestic savings and through rapidly rising foreign direct investment (Table 3.2). Capital accumulation also drove a shift in the factor content of production, promoting growth by 'medium-tech' industries such as electronics and transport equipment, which are capital-intensive relative to traditional manufacturing industries such as food processing and consumer staples.

Capital accumulation, although primarily supporting growth in industry, also had effects in other sectors. Rising demand for labour associated with manufacturing sector growth helped shift the balance of employment creation away from agricultural and natural resource sectors; in Malaysia, for example, manufacturing sectors contributed nearly two-thirds of total job creation in the decade 1987–96 (Athukorala 2001: 20). Industrialization also fuelled urbanization, further reducing direct dependence on agriculture and natural resources. During the1980s and 1990s, Southeast and East Asian developing economies experienced average rural population growth rates of under 0.6 per cent per year, well below replacement rates and far lower than the 1.5 per cent, 1.7 per cent and 2.0 per cent rates experienced by the Middle East/North Africa, South Asia, and Sub-Saharan Africa respectively.[1]

The growth of capital stocks relative to labour was not, however, the only phenomenon responsible for changing industrial structure; the reform of policies governing trade, investment, exchange rates and other areas of economic activity also played a significant role. Among these, the most important single set of reforms was that relating to industrial promotion policy, the centrepiece of each country's development strategy. For about three decades from the 1950s, import-substituting industrialization (ISI) was the prevalent development strategy in the developing world.[2] ISI strategies were initially motivated by observation of the successful industrialization, behind

Table 3.2   Gross fixed capital formation (% of GDP) and foreign direct investment (% of GFCF), developing Asian countries

Country	Item	1961–80	1981–90	1991–2000
China	GFCF	29	29	34
	FDI	0	2	11
Southeast Asia				
Indonesia	GFCF	22	25	26
	FDI	3	1	2
Lao PDR	GFCF	—	9	27
	FDI	—	0	21
Malaysia	GFCF	20	30	36
	FDI	13	11	15
Myanmar	GFCF	12	15	13
	FDI	—	—	—
Philippines	GFCF	20	22	22
	FDI	1	4	8
Thailand	GFCF	22	30	34
	FDI	2	4	10
Vietnam	GFCF	—	12	25
	FDI	—	1	32
South Asia				
Bangladesh	GFCF	20	18	20
	FDI	0	0	1
India	GFCF	16	21	23
	FDI	0	0	2
Pakistan	GFCF	16	17	17
	FDI	1	2	5
Sri Lanka	GFCF	18	25	25
	FDI	1	3	5

Source: As Table 3.1

protective trade barriers, of the German, Japanese and USSR economies in previous decades, as well as by pessimism about the prospects for achieving large-scale export growth based on agriculture and primary industry. ISI policies in general provided support for heavy industry and other 'basic' manufacturing sectors.[3] Due to the scarcity and consequent high cost of capital and skills used intensively by such industries, protection in the home market was considered necessary in order for them to be able to operate above breakeven. ISI policies thus conferred benefits mainly on capital-intensive industries producing for the home market.

As is now well known, the effects of ISI policies were by no means limited to the industries for which they were designed. Rather, their impacts were transmitted to other sectors through factor and product markets, and through their influences on aggregate rates of economic growth.[4] In some countries, relatively mild ISI regimes assisted so-called 'infant industries' with only minor intersectoral effects. However, under more far-reaching ISI strategies, the considerable expansion of capital-intensive industries contributed little to aggregate employment growth, with the result that additions to the labour force caused by population increase were absorbed not by manufacturing, but by agriculture and services. In some countries, interest rate caps on bank lending – intended to complement ISI trade policies by reducing the cost of borrowing for investment – resulted in artificially low capital costs for favoured sectors, with the result that they became less labour-intensive (see, for example, Coxhead and Jayasuriya 1986).

Overall, industrial promotion schemes based on barriers to imports have two main effects on other sectors, other than through long-term and indirect growth impacts. Trade restrictions, by reducing import demand, help support an overvalued real exchange rate. This diminishes the competitiveness of export industries in world markets. At the same time the growth of relatively capital-intensive industries tends, by slowing the overall rate of labour demand growth, to drive down wages for all sectors, and this confers a benefit on labour-intensive industries. In the most inward-oriented ISI regimes the second effect is dominated by the first, and industries producing export goods (or those producing import-competing goods without tariff protection) grow more slowly or not at all. In resource-dependent Asian economies these are mainly agricultural or resource-intensive primary sectors. ISI policies directly and indirectly discriminated against export-orientated industries, yet second-generation industrializing economies in Southeast and South Asia, by contrast with first-generation economies like Korea and Taiwan, provided few or no countervailing measures to export-oriented sectors.

In practice, unless ISI industries transform themselves into successful competitors in international export markets through technical progress or economies of scale, their growth is constrained by the size of the domestic market. Diminished external competition, the lack of scale economies and, in some cases, policy-mandated market power lead to a perpetuation of inefficient production methods and continuing demands for increased protection against more efficient international competitors. Developing country policy makers ultimately face a choice between increasing protection to sustain ISI industries, or reducing it and thereby causing the decline of some ISI sectors (and the possible rise of other industries formerly hurt by protection policy). Governments in developing Asia that repeatedly made the first choice during the early period of modern growth frequently experienced a debilitating cycle of ever-increasing rates of protection, balance of payments crises, foreign exchange controls, and slow growth in manufacturing sector employment (Papageorgiou *et al.* 1991). From the 1950s to the late 1970s, both the Philippines and Sri Lanka provide examples of economies in which ISI policies were maintained in the face of mounting negative effects, measured in terms both of overall economic growth and of the distortion of sectoral resource allocation (Baldwin 1975; Bautista *et al.* 1979; Athukorala and Jayasuriya 1994).

In contrast, in the 1970s a number of other Asian developing countries began to move away from ISI towards growth strategies that placed more stress on industrial exports. So-called export-oriented industrialization (EOI) policies typically encouraged the production of commodities in which countries had a natural comparative advantage, as a way of achieving faster development and industrialization. For most developing countries, this meant that industries made intensive use of unskilled or semi-skilled labour and also, in the case of resource-rich countries, expanded natural resource-intensive commodities. The rapid rates of industrialization and economic growth in the 1980s by the Asian newly industrializing economies (NIEs) are widely attributed to their pursuit of such outward-oriented growth strategies (World Bank 1993).[5] The success of EOI is reflected in the overwhelming predominance of manufactures in the exports of the NIEs (Table 3.3). These economies now depend much less, in a relative sense, on the exploitation of environmental and natural resources to generate employment and foreign exchange. This in turn reduces the cost of adopting 'sustainable' environmental strategies (at least where natural resources are concerned), as compared with countries where incomes continue to depend on agriculture and resource-intensive primary industries.

Intersectoral Consequences of Industrialization Policies

Agricultural development, in the resource-dependent economies of developing Asia, has been and remains a key element of overall economic growth and development. Countries whose agriculture sectors have failed to flourish have, in general, performed poorly in overall economic development (Timmer 1988), for reasons that may be rather baldly summarized as departures from comparative advantage and efficient resource allocation. Despite a fairly widespread and early recognition of the importance of agricultural development, most developing countries pursued policies that effectively retarded it by discriminating against the sector, both directly and indirectly.

Table 3.3   *Total exports (X, % of GDP), manufactured exports (MFG, %
of exports), and trade/GDP ratio (%), developing Asian
countries*

Country	Item	1961–70	1971–80	1981–90	1991–2000	Trade as % of GDP, 2000
China	X	2	4	11	22	44.5
	MFG	—	—	*62*	*83*	
Southeast Asia
Indonesia	X	10	24	25	31	67.0
	MFG	*2*	*2*	*18*	*49*	
Lao PDR	X	—	—	8	23	45.2
	MFG	*7*	*2*	*34*	—	
Malaysia	X	42	46	59	97	219.7
	MFG	*5*	*14*	*34*	*73*	
Myanmar	X	13	6	5	1	1.1
	MFG	*1*	*6*	*6*	*10*	
Philippines	X	16	22	25	42	91.0
	MFG	*6*	*14*	*29*	*60*	
Thailand	X	16	20	27	46	108.8
	MFG	*3*	*16*	*42*	*71*	
Vietnam	X	—	—	14	36	94.1
	MFG	*1*	*11*	*5*	—	
South Asia
Bangladesh	X	7	4	5	11	28.9
	MFG	—	*63*	*68*	*85*	
India	X	4	5	6	11	19.3
	MFG	*48*	*54*	*61*	*74*	
Pakistan	X	9	11	12	16	31.3
	MFG	*41*	*56*	*65*	*83*	
Low & middle	X	12	16	19	25	14.7
income LDCs	*MFG*	*20*	*29*	*44*	*62*	

Note: — = not available.

Source: As Table 3.1

The extent to which ISI interventions in the 1960s and 1970s turned the terms of trade against agriculture has been documented in a set of 18 developing country studies, including several of countries in tropical Asia (Krueger *et al.* 1991). These studies examined the effects of trade, price and exchange rate policies on agricultural prices and output, separating the total effects into components due to direct interventions and those due to the indirect effects of interventions in other sectors, such as industrialization and exchange rate policies. The analysis distinguished separately the effects of interventions on incentives to produce import-competing crops (mainly food) and export-oriented crops. In spite of considerable variation in country experiences, the overall picture that emerged was remarkably consistent:

> Government price interventions discriminated strongly – and increasingly – against the agricultural sector in developing countries during 1960–84. By far the greatest impact came through indirect interventions (industrial protection and macroeconomic policies), which reduce incentives in agriculture relative to other sectors of the economy. (Schiff and Valdés 1991: 10)

Over the period studied, direct interventions (that is, agricultural development policies) taxed agriculture on average at a rate of about 8 per cent, but indirect interventions taxed it by an additional 22 per cent. Among indirect interventions, industrial protection was the dominant influence, lowering relative agricultural prices both directly and also indirectly through its contribution to overvaluation of the real exchange rate (Krueger *et al.* 1988). Instead of laying the foundations for sustained economic growth and poverty alleviation, the negative effects on the agricultural sector of the 'package' of industrialization policies far outweighed the positive effects of any direct agricultural development policies. In the words of Nobel prize-winning agricultural economist T.W. Schultz, 'the modernisation of agriculture was being sacrificed at the altar of industrialisation'.[6]

By what means did industrialization and related macroeconomic policies influence the use of environmental and natural resources in Asia's resource-dependent countries? The short answer is that their influence was transmitted through relative product prices (the main subject of the studies cited above), through factor markets, and through the negative impact of industrialization policies on economic growth and poverty alleviation. The relative price channel itself contains more than one relevant story. Not only did policies penalize the growth of agriculture *as a sector* relative to other areas of the economy, they also introduced substantial differences in incentives *within* agriculture, by discriminating among agricultural products, specifically between importables and exportables. Direct agricultural interventions taxed exportables and protected importables, with the price wedge between the two averaging about 30 per cent (Krueger *et al.* 1988). Since food is predominantly importable, except in a minority of developing countries such as Thailand, direct agricultural policies had the general effect of increasing producer incentives to grow annual crops – cereals and pulses – at the expense of exportables. The latter, in tropical Asia, are overwhelmingly perennials such as tea, coffee, rubber, oil palm and tropical fruits. In addition, by distorting incentives in favour of food production, trade policy interventions tended to raise the price of a key consumption good even as they promoted the expansion of industrial sectors whose growth, since it generated relatively little additional employment, did little to increase wages. The net effect was downward pressure on real wages, exacerbating the effects of rapid labour force growth. The link between falling real wages and rising poverty is simple and direct; and poverty, as discussed in Chapter 1, is one of the major 'drivers' of deforestation. Given rapid population growth, it is not surprising that in the countries with the most severe and persistent import substitution policies, migration to the agricultural frontier peaked during the high tide of protectionism, contributing to a doubling and redoubling of the numbers dependent on frontier agriculture, and increasing pressures for deforestation (see, for example, Cruz 2000).

As already mentioned, the developing world as a whole had begun to turn away from the more extreme forms of ISI from about 1980. In tropical Asia, countries that moved fastest to create a more level sectoral playing field experienced faster overall growth as well as more balanced incentives for resource allocation within agriculture. During the peak years of growth from 1986–96, the more export-oriented Asian NIEs experienced booms in industrial investment and manufacturing output, earning from the World Bank the admiring title of 'East Asian Miracle'. The investment booms produced very rapid growth of non-agricultural labour demand, and the effects of this spilled over, through migration, to labour markets in all sectors. In Thailand and Malaysia, the fastest-growing resource-rich economies of tropical Asia, labour productivity growth in manufacturing caused rural wages to rise sharply and the agricultural labour force to decline not merely in relative terms but absolutely (Coxhead and Jiraporn 1999; Athukorala 2001).[7]

The impact on agriculture of the reforms that generated such rapid growth in the NIEs was twofold. Profitability declined in labour-intensive sub-sectors, but the consequent relative decline in returns to land (together with improved access to rural credit) increased profitability in the production of land-intensive tradables such as plantation crops. In rapidly growing countries with open land frontiers – mainly Thailand, Malaysia and Indonesia – agriculture continued to expand in area; however, growth was heavily biased towards the use of land for perennial crops (Table 3.4). Their expansion took place mainly by conversion of forests (Gérard and Ruf 2001). Widespread burning for this purpose has at times produced catastrophic environmental side-effects, including the well-publicized smoke and 'haze' that enveloped large areas of Southeast Asia in the late 1990s (Schweithelm and Glover 1999).[8] In other Asian countries, mainly

Table 3.4   Agricultural land use trends in developing Asian economies

| Country/Region | % of total land area | | | | | |
| | Arable land[a] | | Permanent crops[b] | | Agricultural area[c] | |
	1980	1997	1980	1997	1980	1997
Cambodia	11.3	21.0	0.4	0.6	11.7	21.6
India	54.8	54.5	1.8	2.7	56.6	57.2
Indonesia	9.9	9.9	4.4	7.2	14.3	17.1
Lao PDR	2.9	3.5	0.1	0.2	3.0	3.7
Malaysia	3.0	5.5	11.6	17.6	14.6	23.1
Philippines	14.5	17.2	14.8	14.8	29.3	32.0
Sri Lanka	13.2	13.4	15.9	15.8	29.1	29.2
Thailand	32.3	33.4	3.5	6.6	35.8	40.0
Vietnam	18.2	17.4	1.9	4.7	20.1	22.1
Low and middle income LDCs	9.4	10.3	1.0	1.2	10.4	11.5
East Asia & Pacific	10.0	12.0	1.5	2.6	11.5	14.6
Latin America & Caribbean	5.8	6.7	1.1	1.3	6.9	8.0
Middle East & North Africa	4.4	5.2	0.4	0.7	4.8	5.9
South Asia	42.4	42.5	1.5	2.1	43.9	44.6
Sub-Saharan Africa	5.4	6.4	0.7	0.9	6.1	7.3

Notes:
[a] Arable area is defined as land under temporary crops, temporary pastures and short-term fallow. Excludes land abandoned as the result of shifting cultivation.
[b] Permanent crops area is defined as land cultivated with crops that occupy the land for long periods and need not be replanted after each harvest (flowering shrubs, fruit trees, nut trees, vines etc.). Excludes areas under trees grown for wood or timber.
[c] Sum of arable area and area under permanent crops.

Source: World Bank (2000a).

net food importers, expansion of overall agricultural area has been more tightly constrained. Moreover, in those countries – especially the Philippines and Sri Lanka – agricultural land use growth has been mainly for food crops. These countries exhibit agricultural development patterns that the Krueger *et al.* studies associated with inward-looking development policy. Recent deforestation, to an even greater extent than elsewhere in the region, has been mainly to produce land for the expansion of short-term food crops and to replace agricultural land abandoned due to degradation.[9]

3.3   AGRICULTURAL DEVELOPMENT AND FOOD POLICY

Of course, industrialization was by no means the sole target of development policy. Agricultural development, and specifically the security of food supply, has long been a major policy concern. Staple foods such as rice and corn are economically and politically important, moreover, by virtue of their prominence in the incomes and expenditures of poor households and the potential consequences of failures of supply. Governments in developing countries frequently enshrine food security – or, more strongly, staple grain self-sufficiency, at the national or even sub-national scale – as a basic plank of development policy. They support R&D for technological progress, provide input subsidies, and target price and supply stabilization through interventions in domestic and international trade. As a result of policies to regulate international trade, domestic markets for staple cereals are at least partially insulated from global markets. In fact, very high levels of protection for cereals have persisted in Asia even after major trade reforms in other sectors, with the result that rice, corn and other staples are now among the most heavily protected sectors in Asian countries (WTO 1999a, 1999b and see similar reports for other Asian countries). Thus although there has been an overall policy bias against agriculture as documented by Krueger *et al.*, within agriculture these policies preserve or even extend a systematic bias favouring food and grains over other crops.

This policy-induced distortion has potentially important implications for the environment. Within the agricultural sector, cereal production is the main activity in developing Asian countries. Rice and corn production account for a very large fraction of cultivated area (Table 3.5) and absorb proportionally similar shares of agricultural labour, investment and purchases of intermediate inputs such as fertilizer. Since the land cultivated to cereals is a very large fraction of total agricultural area, it follows that almost any intervention in cereal markets which affects incentives or the production technology is bound to have environmental impacts through the demand for land, soil nutrients and water, and through the discharge of agricultural effluents into freshwater and coastal ecosystems.[10]

Food Production and the Green Revolution

Throughout its early modern history, large parts of tropical Asia were characterized by relative land abundance and labour scarcity. Transport costs rendered most trade in staple foodstuffs unprofitable or impractical; instead, local land and labour resources were allocated to match demand with local supply. However, beginning in the late nineteenth century, rapid

Table 3.5   Area planted to cereals, 1980–98 average

Country	Cereal area planted ('000 ha)	% of arable land
China	91,525	78
Southeast Asia		
Indonesia	13,422	72
Lao PDR	653	84
Malaysia	695	48
Philippines	6,676	123
Thailand	10,984	64
Vietnam	6,635	118
South Asia		
Bangladesh	10,946	128
India	102,044	63
Pakistan	11,649	57
Sri Lanka	835	96

Note: Due to double-cropping, area may exceed 100 per cent of arable (cultivated) land.

Source: As Table 3.1

population growth applied increasing pressure on the agricultural land base. In the two decades after the Second World War, a period during which the region's population grew very rapidly, the geographic limit of cultivable land was reached or approached in several countries. In the absence of technological progress, domestic food production per capita began to decline and caused net imports to rise (or, in food-exporting countries, net exports to fall). A series of crop failures in 1973–74 caused by drought and disease left the region critically short of rice. Food availability in the largest food-deficit countries, Indonesia and the Philippines, was maintained only by means of emergency imports and infusions of foreign aid, and food prices rose sharply, triggering inflation, economic distress and considerable political unrest.

In the longer term, enhancement of food supply in the food-importing countries came from technical progress abetted by infrastructure investments, price supports and input subsidies. Research directed at producing high-yielding rice varieties, especially that carried out at the International Rice Research Institute (IRRI), an international agricultural research institution based in the Philippines, led to the release of new plant types with properties that greatly enhanced the productive capacity of irrigated rice land. The IRRI 'modern varieties', first released in 1966, made it possible to grow rice at all times of year, and more than once per year on a single plot of land. Above all, the new varieties were highly responsive to nitrogen fertilizer. The 'Green Revolution' technological package of modern rice varieties, irrigation and fertilizer proved capable of yielding double or even triple the quantity of grain produced per crop by traditional cultivars; and by increasing the number of crops grown per year, raised annual output per unit of land even more (Barker and Herdt 1985).[11] Public sector investments in new technologies, price supports for producers, subsidies on fertilizer and other inputs, and irrigation, roads and market infrastructure encouraged farmers to adopt these technologies in the land-scarce Asian economies. Table 3.6, which records adoption rates of modern rice varieties, also indicates a correlation between such adoption, the spread of irrigation and increased fertilizer use in agriculture.

Table 3.6   Adoption of modern rice varieties, irrigation and fertilizer use

Country	Adoption of modern rice varieties (% area planted)			Irrigated land as % of crop land			Fertilizer use (kg/ha)	
	1970	1980	1990s[a]	1961–80	1981–90	1991–98	1984	1994
China	0	14	100[b]	38	38	38	200	309
Southeast Asia								
Cambodia	—	—	11	4	7	7	1	3
Indonesia	10	63	73	15	15	15	72	80
Lao PDR	—	—	2	5	15	18	0	2
Malaysia[c]	28	—	90	6	6	5	105	159
Myanmar	4	41	72	8	10	13	19	12
Philippines	50	74	89	11	15	16	29	64
Thailand	0	12	68	15	19	22	23	64
Vietnam	—	—	80	20	38	43	57	192
South Asia								
Bangladesh	5	21	52	11	23	41	65	120
India	15	45	73	18	25	31	49	80
Pakistan	37	44	42	67	77	80	62	98
Sri Lanka	10	71	91	23	29	30	102	113

Notes:
[a] Various years.
[b] 40% hybrid rice.
[c] West Malaysia only.

Sources: Modern varieties: IRRI (1991, 2001); irrigated area: as Table 3.1; fertilizer use: World Resources Institute, *World Resources 2000–2001*, Washington, DC: WRI

In countries and sub-national regions with adequate irrigation, and where fertilizer and other complementary inputs were available to farmers, rice yields increased rapidly. Higher yields and the greater labour demand generated by more productive land helped transform the region's agricultural economies. In the two decades following the release of the modern rice varieties, rice production in most of the region's developing economies grew rapidly (Table 3.7), while the total land area devoted to its cultivation increased only slightly. In Indonesia, for example, per capita rice availability rose from 83 kg milled rice in 1962–64 to 140 kg in 1986–88 – at the same time as imports were steadily reduced. Once the world's largest rice importer, Indonesia achieved the politically significant goal of rice self-sufficiency in 1985.

Table 3.7   Indices of rice production, area and yield (1970 = 100)

Country	Production		Harvested area		Yield	
	1980	1990	1980	1990	1980	1990
Cambodia	39	63	57	75	68	84
Indonesia	153	227	111	123	139	185
Laos	117	177	110	92	106	193
Malaysia	122	107	80	89	153	120
Myanmar	163	167	100	97	163	172
Philippines	138	172	108	110	128	156
Thailand	125	147	134	149	93	99
Vietnam	115	188	119	125	97	151

Source: IRRI (1991)

The spread of Green Revolution technologies and irrigation enabled grain-deficit countries to increase production on currently cultivated land. However, the yield advantage of the new rice technology depended on the availability of complementary inputs, particularly irrigation, and hence adoption rates in rainfed and upland agriculture remained very low. For this reason the Green Revolution had little *direct* impact on upland agricultural productivity. However, yield gains in lowland irrigated areas almost certainly diminished the pressure for an expansion of food production in uplands, by driving down relative grain prices. Rising labour productivity and labour demand in lowland agriculture also reduced incentives for labour migration to uplands (David and Otsuka 1994; Coxhead and Jayasuriya 1994; Hayami and Kikuchi 2001).

Food Policy

Although the technological advances of the Green Revolution helped alleviate diminishing per capita food production for a time, most countries in the region continue to intervene in domestic food markets and trade, as noted above. These interventions are intended to stabilize consumer prices as well as complement infrastructural and R&D investments and, by maintaining producer incentives, to help offset the prevailing anti-agriculture bias of industrial promotion policies. They were adopted – and by and large persist – for several reasons.

First, food security – and, more specifically, national self-sufficiency in staple cereals – remains a highly sensitive political goal, commanding a great deal of policy attention. In the early years of modern economic development the governments of the region played a dominant role, controlling trade, distribution, prices and even (in some countries) production, through state agencies. These entities, such as BULOG[12] in Indonesia, developed into large and diversified commercial enterprises. Given liberal budgetary support, they featured prominently in efforts to promote rural development. With the support of laws restricting private sector involvement in international trade in grains, the activities of the state food corporations successfully insulated domestic food prices from international markets for significant periods of time (David and Huang 1996; Barker and Herdt 1985).

Second, in spite of infrastructure investments, increasingly intense competition for land encouraged rural-based anti-government movements – some communist, others based on ethnic or cultural divisions – that produced or stimulated armed insurgencies and civil wars in many parts of Asia. The growing shortage of land spilled over into national politics, with calls for land tenure reform as a measure to address income inequity, poverty and the spread of communism. Food price and supply stabilization through policies that subsidized both food producers and consumers alike became instruments to achieve the broader political and military goals of governments in the region.[13]

Even prior to the Green Revolution, many governments attempted to overcome domestic food shortages (and in passing to alleviate civil unrest) by investing in irrigation, land development and productivity-improving infrastructure. In Malaysia, Indonesia, Sri Lanka and the Philippines, government agencies cleared forest, built roads and houses, and sponsored resettlement in frontier areas by rural households from more densely populated regions. Throughout developing Asia, the state undertook major investments in the construction and operation of dams, canal systems and drainage in agricultural lowlands. Like the activities of state grain-trading corporations, these investments seldom recouped even a fraction of their costs: indeed it is unlikely that they were ever intended to do so. They were primarily a means to redistribute income to rural areas. Their effects on land use, however, were enormous. Major irrigation projects allowed intensification and set the stage for subsequent adoption of Green Revolution technologies in the river delta ecosystems. In other areas, land development and resettlement schemes pushed back the agricultural frontier, converting forests to plantations and in some cases to intensively farmed irrigated rice lands.

Environmental Linkages of Agricultural Development Policy

The modern history of cereals production and policy in Asia suggests a number of environmental linkages. Land area expansion often took place at the expense of perennial land uses, including forests. Technical progress – the Green Revolution – that increased the productivity of lowland areas had an effect similar in most respects to an increased supply of acreage. This was complemented by investments in irrigation and other forms of agricultural infrastructure, which further facilitated intensification in traditional lowland and deltaic rice-growing areas. While the direct impacts of these investments and of Green Revolution technologies outside of irrigated areas were much smaller, their indirect effects, through the supply and price of cereal crops, discouraged cereal production in less favourable areas. These efforts should have relieved pressure on the agricultural land frontier.

However, complementary investments aimed at opening new lands to cultivation, especially those associated with internal migration and resettlement schemes, promoted agricultural expansion, usually at the expense of forest lands. Moreover, interventions in international trade and domestic markets strove to raise and stabilize producer prices by means of heavy subsidization. These market interventions had the twin effects of promoting the expansion of food production, sometimes at the expense of other crops, and of de-linking domestic and international cereal prices in the short to medium term. They must be held at least partly responsible for the expansion of area planted to annual cereal crops in the region, especially in the relatively fragile and easily degraded uplands (Coxhead and Shively 1998; Coxhead 2000).

3.4 DEVELOPMENT IN THE UPLANDS

The agricultural development story as told so far has referred to the distinctions within the agricultural sector, particularly the differences between uplands and lowlands, and those between export/industrial crops and non-traded/food crops. Clearly agriculture is not a homogeneous sector; but to understand fully the environmental aspects of agricultural development, it is essential to appreciate the constraints imposed by the geography of developing countries. Distance and terrain matter: the quality and quantity of infrastructure tend to diminish sharply with distance from major ports and cities, and this decline is markedly sharper when high altitude or steeply sloping terrain raises transport and communications costs. The economies of upland regions can be (and frequently are) very different, in both structure and level of development, by comparison with coastal and river delta areas. They are less densely populated and more dependent on agriculture and other resource-based industries; their populations are poorer, less healthy and less well educated. Access to markets for goods, labour, credit and insurance is constrained by higher transport and transactions costs. Formal legal and administrative institutions are relatively weaker, although traditional or customary counterparts are often stronger. Agricultural development in the uplands typically utilizes labour and very limited capital to colonize new lands, or to intensify the use of existing land with new crops or technologies.

Economic development in the uplands is constrained by the reach of markets. As these expand, they create new opportunities for income generation and, in so doing, alter the value of region-specific resources such as forests and agricultural land. They also convey the indirect impacts of policies not specifically directed at upland economies, but directed at other sectors or designed to accelerate overall economic growth. Both the expansion of the market and the impacts – direct as well as indirect – of policies exert strong effects on the pattern of development and resource use at the agricultural frontier.

Expansion of the Market

With growth, the geographic extent of the market increases. Remote areas formerly connected only very weakly or intermittently to the national economy become more completely integrated. This is caused by infrastructure development, movement of people, growth of incomes and the exploitation by traders of arbitrage opportunities. In practice, the expansion of the market brings in areas that are more sparsely settled, usually because of geographic or some other disadvantage. These areas include mountainous and steeply sloped hinterlands, areas that until recently were typically thickly forested.

The expansion of the market can have profound effects on rates and patterns of natural resource exploitation, and on the quality of the environment in uplands and upland watersheds. These effects arise because national and international markets assign monetary values to agricultural and resource products, as well as to the natural environment, that differ from the values they achieve in strictly local markets. Therefore, the expansion of the market results in different rates and patterns of environmental and natural resource exploitation. This occurs through a number of channels.

Economically, market access provides remote communities with the opportunity to specialize in production. This naturally implies a shift in agricultural land use, very frequently from mixed gardens to monoculture. The key mechanism driving such shifts is differences in the valuation of agricultural and natural resource products in external markets and in isolated communities, which in turn imply different valuations of assets such as land, standing forest and even water. Figure 3.1 (adapted from Gersowitz 1989) illustrates the processes at work as the market expands. It shows a stylized spatial economy in which distance from a port located at point A is measured in terms of distances along a road (x) and off-road (y). (To

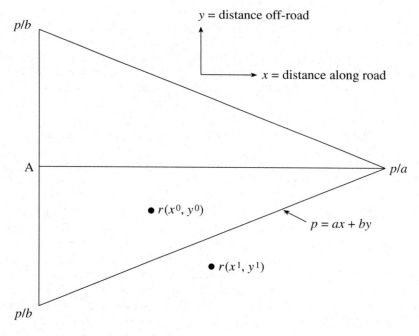

Source: Adapted from Gersowitz (1989)

Figure 3.1   The spatial expansion of the market

focus on the spatial aspect we assume terrain to be uniformly flat.) Transport along the road costs a dollars per kilometre, while off-road transport costs b per kilometre. Empirically, the unit cost of off-road travel is far higher than the on-road cost, which is why most feeder roads approach highways at angles very close to 90°. Suppose that a single agricultural commodity can be produced and sold in the port at price (net of production costs) p. Since transport costs reduce the actual price received by producers away from the port, there is a *boundary of cultivation for the market* given by the triangle whose edges are the points at which price net of transport cost is zero. Outside the triangle, agricultural production takes place for subsistence only.

Clearly the area of the triangle – that is, the extent of the market – depends on the commodity price at the port and on transport costs. A rise in p or a reduction in either a or b (due to lower fuel prices or road improvements, for example) will cause the market to expand. Farmers formerly producing for subsistence only will begin producing for the market. In a more general setting in which several different crops can be produced, each will have its own specific boundary of profitable commercial cultivation. In this setting a change in transport costs or in the prices of farm inputs or outputs not only shifts the extent of the market but will also induce farmers to alter the mix of outputs they produce. Thus the spatial expansion of the market can be one source of the composition effect of trade reforms or world market changes referred to in Chapter 2.

Market expansion alters the valuation of location-specific resources used in production. In the subsistence economy, resources (such as standing trees, soil quality and even labour) will have values linked only to the subsistence requirements of local households. As market expansion brings former subsistence farmers into commercial production, the valuation of these resources will alter to reflect returns obtainable from the new uses. Thus a fixed resource r at location (x^0, y^0) in Figure 3.1 will have a different value from that of the same resource at location (x^1, y^1), outside the boundary of cultivation for the market. Under some conditions the value of a fixed resource may increase; under others its value may fall.

Thus as the market expands into agricultural hinterlands, we expect, and observe, changes: in land use between forest and agriculture; in the mix of agricultural crops produced; in technologies; and in the valuation of natural resource stocks. The environmental implications of the expansion of the market are very important in tropical countries, where the frontier is located within environmentally sensitive forest and upper-watershed areas. These spatial phenomena must be taken into account in the analysis of a composition effect, as discussed in Chapter 2.[14]

Impacts of Development Policies in the Uplands

The thrust of economic development policies – notably, though not
exclusively, policies related to trade and the macroeconomy – exerts
tremendous influence over the allocation of natural resources and the rate
of environmental degradation in developing countries (Binswanger 1990;
Munasinghe and Cruz 1995; Repetto and Gillis 1988; Pearson and
Munasinghe 1993). Economic policies have the power to induce or retard
composition effects (and, in the longer run, scale effects) associated with
economic growth. A point that is often overlooked, however, is that they do
so not only directly, in the sector at which they are targeted, but also indirectly, through economy-wide adjustments in the markets for goods, services and inputs. Accordingly, policies directed at specific sectors such as
manufacturing industry or lowland agriculture can affect resource valuations, patterns of land use and production, and associated environmental
outcomes in other industries and in geographically distinct or remote areas
such as uplands.

Market expansion, and the changes it engenders in the structure of
upland production, is not independent of national development policies.
The price that determines the boundary of cultivation for the market may
be subjected to policy interventions that change both its level and its variability. In the Philippines, for example, the expansion of corn and temperate climate vegetables into upland and highland areas has received
significant support from policies that raised and stabilized their prices, thus
greatly increasing the area over which they could profitably be grown for
external markets.

Policies directed at other sectors operate also through agricultural
product and factor markets, including markets for labour and credit. In the
Philippines, much of the impetus for migration to upland areas since the
1950s has come from the very slow growth in real incomes in lowland agriculture and non-agricultural sectors, thus rendering the expected income to
be derived from land colonization and upland farming relatively attractive.[15] More recent empirical work indicates that higher wages in non-
agricultural and lowland employment would have significant effects on
land use in Philippine uplands (Coxhead *et al.* 2002), although the
short–medium-run impact on resource depletion and the environment,
which depends on farmers' adoption of soil-conserving technologies, is less
clear (Rola and Coxhead 2002; Shively 1999).

3.5   FOUR REPRESENTATIVE ECONOMIC TYPES

The discussion so far suggests the existence of a common set of stylized facts about the structural features of Asian developing economies in relation to environment and natural resources. There is, however, a wide diversity of structure and experience, as can be seen in comparisons of individual country data. In most developing economies, environmental outcomes over time reflect the secular income growth path followed, as well as associated changes in the structure of production, domestic demand and trade. However, the pace of aggregate growth and the nature of structural change are critically influenced not only by initial conditions and external shocks, but also by the specific development strategies pursued. These policy differences in turn interact with heterogeneity in endowments to produce varying mixes of scale, composition and technique effects. This can be seen quite dramatically in the wide differences observed in policy-related economic and environmental variables not only between developing and developed economies, but also among developing economies themselves. This in turn implies that a single model cannot be used to address environmental issues among developing countries, and analytical models, if they are to be empirically relevant, should incorporate key differences in factor endowments, economic structure and policy.

The basic open economy models presented in Chapter 2 were very simple in this respect. By abstracting from many real-world complexities, they helped to highlight and make clear some fundamental propositions about the links between policy and environmental outcomes. But expositional simplicity and transparency comes at a price: the number of ways in which such models can be used to address empirically important issues is limited. Developing countries present a number of important contrasts and specific features where natural resources and the environment are concerned. Our review of developing Asian economies suggests the importance of attempting to construct model variants that more closely reflect the stylized facts of the development–environment relationship and its economic 'drivers' in different types of economies. This motivates us to construct models of several representative economic types.

Each representative economy described below is a variation on a common stylization that attempts to capture the main features discussed in the foregoing sections. These include spatial variation in resource endowments (modelled in the form of an upland region that is not only spatially, but also economically and technologically, distinct from lowlands); a lowland region that produces both agriculture (by assumption, under relatively more favourable conditions) and manufactures; and environmental phenomena that are measured in terms either of the loss of forest cover, or of the degradation of agricultural land in uplands, or both. In Chapter 4, we present formal models that incorporate all of these phenomena. Here, we simply provide a sketch of each representative economy, highlighting its key distinguishing characteristics. Each representative economy embodies alternative sets of assumptions about economic structure that we expect, on the basis of the review in sections 3.3–3.4, to condition the ways in which it will respond to an economic stimulus such as a terms of trade shock or policy innovation. As will be shown in the next chapter, these hypothetical economies, as well as further variations on the basic model, can be readily implemented in both analytical and applied general equilibrium models by varying the values of key structural parameters.

The 'Jeepney' Economy: Net Food Importer with ISI Policies

The first representative economy captures the main features of food-importing developing countries during the ISI period. Among developing Asian economies, we may think of this, for example, as a stylized description of the Philippines in the period before the trade and economic policy liberalizations of the 1990s: hence the name, which alludes to the Philippines' ubiquitous backyard-built, all-purpose vehicle based on the Second World War military jeep. The model could also be applicable for some purposes to sub-national economies, most notably that of the Indonesian island of Java prior to sweeping economic reforms begun in the 1980s. Its main features are a policy bias in favour of import-competing industries, which are relatively capital-intensive and generate little in the way of job growth, and a persistent deficit, at world prices, in the production of staple foods. Both the ISI sectors and the food sector are protected, although by different policy instruments. Imports of manufactures are subject to tariffs, which raise the prices received by domestic producers above those in world markets and thus distort the domestic terms of trade in favour of manufactures. Food policy stresses self-sufficiency over cheap prices. Under free trade, the country would be a net food importer because in the absence of interventions its autarky price would be higher than the world price, but food imports are limited by quantitative restrictions (in the cases of the Philippines and Indonesia, grain trade is the monopoly of a state corporation). As a result, food is effectively non-traded, with prices reflecting domestic supply and demand.[16]

Both kinds of policy – tariffs on industrial importables and the protection of domestic food producers – indirectly penalize the producers of tradable goods, including exporters of agricultural and natural resource products. One outcome is that the conversion of forest to agricultural land at the frontier is undertaken primarily for the purpose of producing more food, rather than for establishing perennial export crops such as oil palm, coffee or rubber. Food crops are favoured not only because food policy raises their relative prices; manufacturing protection also depresses wages, which further increases the relative profitability of labour-intensive activities such as food production.

Finally, in this economy the incentives provided by development policy promote private investment in (import-competing) manufactures. Most costs in the agricultural sectors are for the use of land and labour rather than for intermediate inputs such as fertilizer. In lowland agriculture – the primary food-producing region – public expenditures on R&D and infrastructure enhance productivity. Given the historical bias of sectoral policies, it is useful to explore the impact of technological progress in lowland food production, since this is historically the outcome of subsidized investments and inputs. In the jeepney economy it is interesting to investigate the effects of tariff liberalization and the reform of food policies, as well as those of technical change in lowland agriculture resulting from R&D investment (the Green Revolution).

The 'Tuk-tuk' Economy: Net Food Exporter with EOI Policies

The tuk-tuk economy is similar to the jeepney economy in that food production is a major agricultural activity. It differs, however, in that it has natural comparative advantage in food production, and its industrial growth is based much more heavily on the expansion of labour-intensive, export-oriented manufactures. This can be construed as a stylized picture of Thailand, at least after the 1970s.[17] Since this economy is a net food exporter, the food sector is not protected and international trade is permitted more or less freely; food prices may still be subject to some domestic policy objectives so that world market influences may be modified at times, but food policies by themselves are unlikely to increase producer incentives relative to other sectors.[18] Because the manufacturing sector is both large and labour-intensive, growth of its output generates a large increase in labour demand. This raises the opportunity cost of agricultural labour, since higher industrial labour demand is satisfied by migration from agricultural sectors. In uplands, higher labour costs tend to reduce the profitability of forest clearance for agriculture and to increase the relative returns to the less labour-intensive plantation crops rather than food production. Therefore, higher labour costs tend to reduce deforestation, though this may be offset to some extent by the switch to relatively land-intensive plantation crops. In the tuk-tuk economy, it is important to address issues such as the environmental effects of an investment shock in manufacturing.

The 'Becak' Economy: Exportable Plantation Crops with ISI Policies

A third stylization is that of an economy pursuing ISI in manufacturing, while earning foreign exchange from agricultural and natural resource sector exports. This can be thought of as, for example, a stylized picture of an economy like that of Indonesia after the 1970s, or Sri Lanka prior to trade policy reforms, or Malaysia at an earlier stage of its development.[19]

While food production may dominate land use in lowlands, in uplands it is plantation crops that are prevalent. Although this economy is structurally very similar to the jeepney economy, three important features set it apart. First, the dominance of plantation crops in uplands means that changes in the food sector (such as technological progress in lowland food production) are unlikely to exert much influence over upland land use and deforestation. Rather, it is changes directly affecting profitability in plantation crop production that are likely to have the greatest effects on agricultural expansion. Second, the plantation sector may have access to capital, broadly speaking, that is sector-specific. This includes new technological opportunities achieved through crop-specific research, and possibly foreign financing for productive investments as well. Third, for some purposes it is convenient to reinterpret the 'plantation' sector as meaning commercial forestry, in which case we must distinguish between two types of forestry activity in uplands: formal sector forestry, with defined property rights, products which are sold, and the possibility of investment; and informal sector forestry, in which the key features are open access, non-marketed outputs and no capital reinvestment.

In this economy interesting issues for study include the deforestation effects of increased foreign investments in plantation crops, as well as questions about the effects of terms of trade, trade policy and growth in other factor endowments.

The 'Proton' Economy: Exportable Plantation Crops with EOI Policies

Finally, it is useful to define a fourth representative economy in which industrial production is predominantly for export rather than for the domestic market, and in which, as in the becak economy, upland agriculture is overwhelmingly devoted to plantation crops or timber production, both for export.[20] In this economy food is likely to be a net import (as it is in present-day Malaysia), with extensive government regulations on its price as well as subsidies for domestic food producers, located mainly in lowlands.

Figure 3.2 provides a schematic summary of each of the four representative economies in terms of its main distinguishing features. Naturally, although the diagram may give the impression of precision in terms of sectoral orientation, food markets and upland land use, it should be understood that these are stylizations of very imprecise underlying phenomena. Finally, Table 3.8 summarizes the major types of economic 'shocks' that are of obvious interest in a study of the general equilibrium determinants of land allocation and natural resource use changes. Again, the list is hardly exhaustive; rather, it captures the main types of shock that might be thought to drive an environmental composition effect.

3.6 SUMMING-UP AND CONCLUSIONS

A generic economic model of the kind presented in Chapter 2 can yield a wide range of insights as to the environmental and welfare implications of policy and other shocks in a developing economy. Clearly, however, the precise impact of a shock depends on the structure of the economy in which

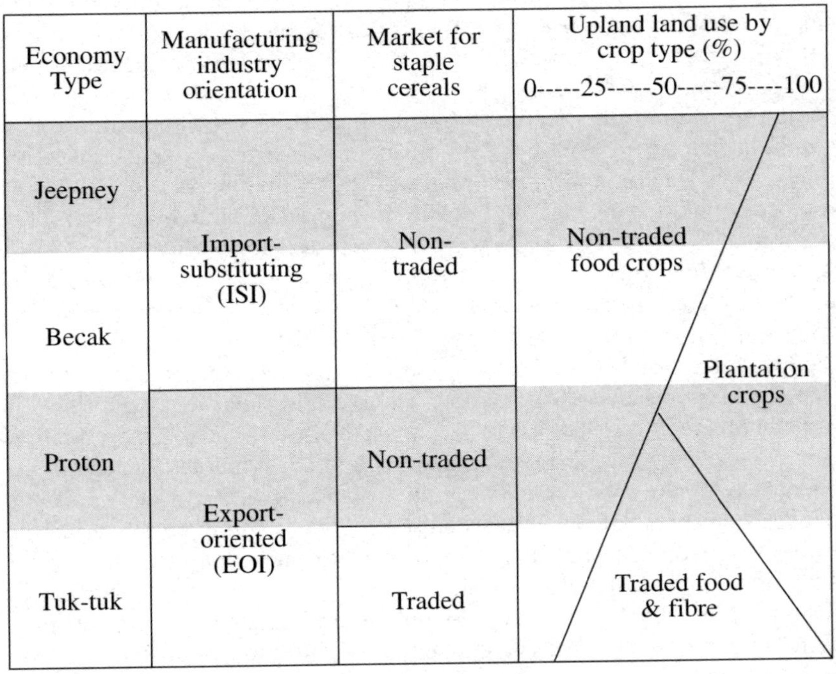

Economy Type	Manufacturing industry orientation	Market for staple cereals	Upland land use by crop type (%) 0-----25-----50-----75----100
Jeepney	Import-substituting (ISI)	Non-traded	Non-traded food crops
Becak			Plantation crops
Proton	Export-oriented (EOI)	Non-traded	
Tuk-tuk		Traded	Traded food & fibre

Figure 3.2   Schematic summary of economic structure in representative economies

*Table 3.8:	Illustrative economic shocks*

Shock	Characteristics
Terms of trade	Rise in price of manufactured good
Labour force growth	Increase in aggregate labour endowment
Manufacturing investment	Increase in manufacturing sector capital stock
Trade liberalization	Tariff reduction
Green Revolution	Technical progress in lowland food sector
Plantation sector investment	Increase in capital specific to exportable tree crop sector

it occurs. In this chapter we have identified some key features of developing Asian economies that are relevant to the assessment of the environmental implications of economic shocks. The structure of an economy, and the historical and institutional circumstances that it embeds, may determine whether a given economic shock has a positive, negative or negligible effect on key environmental variables such as the rate of deforestation, the expansion of upland agriculture or the intensification of agricultural land use.

On the basis of an empirical review, in this chapter we have identified several common features of resource-based developing economies, and some other important features that distinguish one from another. The common features include aspects of economic structure that are determined by a factor endowment set which is initially heavy on natural resources and unskilled labour but light on capital and human capital. This economic structure also reflects past policy decisions which, in general, promoted the growth of import-competing manufactures and weakened links between domestic and international markets for staple cereals. The common features also include spatial characteristics, specifically a fundamental distinction between lowlands and uplands. The differences between these two regions are based on specific land quality characteristics (including climatic features) that make uplands less efficient areas for production than lowlands. Thus in our stylization 'upland' connotes 'marginal': it encompasses the frontier between intensive cultivation and the forest, between commercial and subsistence production, and between private property and open access. In nearly every developing economy, agricultural development has included an element of expansion at this margin in response to emerging market opportunities, and taking advantage of institutional weaknesses, with accompanying degradation of forest and land resources.

Our review also highlights structural differences among economies that can reasonably be expected to play a part in conditioning responses to shocks. Among these, two in particular stand out: the trade orientation of manufacturing sectors, and the extent to which domestic food prices are responsive to international price shocks. These structural differences, in turn, imply variations in the relative importance of certain policy regimes. An informal discussion and comparison of the four representative economies constructed by varying these two assumptions only (Table 3.8) suggests two preliminary conclusions. First, institutional weaknesses matter a great deal, both directly and in interaction with economic policies. Second, there may be very few predictions of environmental outcomes associated with particular economic shocks that are *generally* true, even when we take account only of one or two ways in which economic structure may vary across nations.

NOTES

1. As a consequence, rural population density (persons/sq. km) peaked in Asia during the 1970s, whereas it has increased every decade in the other developing regions (source of basic data: World Bank, *World Development Indicators 2001*).
2. The literature on these two development strategies is vast, and only a brief summary highlighting their main features is given here. For a review of this literature and the historical experience, see Papageorgiou *et al.* (1991) and Rodrik (1995). In practice, many countries pursued hybrid policies that combined some elements of import substitution and export orientation, and many moved from an early phase of import substitution to more liberal trade and export orientation. This has given rise to continuing controversy over the role of trade policy in successful growth, and whether the dichotomy is not overdrawn, with some arguing that an initial import substitution phase can be seen as providing a platform from which subsequent export-orientated industrialization can 'take off'. Here, we do not aim to get into this controversy, but to introduce the elements of these strategies that are important for our subsequent discussion of how environmental outcomes may be influenced by the interaction of trade policies and economic structure.
3. Labour-abundant developing countries have natural comparative advantage in labour-intensive industries, and in the absence of trade policies tended to import capital-intensive products. Protection, by promoting import-substituting production, thus favours relatively capital-intensive industries.
4. See Corden (1971) and Dornbusch (1974) for theoretical expositions of these effects.
5. This shift to export promotion was often accompanied by continued protection of selected import-substituting industries. For example, countries such as Thailand and Indonesia adopted policies intended to promote export growth by natural resource and labour-intensive sectors through a variety of means ranging from 'competitive' exchange rate depreciations (Warr 1984) to export-processing zones (Warr 1989) while maintaining high levels of protection for ISI sectors such as the automotive industry.
6. From his foreword to Schiff and Valdés (1991: vii).
7. See Chapter 8 for a more detailed examination of the Thai case.
8. 'The 1990s has seen the rise of tree plantations as the most powerful force behind the conversion of forest lands in [the Indonesian islands of] Sumatra and Kalimantan. The government supported the development of pulp wood and palm oil plantations, using incentives such as free land, subsidised capital, and free use of standing timber. Rising domestic and international demand for palm oil, pulp, and paper . . . has given additional impetus to the growth of these industries' (Schweithelm and Glover 1999: 6).

9.   The data on 'arable' land in Table 3.3 exclude such permanently abandoned land and so understate the extent to which land conversion from 'other' uses, including forest, to agricultural production has occurred.

10. Although beyond the scope of this book, the case of China deserves mention at this point. Paradoxically, the opening of the Chinese economy since 1980 has generated enormous local pressures for self-sufficiency in staple foods, among other commodities (Young 2000), as well as empowering provincial authorities to adopt policies aimed at that goal. The result has been massive expansion of food production not only in areas (such as the river deltas) that have obvious comparative advantage, but also in hinterland and upland regions ecologically unsuited to intensification. Intensification of pastoral lands in Northwest China, for example, is contributing to desertification, as well as to a huge increase in the number of dust storms annually sweeping over Beijing and the eastern seaboard, and beyond to countries around the Pacific Rim (*Far Eastern Economic Review* July 2001; see also Lin and Zhang 1998).

11. Modern varieties of rice are also stiff-strawed and of short stature, to increase light use efficiency and reduce grain losses when plants bend (or 'lodge') under the weight of their grain during monsoon rain and winds. They are rapid-maturing and non-photoperiod sensitive, meaning that plant growth and grain maturity occur in a fixed number of days rather than in response to seasonal changes in day length and temperature, and allow more than one cropping cycle per year.

12. Badan Urusan Logistic, or National Logistical Agency.

13. A memoir by Salas (1987) provides a lively account of Philippine efforts to eliminate rice imports through state support of technology, infrastructure and prices during the Marcos regime (1965–86). His narrative makes it clear that efforts to achieve rice self-sufficiency were aimed as much at political as at developmental goals.

14. Of course, farm-specific characteristics – human capital endowments, risk aversion and so on – will also constrain entry to the market. Accordingly, the spatial boundary shown in Figure 3.1 is probably best thought of as a broad and rather fuzzy band rather than as a dimensionless line.

15. This was documented in a study by Cruz and Francisco (1993: 26), who concluded that 'migrants [to upland areas] are motivated more by lack of other livelihood options than by the attractiveness of destination lands'.

16. This characterization does not preclude international trade in food (and indeed, both countries mentioned do engage in this). But such trade as does take place is small in volume relative to the domestic market, and as the result of this, product differentiation and domestic market interventions, the international and domestic prices are effectively independent.

17. The tuk-tuk, a highly manoeuvrable and colourful three-wheeled motorcycle taxi, exemplifies the exuberant and fast-paced spirit of urban Thai culture.

18. In Thailand, the major food-exporting country in the region, rice exports were taxed for government revenue purposes and at times to lower domestic prices; government policies almost always had the effect of depressing domestic prices, though some (limited) subsidies reduced the net negative impact on the sector (see Siamwalla and Setboonsarng 1990).

19. The becak is a bicycle taxi (or rickshaw) common in rural Indonesia.

20. 'Proton' is the name of Malaysia's 'national' car, produced as a joint venture with a leading Japanese maker.

4. Deforestation and upland land degradation in an open economy: empirical and analytical foundations

4.1 INTRODUCTION

In Chapter 2 we discussed the general equilibrium modelling of environment, policy and development with reference to a highly abstract model of an economy subject to environmental damage. In Chapter 3 we considered some special characteristics of Asian developing countries not captured in such generic models, and ways in which these structural features might condition environmental and economic responses to policy and other changes. In this chapter we return to a formal modelling approach in order to focus on the likely effects of market and policy changes affecting developing Asian countries; specifically, in the 'representative' economies described in section 3.5. In constructing models of the representative economies we retain the emphasis on natural resource issues, primarily deforestation and land degradation (though the models can be extended with relative ease to address other environmental issues, such as industrial emissions). The focus on natural resource issues is not intended to imply that other types of environmental problems are unimportant. Rather, it is because a high degree of stylization and simplification is necessary in order to provide a coherent yet concise problem statement for modelling purposes. The trade-off permits us to identify and explain the main economic processes, generate predictive statements, and motivate the more detailed, yet less transparent, extensions and empirical applications found in Chapters 5–8.

4.2 MODELLING TRADE AND ENVIRONMENTAL PROCESSES: STYLIZED FACTS

We begin in this section with a model that can be used to explore and understand, in stylized form, environment–economy interactions in open developing countries. In designing such a model, our goal is to capture key aspects of economic structure as well as the environmental processes discussed in earlier chapters, that is, deforestation and the degradation of upland agricultural land, and their intersectoral effects. Obviously, to model these environmental processes and describe the general equilibrium of the economy require many simplifications and generalizations, both about the economy as a whole and about the many features of the economy that interest us less directly. Our response to this challenge is to build on the approach used in Chapter 2, that is, to characterize the economy as consisting of a few key sectors producing distinct products and using distinct technologies. By assumption, these sectors are linked through markets for products and factors of production, and also (in some cases) through externalities associated with environmental damages. Since product and factor markets may also extend beyond the domestic economy through trade, migration and international investment, our specification of factor and product markets ensures both that we capture important linkages among sectors and that we guarantee both internal and external balance, that is, that national income is equal to expenditure and the trade deficit is zero, with full employment of factors.

As the discussion in earlier chapters has indicated, there are some features of developing, resource-intensive economies that must be captured in some form if modelling is to be linked in a useful way to empirical analysis and policy formulation. In the remainder of this section we introduce five key features that cause our model to depart from a generic neoclassical structure. These are the spatial differentiation of factor endowments and production; the absence of property rights in some resources; interregional labour migration; food markets and pricing; and environmental externalities.

Spatial Characteristics

In developing countries geography is a major feature of economic life: even more so than in wealthy countries, where infrastructure and technology are widely and effectively deployed to compensate for geographical heterogeneity. Sub-national regions of developing countries are frequently referred to by their geographic characteristics, whether distance from major centres ('the provinces'), altitude ('uplands', 'highlands') climatic features ('dry zone') or related conditions. In short, geomorphological, climatic and even cultural differences, as well as economic distinctions, serve to identify separate zones within a country. A major division in nearly all agricultural or resource-based economies (albeit with various names) is that between *lowland* (mainly flat, low-altitude areas with irrigation or water impoundment structures serving wide areas) and *upland* (mainly hilly or steep land, unirrigated, and including mid- to high-altitude areas). We propose to adopt this dichotomy as a stylization of spatial differences within a developing country. The key point captured by this division is that upland and lowland land are distinct, and that one cannot be transformed into the other. Land, as a factor of production, is regionally immobile.

In most developing countries, centuries of deforestation and agricultural expansion in *lowland* regions – coastal plains and deltas, and the inland flood plains of major river valleys – have transformed these areas to permanent agricultural systems. Lowland agricultural technologies typically rely heavily on land-improving technologies and investments, especially irrigation and water impoundment structures and yield-increasing improved cultivars. Deforestation and even soil erosion are relatively minor issues in such intensively farmed lowland areas (Lindert 2000), although other land use-related environmental problems, especially long-term land quality degradation (Cassman and Pingali 1995) and health-related side-effects of agricultural chemical use (Rola and Pingali 1993) are of considerable importance in some countries.

Uplands, which we define as all other cultivated and cultivable lands, exhibit a different range of environmental processes, among which soil erosion and deforestation are by far the most prominent.[1] These phenomena are observed both directly, and through their secondary manifestations in the degradation of watershed function and the rising costs of activities such as irrigation and hydroelectric power generation that depend on reliable supplies of clean water. Upland agricultural production, by and large, involves less fixed investment in land (with some famous exceptions, such as the rice terraces in Banaue, Philippines), and in other ways also are generally less intensive in the use of non-labour inputs. National and international investments in yield-increasing agricultural technologies – the Green Revolution – have had their greatest successes in lowland areas with superior water availability and control (Lipton with Longhurst 1989; David and Otsuka 1994), and these persistent differences in technology and productivity lie at the heart of our upland–lowland spatial distinction. Technologies for cereal production in uplands rely more heavily than in lowlands on unimproved seed varieties, *in situ* soil fertility and rainfall, and thus require much less labour per unit of output produced. Lowland production, in contrast, is strongly associated with the adoption of improved seed varieties and a higher use of complementary inputs such as fertilizer. New cereal technologies are land saving relative to traditional methods, and, with the exception of fully mechanized systems, the share of labour in total production cost is correspondingly higher (Coxhead 1992; Hayami and Kikuchi 2001; Coxhead *et al.* 2002). Uplands also have endowments of forested land and are the location for production of many perennial crops.

Property Rights and Forest Land Conversion

Finally, our definition of upland also takes in frontier areas on the boundary between agricultural cultivation and areas of permanent cover such as forest or agricultural systems based on long-term forest–fallow rotations. We assume that all upland agricultural land is 'created' by the use of labour to clear forest or other permanent cover, along with associated tasks such as burning and the removal of rocks and stumps; we refer to this process as deforestation or land- clearing.[2]

How is forest land acquired for this purpose? Frontier areas in developing countries tend to be geographically remote and to lie near, or in some cases beyond, the effective boundaries of national economic and legal institutions. While remoteness has a number of important implications for the kinds of goods produced and technologies used, perhaps its most striking feature in developing countries is that property rights in land beyond the zone of permanently settled agricultural cultivation are frequently poorly defined or enforced. At the limit, there is no constraint on the colonization and use of forest land; it is an *open access* resource. This characteristic of the agricultural frontier in uplands enables very different forms of economic behaviour compared with lowlands, where land ownership and use rights are generally better defined and more effectively enforced. Specifically, if property rights are absent or unenforceable, then users of the land face a different set of incentives with respect to forest clearing than others in the economy who benefit from the existence of standing forest. When forest clearing is unrestricted, private producers will clear a greater area than is socially optimal, generating a negative externality for society as a whole.

Migration

Overlapping the spatial features just discussed, several aspects of *intersectoral* markets have important implications for developing economies with large natural resource sectors. Labour mobility is one such aspect. Traditional analyses of the causes of deforestation and agricultural expansion in uplands attribute much resource degradation to the activities of migrants: sometimes from lowlands; more frequently from other upland areas where the resource base has been depleted by past activities. At the level of the economy, however, the labour market plays other important roles. When labour is mobile among sectors, it moves in response to changes that alter its relative productivity. Asia's Green Revolution provides an excellent example. As described in Chapter 3, the technical innovations of the Green Revolution, which had disproportionately large effects on rice yields in lowland irrigated areas relative to uplands, promoted wider adoption by farmers. Consequently, labour productivity rose faster in lowlands than in uplands during the Green Revolution, and this elicited an intersectoral and interregional migration response in which agricultural workers left upland areas for jobs in lowland agriculture (Kikuchi and Hayami 1983; David and Otsuka 1994). In countries and regions experiencing high adoption rates of the new cereals technologies, the associated labour demand growth must have offset, to some extent at least, prevailing economic pressures driving rural migrants into upland areas.

Looking beyond agriculture, there is abundant evidence of 'down-slope' migration in developing Asian countries during phases of rapid growth in labour-intensive non-agricultural sectors. The decade-long investment boom that began in about 1986 in Thailand fuelled tremendously rapid growth of labour-intensive, export-oriented manufacturing industries. Agriculture, historically the mainstay of the economy and the primary employer, captured only a tiny fragment of the investment boom and, as the most labour-intensive sector, found itself increasingly unable to compete with wages offered in other industries. From 1989 to 1995 industry absorbed nearly 3 million workers out of a total agricultural labour force of about 20 million; as a result, planted area began to decline – most rapidly in upland areas – and agricultural output growth rates decelerated substantially (Coxhead and Jiraporn 1999). In order to capture these phenomena, which are central features of structural change in developing countries, we distinguish between the spatial migration of labour between upland and lowland regions, and the more general movement of labour among sectors, which we describe as *intersectoral mobility*. This choice of terms reflects our assumption that within each region (upland and lowland) the intersectoral movement of labour does not have a significant spatial component, while the interregional movement (up-slope or down-slope) does. The significance of the distinction between intersectoral and interregional mobility becomes clearer when interregional migration costs are significant.

Domestic Markets for Staple Cereals

Modelling intersectoral relationships also requires careful attention to the market for staple foods. As shown in Chapter 3, in most developing Asian countries most upland agriculture is devoted to staple food production, whether cereals, coarse grains or starches. The markets for such goods are sufficiently idiosyncratic that it would in most cases be a serious mistake to model them symmetrically with other types of goods – or even with other agricultural products. First, staple food production is a major area of economic activity, employing a large share of the agricultural labour force and occupying much, if not most, agricultural land. Second, among poor populations, expenditure on basic foodstuffs is a large part of total spending, often accounting for more than 50 per cent of daily caloric requirements (IRRI 2001), and demand for them is typically highly inelastic with respect to price. Income elasticities are also low, an empirical regularity known as Engel's law. Third, as discussed in Chapter 3, food self-sufficiency is a prominent feature of the state's economic development strategy in most poor countries, and the cereal grain sector is typically the target of a wide range of policy interventions involving regulation of both domestic and international trade. The food market is thus prominent in factor incomes and household expenditures, government finances and international trade: all four of the criteria that Timmer (1986) identifies as meriting a general equilibrium modelling treatment.

In international markets, most grains are traded and priced as undifferentiated commodities. For example, corn from one location is usually a very close substitute for corn from another, so consumers for the most part are indifferent between imported and domestically produced corn. This implies that excess demand or supply in grain markets is offset by international trade, with the result that its price is approximately equal to the domestic-currency equivalent of the world price, adjusted by transport costs and trade taxes (the *law of one price*). But it is a striking fact that staple food prices in many developing countries do not reflect prevailing international prices; in the short and medium run at least, the law of one price is frequently violated. In fact, it is domestic market conditions that are the key determinants of food prices. In some countries – or some sub-national regions – this is due to transport costs that make trade in food unprofitable. In others, it is food policy that breaks the link between international and domestic markets. Sometimes government agencies assume part or all of the responsibility for food marketing and actively intervene in markets to defend a target price. Regulatory barriers to profitable food trade, whatever their source, prevent international arbitrage and thus cause domestic food prices to respond to domestic demand and supply factors. In the extreme case, they behave as though food were a *non-traded* good: that is, one whose price is determined entirely in the domestic market. So widespread is this phenomenon in developing countries that to model food as a 'pure' traded good with a price set only in international markets (even when adjusted for tariffs and other trade costs) constitutes a serious misspecification.[3]

Economic models in which food markets play a prominent role must therefore be cognisant not only of the spatial differences in food production technologies noted earlier in this section, but also of the implications of different specifications of the market-clearing mechanism. In contrast to traded-goods markets, in which excess demand or supply can be eliminated through imports or exports, the market for food as a non-tradable clears with an endogenous price. When the food market is 'large' in relation to economic aggregates such as employment, national income, consumer expenditures or government budgets, endogenous changes in the supply or demand for food can have significant general equilibrium effects. These effects are very important elements of the analysis that evolves as we develop the basic model in section 4.3.

Intersectoral Externalities

In section 4.2 we noted that a consequence of open access to forests is that producers will clear forest at a rate greater than would be socially optimal, as they ignore consumer benefits derived from standing forest. Such environmental externalities may also have intersectoral or interregional dimensions. In developing country agriculture, the loss of watershed function and the transport of soil and other solids introduced to the water system by agriculture-related soil erosion confer negative externalities on downstream water users, including irrigated lowland agriculture and non-agricultural activities such as hydroelectric power generation. These external effects are notoriously difficult to measure (see Chapter 2), especially as their causes (removal of permanent land cover and soil disturbance through cultivation) and effects (changes in the volume and seasonal distribution of water delivery, siltation of reservoirs and canals, accelerated wear of turbines) are separated by both space and time and are modified by many intervening factors. However, possible intersectoral effects should not be ignored simply because they cannot easily be quantified. They should be recognized, and the consequences of their existence examined, while noting the limitations imposed by the considerable information deficiencies that make quantification particularly difficult. In section 4.6, we consider a relevant subset of intersectoral externalities and trace their general equilibrium implications.

4.3   THE BASIC MODEL

Stylized Facts and Assumptions

In this section we present a relatively simple model that captures the key stylized facts just discussed, and generates predictions of changes in key economic and environmental variables when the economy is subjected to certain kinds of exogenous 'shocks'. As indicated above, we incorporate spatial features by positing two regions, upland and lowland. Within each region we allow for the production of two goods. This rather abstract specification is capable of a number of interpretations in light of empirical realities of the kinds introduced in Chapter 3. For the present, however, we assume that one sector in the lowland region produces manufactures, and the other an agricultural product (food), while one sector in the upland region produces food and the other a non-food agricultural product. Food is thus produced in two spatially separate sectors with distinct types of land; by implication, regional food production technologies are distinct.

We assume in this chapter that manufactures and the non-food upland product are freely traded (or traded subject to an *ad valorem* tariff) with the rest of the world at given world prices, but that food is non-traded. Total food supply from lowlands and uplands must be just equal, in equilibrium, to total domestic demand, and its price adjusts relative to the prices of the traded goods to ensure that this market-clearing condition is satisfied.[4]

For factor markets, the critical information required for modelling purposes is the elasticity of aggregate supply and the degree of intersectoral mobility in response to differences in relative returns. We make the following assumptions. The lowland sectors each use labour and a sector-specific factor (capital in manufacturing, land in agriculture). The two upland sectors both use labour and agricultural land. Labour is assumed to be fully employed and freely mobile among sectors and regions. As discussed above, land is region-specific; within uplands, however, agricultural land is 'mobile' (that is, it can be reallocated) between the food and non-food sectors. Agricultural land in uplands is in elastic supply, being created by clearing forest, an activity which requires only labour. We assume open access to forest land, so there is no non-economic constraint on the amount of land that can be converted by forest clearing. In lowlands, the supply of land is assumed to be exogenously given. Finally, manufacturing sector capital is assumed to be specific to that sector (that is, can be used only in that sector), and its supply grows at an exogenous rate. The schematic diagram in Figure 4.1 summarizes the domestic economy, highlighting interregional and intersectoral linkages that operate through the markets for mobile factors and non-traded food.

For analytical purposes it is convenient to summarize the features of the model in relation to the standard models used in trade theory and environmental economics. Relative to a standard *n*-sector extension of the Heckscher–Ohlin (H–O) model, the workhorse of neoclassical trade theory, our model embodies the following departures:

1. We assume that the flow of services provided by standing forest is a public good; by assumption there is no market for these services, which

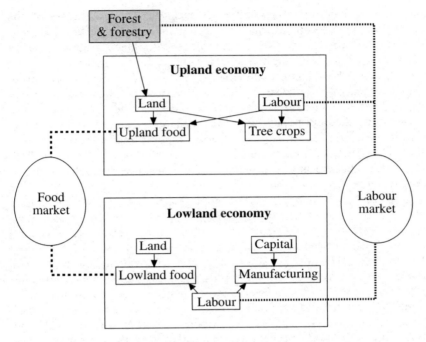

Figure 4.1   A stylized two-region economy with non-traded food and interregional labour mobility

are lost, *pro rata*, when forest is cleared to make land (this is the source of the only externality in most versions of the model).

2. One factor of production (agricultural land in uplands) is endogenously supplied, by contrast with the H–O assumption of fixed domestic factor endowments. The model may equivalently be interpreted as representing a four-good economy with one intermediate good (land in the upland region), produced using only labour.

3. Whereas the standard H–O model assumes all goods are traded at given world prices, in our model at least one good is non-traded, so its price is determined endogenously in domestic markets.

4. Because of the assumption of regionally distinct land endowments, one of the goods (food) is produced using two different technologies, or (equivalently) using land of different quality in separate regions, as discussed at the start of the previous section.

In the H–O model with complete markets, fixed factor endowments and all goods traded at world market prices, the production and consumption sides of the economy are functionally separate. The two halves of the economy are linked only through an aggregate budget condition that constrains total expenditure on goods to total national income; that is, a sum no greater than the value of payments to productive factors, or value-added. This separability greatly simplifies the analytics, since it means that changes occurring on the supply (or production) side of the economy can be analysed independently of incomes and consumer preferences. The classic trade-theoretic papers on growth, structural change and distribution (Jones 1965, 1971) all employ separability. In our model, however, assumptions (1), (2) and (3) each constitute a source of non-separability. This means that the consumers' problem and the producers' problem must be solved simultaneously.

Some of the above departures from H–O are shared with other models of trade and deforestation in that part of the environmental economics literature in which spatial features are explicitly modelled. Features (1) and (2) are both present in models by Lopez and Niklitschek (1991) and Deacon (1995). Feature (3), non-tradability, is not possible in the Deacon model, which contains only two goods and no traded factors, and is not exploited in the three-good Lopez and Niklitschek model. This means that domestic demand and supply conditions have no impact on *any* product prices in their models. Feature (4), spatially distinct production of a good, is feasible in our model because we assume that more than one good is produced in each region, a characteristic not shared with earlier models. The structural assumption that food is both non-traded and produced in more than one region is a fundamental difference between our approach and that of earlier models. In the latter, the regional economies (analogous to our uplands and lowlands) are linked only through the labour market. Shocks that alter labour productivity in one region then have direct and unambiguous effects in the other, through migration. The addition of a new link, the food market, provides for a much richer approximation of the stylized facts of developing countries, and results, naturally, in somewhat greater complexity and ambiguity of results.

Assumptions (3) and (4) were both embedded in our earlier work (Coxhead and Jayasuriya 1994, 1995), but assumptions (1) and (2), which come from the natural resource modelling literature, were not. The inclusion of food as a non-traded good enables the empirically important influence of domestic demand and supply factors on commodity prices to be explicitly incorporated without sacrificing the convenience of a small-country model. The natural resource literature lacks a structured consideration of the role of endogenous prices and spatial asymmetries in production. On the other hand, models in Coxhead and Jayasuriya (1994, 1995) did not consider deforestation or aggregate agricultural land expan-

sion. The model we are about to present is thus a synthesis and consolida-
tion of previous efforts (most of the earlier models just referred to can now
be generated as special cases) as well as an extension incorporating innovations that permit the study of technical progress, intersectoral externalities
and policy reforms of types relevant to many developing countries.

The model just sketched captures, in stylized form, the main economic
and physical links among regions and sectors in which environmental
damages occur, and the rest of the economy. It is intended to serve as a
vehicle for understanding both the broad economic implications of
deforestation and land degradation, and the environmental consequences
of economic changes originating not only within the uplands but also in
other sectors and regions. In the remainder of this chapter we first present
the necessary theoretical tools and then construct the model. In the course
of this exposition we expand on each aspect noted in the thumbnail sketch
just provided. The chapter concludes with a reflection on the advantages
and limitations of the modelling approach we have adopted.

Modelling Tools and Solutions

The modelling problem is compactly addressed using duality (Woodland
1982; Dixit and Norman 1980). Since the exposition requires some notation, Table 4.1 provides a summary of the main symbols, functions, abbreviations and parameters.

In each region, upland and lowland, a representative price-taking producer is assumed to maximize the revenue obtainable from regional factor
endowments, subject to the technological feasibility of the desired production plans. In uplands, two goods are produced, food (subscripted n, a
mnemonic for non-tradable) and non-food, or tree crops; the vectors of
upland prices and outputs are denoted $\mathbf{P}^U$ and $\mathbf{Y}^U$ respectively. We choose
units such that the price of non-food crops is unity, so p is the relative price
of food to tree crops in uplands. These goods are produced using a vector
$\mathbf{V}^U$ of upland inputs, containing labour (L^U) and upland land (T). Land,
however, must be cleared for production, and therefore some labour must
be devoted to this purpose. Following Lopez and Niklitschek (1991), we
suppose that each unit of land requires the input of a constant quantity α
of labour; thus $T = \alpha L$.[5] The upland producer's problem is then captured
by a revenue function:

$$R(T, L^U - \alpha T, p) = \max_{T,Y} \{\mathbf{P}^U \cdot \mathbf{Y}^U | \mathbf{V}^U\}.$$

The revenue function is non-decreasing and homogeneous of degree 1 in
$\mathbf{P}^U$ and $\mathbf{V}^U$. Partial derivatives of R with respect to the *j*th price give output

Table 4.1   Summary of algebraic notation used in Chapter 4

Symbol	Definition
p	Relative price of food[a]
q	Relative price of manufactures[a]
$\mathbf{P}^U$	Vector of upland prices $(p, 1)$
$\mathbf{P}^L$	Vector of lowland prices (p, q)
w_i	Relative price of factor i[a]
$\mathbf{V}^U$	Vector of upland factor endowments (L^U, T)
$\mathbf{V}^L$	Vector of lowland factor endowments $(L - L^U, \mathbf{K}) = (L - L^U, K_n, K_m)$
L^U	Labour used in upland region
L	Total labour endowment
T	Upland land endowment
K_n	Land endowment in lowland agriculture
K_m	Fixed capital in manufacturing
P	Consumer price vector $(p, q, 1)$
F	Forest land
D^v	Determinant in model variant v
Z_i	Excess demand for commodity i
A	Total factor productivity parameter for lowland agriculture
$\tilde{K}_n$	Physical endowment of lowland land
m	Income elasticity of food demand
$R(T, L^U - \alpha T, p)$	Upland region revenue function
$S(\mathbf{K}, L - L^U, p, q)$	Lowland region revenue function
$E(\mathbf{P}, T, u)$	Expenditure function
$E_T(\mathbf{P}, T, u)$	Negative of willingness to pay for standing forest
α	Unit labour input for forest clearing
B	Productivity parameter for lowland land
q^*	World price of manufactures
t	Tariff on manufactured imports

Note: [a] Numéraire price is that of tree crops.

supplies, which we denote by $R_i = \partial R(\mathbf{P}^U, \mathbf{V}^U)/\partial p_i > 0$. The derivative of the revenue function with respect to each factor endowment gives the shadow price of that factor; thus for upland land with price w_T, $w_T = \partial R(\mathbf{P}^U, \mathbf{V}^U)/\partial T$. By the assumption of a strictly convex technology set, the revenue function is strictly convex in $\mathbf{P}^U$ and strictly concave in $\mathbf{V}^U$, that is, $R_{jj} > 0$ for all j in $\mathbf{P}^U$, and $R_{ii} < 0$ for all i in $\mathbf{V}^U$.

Like the uplands, the lowland region also contains two sectors, producing food (n) and manufactures (m). The lowland output vector is $\mathbf{Y}^L$. The lowland price $\mathbf{P}^L$ has elements p and q, where the latter is the price of manufactures. Lowland food is produced on irrigated land, that is, land of fundamentally different quality from that used in uplands. However, the output of the lowland food sector is a perfect substitute in consumption for food produced in the uplands and is freely traded between regions, so there is only one economy-wide price for this good. Each industry uses a sector-specific factor (irrigated land and manufacturing capital), which we summarize as a vector $\mathbf{K} = (K_n, K_m)$, and labour. Thus the lowland producer's problem is to maximize revenues, taking prices and factor endowments as given, a problem captured by the lowland region revenue function:

$$S(\mathbf{K}, L - L^U, p, q) = \max_Y \{\mathbf{P}^L \cdot \mathbf{Y}^L \mid \mathbf{V}^L\}.$$

This revenue function has the same properties as those of the upland region. Its derivatives with respect to $\mathbf{P}$ give supply functions $S_i(\mathbf{P}^L, \mathbf{V}^L)$, $i = n, m$, which are non-decreasing and homogeneous of degree in $\mathbf{P}^L$ and $\mathbf{V}^L$. By the assumption of a strictly convex production technology, $S(\cdot)$ is convex in $\mathbf{P}^L$ and concave in $\mathbf{V}^L$.

The model permits analysis both of environmental outcomes and of economic welfare. Since the model is non-separable between supply and demand sides, however, the welfare analysis of commodity price shocks, technical progress and other supply-side phenomena requires an explicit model of consumer behaviour. In this basic version of the model we suppose utility to be derived both from the consumption of goods and from the existence of standing forest. The benefits from standing forest may be thought of as derived from biodiversity, watershed function, recreational use and/or existence values. These benefits are lost when forest is cleared for agricultural production; but because the forest-clearing decision takes no account of consumer preferences (output from forest-clearing activity is not marketed), the quantity of land cleared is exogenous to the consumer. The consumer's problem is to maximize utility subject to income and the quantity of standing forest. We assume utility to be separable between forest and marketed goods.

We can summarize aggregate consumption using an expenditure function $E(\mathbf{P}, F, u) = \min\{\mathbf{P} \cdot \mathbf{C} \mid u\}$, where u stands for aggregate utility, F is the quantity of forest land, and the vectors $\mathbf{P}$ and $\mathbf{C}$ contain prices and quantities of food, tree crops and the manufactured good. The consumer's enjoyment of the benefits of forest is quantity-rationed, so $E(\mathbf{P}, F, u)$ is a *conditional expenditure function* (Neary and Roberts 1980; Woodland 1982). For analytical convenience we substitute the quantity of upland agricultural land, T, defined as $1 - F$, where total upland area is normalized to unity. Since there is no market for forest, the marginal effect of a change in T, denoted E_T, is the virtual price of land cleared for agriculture, or the negative of the marginal amount the consumer is willing to pay to preserve standing forest. Therefore, we have $E_T \leq 0$.

As its definition indicates, the expenditure function gives the minimum expenditure necessary to achieve a target level of utility, u. It is non-decreasing and homogeneous of degree 1 in **P**. Partial derivatives of E(**P**, T, u) with respect to the jth price give compensated commodity demands by consumers, which we denote by $E_i = \partial E(\mathbf{P}, T, u)/\partial p_i > 0$. We assume strictly convex preferences, so E(·) is strictly concave in **P**. We assume that goods other than forest are substitutes in consumption, so $E_{ij} \geq 0$, $\forall$ i,j in **P**. Since utility is separable between marketed goods and forest, $E_{iT} = 0$.[6]

In equilibrium, total expenditure in the economy is equal to total income from both regions:

$$E(p, q, T, u) = R(T, L^U - \alpha T, p) + S(\mathbf{K}, L - L^U, p, q). \qquad (4.1)$$

We make the assumption that the food market clears not only across regions, but entirely within the domestic economy, as food is not internationally traded. The sum of regional supplies must therefore be equal to domestic demand, or:

$$R_n + S_n = E_n. \qquad (4.2)$$

As noted, a typical feature of upland land is that, at the margin, it is 'freely' accessible for conversion to agriculture, often for little more than the cost of the labour required to clear and prepare it and establish property rights to it. In fact, the act of forest clearing itself confers *de facto* use rights in many frontier areas. In constructing the model we assume that upland producers take no account of the social cost of deforestation. Thus (again following Lopez and Niklitschek 1991) we assume that upland producers devote labour to the clearing of forest to create agricultural land until the marginal value product of such land is just equal to the marginal cost of labour used to clear it, or:

$$R_T - \alpha R_L = 0. \qquad (4.3)$$

This formulation embodies the assumption that private producers do not consider social costs in their forest-clearing decisions. Because of this, in equilibrium there will typically be a greater amount of deforestation in uplands than is socially optimal.[7] Since consumers derive utility from standing forest, the rate of forest conversion for agriculture that is optimal for upland producers will confer a negative externality on society as a whole.

If we assume that labour is freely mobile between upland and lowland regions, that is, that it migrates between regions in response to changes in regional and sectoral labour productivity, then in equilibrium we have:

$$R_L - S_L = 0. \qquad (4.4)$$

The solution to equations (4.1)–(4.4) provides values for changes in the choice variables T and L^U as well as the relative price p and a money-metric of aggregate welfare change. These allow us to solve for changes in the sectoral allocation of upland land as well as net labour migration, employment by sector, factor prices and sectoral outputs. These in turn permit the construction of *ex post* measures of changes in other important indicators such as consumer welfare.

4.4 DEFORESTATION, AGRICULTURAL INTENSIFICATION AND MIGRATION

Approaches to Comparative Statics

With the model just developed we can now identify economy-wide driving forces behind the two main sources of environmental problems in uplands: agricultural land expansion, which is associated with deforestation; and intensification, which is associated with soil depletion and erosion. We can simultaneously identify the causes of interregional labour migration, which is represented as an endogenous response to external stimuli, rather than as an autonomous occurrence. One fundamental insight to emerge is that in any upland agricultural system connected through markets to a broader economy, it is not strictly correct to point to population pressure as an autonomous cause of upland land use changes. Rather, we find that the net migration rate is a response to the relative returns to labour in upland and lowland regions, and, within uplands, between more and less intensive forms of agricultural land use. A second fundamental insight is that when relative product prices in the upland region are endogenous, then the structure of upland production depends on economy-wide conditions even when labour is immobile between regions.

The signs and magnitudes of comparative static results from the model depend on values of the second derivatives of the revenue functions, especially that for the upland economy. In terms of the two-good, two-factor upland revenue function, the second derivative $R_{jL} > 0$ indicates that sector j is labour-intensive relative to sector k, from which it also follows that $R_{kL} < 0$, $R_{jT} < 0$, and $R_{kT} > 0$.[8] By Young's theorem, the same signs hold for each derivative with the order of subscripts reversed: $R_{Lj} > 0$, and so on, indicating the factor productivity effects of increases in each sector's price.

It can now readily be seen how the assumed structure of upland production will condition comparative static results. In the discussion of 'representative' economies in Chapter 3, several possible characterizations of upland economic conditions were explored. For the rest of this chapter we shall impose as a 'default' assumption that production in the upland food sector is labour-intensive relative to non-food, or $R_{nL} > 0$; $R_{nT} < 0$. As noted in Chapter 3, this assumption captures stylized features of typical agricultural systems in many developing countries. It is consistent, for example, with semi-subsistence or commercial food crop production systems that compete for land with perennials such as rubber, timber, pasture or even coffee.

The model contains three final goods: tree crops, food and manufactures. The non-food upland crop is chosen as a numéraire, with its price equal to 1 by choice of units. The food price is determined endogenously by (4.2), and the manufacturing price in terms of non-food, q, is exogenously given. Given our choice of numéraire, for a constant food price, a rise in q also represents an exogenous improvement in the terms of trade between lowland and upland regions, a property that we shall exploit at several points in the following discussion.

The effect of a change in some exogenous variable on the food price, the regional allocation of labour, deforestation and aggregate welfare depends on the ways in which sectors and regions are linked through the markets for labour and food. It also depends on key aspects of economic structure, as just discussed, and in particular on whether the manufacturing sector produces *importables* (tradable goods for which there is excess domestic demand in the initial equilibrium) or *exportables* (tradables for which there is excess domestic supply). We assume in the base case that manufactures are importables, but once again, the implications of alternative assumptions are considered at relevant points. Varying the assumptions about the factor intensity of upland production and the net trade position of manufactures amounts to the use of the model to describe, in stylized form, the different types of developing economy as introduced in Chapter 3.

In the labour market, we consider two extreme cases: perfect interregional labour mobility, and complete immobility. In an empirical sense, the former may be considered to depict a medium- to long-run case, whereas the latter represents the short run.

Few comparative static results obtained in a full general equilibrium context are unambiguous in sign without the imposition of additional restrictions on model structure. As the point of comparative statics is to identify the economic relationships that give rise to a particular result, in the following analyses we isolate each mechanism in turn by holding others constant. First, we suppose for analytical purposes that the price of food is exogenously fixed (or equivalently, that the law of one price applies in the food market as in those for other goods), so that the only endogenous price linking the two regions is that of labour. Subsequently, we restore the original assumption of non-traded food with an endogenous price and now suppose that labour is regionally immobile. This permits us to focus only on the forces that operate when the food market must clear domestically. Considering the same set of exogenous shocks under each pair of assumptions reveals the ways in which income and substitution effects in product markets transmit the effects of a shock between regions. In Appendix 4A we consider the effects of shocks when both food and labour markets clear simultaneously.

Comparative Statics When Food is a Traded Good and Labour is Regionally Mobile

When the food market clears through international trade rather than domestically, equation (4.2) does not hold. This restriction yields a model structure and comparative static results very similar to those of Lopez and Niklitschek (1991). For a change in each exogenous variable p, q, L, and K, solutions can be obtained by taking the total differentials of (4.3) and (4.4) and solving as a simultaneous system:

$$
\begin{bmatrix} R_{vv} & (R_{LT} - \alpha R_{LL}) \\ (R_{LT} - \alpha R_{LL}) & (R_{LL} + S_{LL}) \end{bmatrix} \begin{bmatrix} dT \\ dL^u \end{bmatrix} =
$$

$$
\begin{bmatrix} -(R_{nT} - \alpha R_{Ln})dp \\ S_{Lq}dq - (R_{Ln} - S_{Ln})dp + S_{LL}dL + S_{LK}dK \end{bmatrix} \tag{4.5}
$$

By Young's theorem we have $R_{ij} = R_{ji}$ and $S_{ij} = S_{ji}$ for all prices and quantities i, j. By the concavity of the revenue function in factor endowments we have $R_{LL} < 0$ and by assumption $R_{LT} > 0$. If the upland food sector is labour-intensive relative to non-food then $R_{Ln} > 0$; in lowlands, $S_{Ln} > 0$ by the assumption that labour is the only mobile factor within the region. The determinant of the coefficient matrix, D^L, is positive by the strict concavity of the revenue function.[9]

Considering a small change in each exogenous variable in turn, we obtain the following results. An increase in the price of the manufactured good, for example, gives:

$$
dL^U/dq = R_{vv}S_{Lq}/D^L < 0 \tag{4.6a}
$$

$$dT/dq = -(R_{LT} - \alpha R_{LL})S_{Lq}/D^L = -\beta\left(\frac{dL^U}{dq}\right) < 0 \qquad (4.6b)$$

where:

$$\beta = \left(\frac{R_{LT} - \alpha R_{LL}}{R_{vv}}\right) < 0$$

Higher labour productivity in lowlands causes down-slope migration; higher labour costs and diminished upland labour supply both cause the quantity of upland cleared for agriculture to diminish. A similar result emerges when there is exogenous growth in lowland non-labour factor endowments K_j, $j \in (n, m)$, regardless of the sector in which they are located:

$$dL^U/dK_j = R_{vv}S_{LK_j}/D^L < 0 \qquad (4.7a)$$

$$dT/dK_i = -\beta\left(\frac{dL^U}{dK_i}\right) < 0 \qquad (4.7b)$$

From these results it is also easy to anticipate that technical progress in either lowland sector relative to uplands would have a similar effect, causing labour to migrate to the sector where its productivity is higher, and thus reducing incentives to clear forest for upland cultivation (see section 4.5).

Conversely, an increase in the aggregate labour endowment causes upland agriculture and employment to expand, and promotes deforestation:

$$dL^U/dL = R_{vv}S_{LL}/D^L > 0 \qquad (4.8a)$$

$$dT/dL = -\beta\left(\frac{dL^U}{dL}\right) > 0 \qquad (4.8b)$$

None of the results in (4.6)–(4.8) depend critically on the sectoral structure of upland production. Any shock that causes down-slope (or up-slope) migration also causes land-clearing activity to decline (or increase), just as in Lopez and Niklitschek (1991). This is not true, however, of an exogenous change in the price of food:

$$dL^U/dp = [(R_{nT} - \alpha R_{Ln})(R_{LT} - \alpha R_{LL}) - R_{vv}(R_{Ln} - S_{Ln})]/D^L \qquad (4.9a)$$

$$dT/dp = [(R_{LT} - \alpha R_{LL})(R_{Ln} - S_{Ln}) - (R_{nT} - \alpha R_{nL})(R_{LL} + S_{LL})]/D^L \qquad (4.9b)$$

A rise in the price of food causes resources to be reallocated to food crop production. Food, however, is labour-intensive, so the food price increase raises wages through Stolper–Samuelson effects. This in turn makes land clearing more costly. Thus net migration may go in either direction, and the sign and extent of any change in land clearing cannot be ascertained. However, if the labour productivity effects of a food price increase are as high or higher in the lowland labour market as in uplands (that is, if $S_{Ln} \geq R_{Ln}$), then $dL^U/dp < 0$ and $dT/dp < 0$ when upland food production is labour-intensive.[10]

From the foregoing we see that when food is produced in more than one region, an increase in its price may result in either an expansion or a contraction of upland agricultural cultivation, depending on the structure and technology of the food sectors. There are some clear limiting cases: for example, upland area will expand if lowland supply response is very inelastic, and it will contract if wages increase sharply and cause land-clearing costs to become prohibitively high. These cases, in turn, hint at some possible policy approaches to the deforestation problem when food price policy promotes upland development.

The structure of our model also provides for a measure of aggregate welfare change. Once the change in the deforestation rate has been established, the total differential of (4.1) provides a solution for the effect of the positive terms of trade shock on aggregate real incomes and the flow of non-marketed benefits from standing forest. Denote the excess demand for manufactures by $Z_q = E_q(p, q, T, u) - S_q(K, L - L^U, p, q)$, noting that $Z_q > 0$ for a net import and $Z_q < 0$ for a net export. Taking an increase in q as an example we obtain:

$$E_u \frac{\partial u}{\partial q} + E_T \frac{\partial T}{\partial q} = -Z_q < 0. \qquad (4.10)$$

Since E_u is the inverse of the marginal utility of income, the first term on the left-hand side provides a measure of change in real expenditures. If there were no externality (that is, if willingness to pay for standing forest were zero), then this term would measure the pure welfare loss from a small change in q, which would be the real income decline due to the terms of trade change. When $E_T < 0$ and $\partial T/\partial q < 0$, the welfare loss associated with reduced real expenditure on marketed goods is partially compensated by the benefit of increased forest services; this is because higher wages induced by the rise in q reduce deforestation.[11] We can compute equivalent comparative static results for each of the other exogenous changes just considered.

Comparative Statics When Labour is Immobile but Food is Non-traded

The results provide some strong predictions about the interregional impacts of exogenous changes on the structure of production and environmental change in uplands, when the food market clears through trade at a constant price. We now suppose that food is non-traded, which creates the possibility that exogenous shocks may have additional welfare effects through endogenous commodity price changes. To focus on this story alone, assume for the moment that labour is immobile between regions. Then (4.4) does not hold, and the comparative static results are obtained by solving the system of equations obtained by total differentiation of (4.1)–(4.3):

$$
\begin{bmatrix}
E_u & 0 & E_T \\
-\mu E_u & -Z_{nn} & (R_{nT} - \alpha R_{Ln}) \\
0 & (R_{nT} - \alpha R_{Ln}) & R_{vv}
\end{bmatrix}
\begin{bmatrix}
du \\
dp \\
dT
\end{bmatrix}
$$

$$
=
\begin{bmatrix}
-Z_q dq + R_L dL^U + S_K dK + S_L dL \\
Z_{nq} dq - R_{nL} dL^U - S_{nK} dK - S_{nL} dL \\
0
\end{bmatrix}, \qquad (4.11)
$$

where $Z_{ij} = (E_{ij} - R_{ij} - S_{ij})$ for $i, j \in (p, q)$. For example, $Z_{nn} = (E_{nn} - R_{nn} - S_{nn})$ <0 is the derivative of excess demand for food with respect to its own price, and $Z_{nq} = (E_{nq} - S_{nq}) > 0$ is the derivative of Z_n with respect to q. The parameter $\mu = E_{nu}/E_u$ measures the income effect on the demand for food. The determinant of the coefficient matrix in this system can be written:

$$
-E_u D^p = -E_u \{ Z_{nn} R_{vv} + (R_{nT} - \alpha R_{Ln})^2 + m E_T (R_{nT} - \alpha R_{Ln}) \} < 0. \quad (4.12)
$$

Once again considering the effect of a terms of trade shock, we have:

$$
dp/dq = -(Z_{nq} - \mu Z_q) R_{vv}/D^p \quad > 0 \text{ if } \mu = 0 \qquad (4.13a)
$$

$$
dT/dq = (Z_{nq} - \mu Z_q)(R_{nT} - \alpha R_{Ln})/D^p \quad < 0 \text{ if } \mu = 0 \qquad (4.13b)
$$

Assume for the moment that there is no income effect, that is, that $m = 0$. When the price of the manufactured good increases, the substitution effect raises the domestic price of food. In uplands, a higher food price raises the return to labour, so increasing the cost of clearing new land. Thus, when food production is labour-intensive relative to other upland agriculture, the decline in the foreign terms of trade reduces deforestation even without interregional migration! Indeed, when labour is immobile, any change that raises the relative price of food must reduce T, since it is clear from (4.11) that $\text{sign}(dT/d\lambda_j) = -\text{sign}(dp/d\lambda_j)$ for all $\lambda_i \in \{q, L^U, K, L\}$.

Since $Z_q > 0$ for an importable, the pure income effect of a change in q will have the opposite effects. Reduced national income will cause the price of food to fall. In uplands this will increase the relative profitability of non-food, causing upland food to contract. Because upland food production is labour-intensive relative to non-food, the price of labour must fall in order for labour to remain fully employed. This reduction in the price of labour reduces the cost of deforestation, thereby stimulating further land-clearing activity.[12]

We now turn to the effects of exogenous increases in the endowments of sector-specific factors in lowlands. Equation (4.14) provides the results for K_i where $j = n$ indicates land in lowland agriculture, and $j = m$ indicates manufacturing capital:

$$dp/dK_j = -(S_{nKj} - \mu S_{Kj})R_{vv}/D^p \qquad (4.14a)$$

$$dT/dK_j = -(S_{nKj} - \mu S_{Kj})(R_{nT} - \alpha R_{Ln})/D^p. \qquad (4.14b)$$

For the case of an increase in lowland agricultural land, we have $S_{nK_n} > 0$. Since $D^p > 0$, the increase in lowland land reduces the price of food. However, it also generates extra income, which increases the demand for food (assuming $\mu > 0$). Thus the net food price effect of an increase in lowland land may take either sign. In practice, however, such income effects are typically dominated by substitution effects, so we expect the price-depressing effect to dominate.[13] If the food price falls (the bracketed term in (4.14a) is positive), this causes upland resources to shift to non-food crops and upland food production to contract. Because the latter sector is relatively labour-intensive, the associated release of factors generates downward pressure on wages to maintain full upland employment. Equation (4.14b) shows that when labour is regionally immobile, an increase in the lowland land endowment results in deforestation. If labour is allowed to migrate to lowlands, then the downward pressure on wages will be lower (as in equation (4.7)); but to the extent that wages do fall, there will be an increase in deforestation since land-clearing costs have fallen. Because we can expect greater down-slope migration in the long run, the associated wage decline will be lower and pressures for deforestation will diminish accordingly.

For the case of an increase in manufacturing capital, we have $S_{nK_m} < 0$. In this case both the factor market and income effects tend to raise the price of food. In uplands, there is an unambiguous reduction in land clearing, since capital growth in manufacturing results in both increased total food demand (the income effect) and reduced lowland food supply (the resource movement effect). In the longer run, down-slope migration will further enhance the pro-forest effect of this change. This analytical result indicates that investment in non-agricultural sectors can have strongly pro-environment effects at the forest margin.

Maintaining the assumption of interregional labour immobility, we can also explore the effects of exogenous growth of each regional labour force. The results for an exogenous increase in L^U are shown in equation (4.15). The increase in the labour endowment has the predictable effect of reducing wages in terms of both goods' prices; this raises the profitability of food and non-food production, so the demand for cleared land increases, leading to further deforestation (equation (4.15b)). Because the food sector is labour-intensive, its output will expand, so driving down its price (equation (4.15a)). As in earlier cases, the income effect exerts a countervailing influence, although empirically this is unlikely to dominate the overall result:

$$dp/dL^U = (R_{nL} - \mu R_L) R_{yy} / D^p \quad <0 \text{ if } \mu = 0 \qquad (4.15a)$$

$$dT/dL^U = -(R_{nL} - \mu R_L)(R_{nT} - \alpha R_{Ln}) / D^p \quad >0 \text{ if } \mu = 0. \quad (4.15b)$$

Finally, with no change in L^U, an increase in the lowland labour force is given by an increase in L. The results for food price and land clearing in uplands are shown in (4.16). At constant prices, the increase in L will expand output in both lowland sectors. The increase in food supply reduces the food price (subject to the countervailing income effect); in uplands, this price change causes resources to switch to non-food production. Lower profitability in upland food causes the sector to contract and release factors to the non-food sector. Because food is labour-intensive, the wage is driven down and deforestation increases:

$$dp/dL = (S_{nL} - \mu S_L) R_{yy} / D^p \quad <0 \text{ if } \mu = 0 \qquad (4.16a)$$

$$dT/dL = -(S_{nL} - \mu S_L)(R_{nT} - \alpha R_{Ln}) / D^p \quad >0 \text{ if } \mu = 0. \quad (4.16b)$$

An interesting pattern emerges from the cases in (4.14)–(4.16), in which there is growth of region-specific factors with labour immobility. Naturally, an increase in upland labour promotes deforestation in direct fashion (income effects aside). However, since upland and lowland food markets are integrated, factor growth in lowlands also has direct impacts on uplands. Any lowland shock which alters the food price changes relative factor rewards in uplands and thereby influences the rate of deforestation. Interregional labour mobility mutes the upland impact of any exogenous change, because labour mobility, in effect, increases the elasticity of labour supply to both regions.

In the analysis so far, we have examined interregional food and labour market adjustments separately. Appendix 4A provides comparative static results for the case in which labour markets are integrated and food is non-traded. As might be expected, these results include a number of terms which capture the interactions between the two markets; consequently, they yield few clear analytical insights without information on the numerical values of specific parameters governing the relative magnitudes of each type of effect. Such cases are explored in numerical simulations in Chapters 6–8.

Finally in this section, it is important to note that while our emphasis in interpreting the comparative static results has been on factors promoting or retarding deforestation, it is impossible to argue that land clearing for the non-food sector is the only source of environmental concern in uplands. Indeed, soil erosion, primarily from food production involving short-term crops and more frequent disturbance of topsoils, is a major environmental problem in uplands. Changes in the structure of upland production must therefore be interpreted as generating more than one type of environmental effect, and the expansion of one upland sector may diminish one kind of damage only at the cost of increased damage of another kind. We return to this point in section 4.6.

4.5   TECHNICAL PROGRESS AND THE GREEN REVOLUTION[14]

Technical progress in agriculture is another phenomenon that may cause environmental problems in tropical uplands. In an analogy with relative price changes, relative rates of technical progress between upland and low-lands, and within uplands, have potentially significant impacts on net migration, deforestation and the intensity of agricultural land use. However, environmental effects depend greatly on the form of technical progress and on the sector(s) in which it occurs. Because technical progress, like price changes, alters the composition of production within and between regions, its environmental effects then depend on the relative propensity for environmental damage associated with each of the expanding and contracting sectors.

Where technical change is concerned, the most empirically important questions relate to the effects of technical progress in lowland agriculture, because of the major impact of the Green Revolution. At constant prices, an exogenous productivity increase in the lowland food sector causes its output to expand. With no change in food demand this will tend to depress the food price, thereby reducing the profitability of producing food in uplands, since upland food producers have experienced no corresponding productivity growth.

For brevity, consider a form of technical progress which at constant prices increases the productivity of all factors used in lowland agriculture in equal proportion. This (a Hicks-neutral technical change) is thus equivalent to an equiproportionate reduction in unit costs or, equivalently, an increase in the price received by lowland food producers.[15] Defining a total factor productivity measure A for the lowland food sector, we have:

$$S(K, L - L^U, Ap, q)$$

with $dS = pS_n dA > 0$ when other variables remain constant, confirming the equivalence to lowland producers of neutral technical change and a price increase. Following our earlier analysis, if we first assume labour to be mobile but the food price to be exogenous, the effects of adopting Green Revolution technologies (holding other exogenous variables constant) is obtained by adapting (4.5):

$$\begin{bmatrix} R_{vv} & (R_{LT} - \alpha R_{LL}) \\ (R_{LT} - \alpha R_{LL}) & (R_{LL} + S_{LL}) \end{bmatrix} \begin{bmatrix} dT \\ dL^U \end{bmatrix} = \begin{bmatrix} 0 \\ pS_n dA \end{bmatrix}, \qquad (4.17)$$

where $D^L > 0$ as before, and from which we obtain solutions for changes in migration and tree-cutting:

$$dL^U/dA = pS_n R_{vv}/D^L < 0 \qquad (4.18a)$$

$$dT/dA = -pS_n(R_{LT} - \alpha R_{LL})/D^L < 0. \qquad (4.18b)$$

When the food price is exogenously fixed, technical progress in lowland agriculture raises labour productivity in lowlands, and since relative product prices are fixed, both upland sectors contract. There is down-slope migration and an *unambiguous* reduction in deforestation.

Now assume that labour cannot migrate but that food is non-traded and therefore its price is endogenously determined. Adapting (4.11), and holding changes in other exogenous variables constant, we have:

$$\begin{bmatrix} E_u & 0 & E_T \\ -\mu E_u & -Z_{nn} & (R_{nT} - \alpha R_{Ln}) \\ 0 & (R_{nT} - \alpha R_{Ln}) & R_{vv} \end{bmatrix} \begin{bmatrix} du \\ dp \\ dT \end{bmatrix} = \begin{bmatrix} S_n p dA \\ -S_{nn} p dA \\ 0 \end{bmatrix}, \quad (4.19)$$

where $D^p < 0$. Solving for changes in p and T:

$$dp/dA = (\mu S_n - S_{nn}pR_{vv})/D^p \quad <0 \text{ if } \mu = 0 \qquad (4.20a)$$

$$dT/dA = (S_{nn} + \mu S_n)(R_{nT} - \alpha R_{Ln})/D^p > 0, \qquad (4.20b)$$

With immobile labour, the Green Revolution technology depresses the food price (again assuming the income effect to be small), and in uplands, the lower relative price of food alters the structure of production towards non-food crops. Less labour is used in upland food production, wages fall, and there is more land clearing, for a given upland labour force.

Comparing the results in (4.18b) and (4.20b), it is clear that the nature of any change in deforestation depends on the relative strength of the food market and labour market effects. In practice, the food market is likely to adjust to any change in regional economies faster than the labour market, so, in the short run, the Green Revolution's food price effect encourages upland farmers to switch to less labour-intensive crops. In the longer run, however, labour mobility may dominate the outcome, and with migration away from upland areas, all forms of upland activity, including deforestation, should contract. This result is analytically as well as empirically important. Analytically, it indicates a form of economic growth that is more likely than most to deliver unambiguous environmental benefits in uplands. Empirically, the result suggests that the Green Revolution in the large lowland food sectors of Asian developing countries could have substantially reduced both deforestation and the rate of agricultural land degradation in uplands.[16]

The above results also yield insights into the distributional consequences of the Green Revolution. Suppose that only food is produced in uplands. The price-depressing effect of lowland technical progress unambiguously lowers the returns to factors specific to uplands (including labour if migration is infeasible). In this scenario the Green Revolution results in the unambiguous 'immiserization' of upland communities. In our model, with diversified upland production, and especially with labour mobility between regions, immiserization is not a *necessary* outcome. In fact, our model predicts that the Green Revolution creates inducements for down-slope migration, consistent with empirical evidence (Hayami and Kikuchi 2001).

Other forms of technical progress merit brief consideration. We do not present the formal derivations, but these are easily derived from the basic model in the same way as for the Green Revolution story.

Factor-neutral productivity growth in non-food upland crops increases the profitability of their production relative to food. Land and labour are drawn from upland food to non-food, and food production tends to expand in the lowland. With no income effects, the magnitude of the reduction in upland food area is governed by the size and supply responsiveness of the *lowland* region. If the supply response of the lowland food sector is low, then the reduction in upland food area will be correspondingly small. Either way, the lower labour-intensity of non-food means that technical progress in the sector is likely to promote deforestation.

Finally, technical progress in upland food increases the relative profitability of producing that crop in uplands, so land and upland labour switch from non-food to food production. At constant food demand, this form of technical progress results in a lower food price. The losers in this case are farmers in lowlands, where technical change has not reduced unit costs. If there is no interregional migration, expansion of upland food may take place at the expense of non-food production rather than by expanding agricultural land through increased deforestation. In the longer run, however, whether the cleared area rises or falls will be determined by the extent of the two interregional effects of technical progress, the fall in the food price versus incentives for up-slope migration caused by the productivity-increasing change.

It is sometimes argued in discussions of upland agricultural development and the environment that making improved technologies available to upland farmers will inhibit land expansion and deforestation, because more intensive employment of the existing labour force on existing land will raise the opportunity cost of further land clearing. It should be clear from the previous discussion that this argument will be robust only under certain conditions. In particular, any relaxation of the labour constraint through migration will undermine it, as will any tendency in the food or non-food crop markets for prices to be unresponsive to local supply shocks. Extrapolating somewhat beyond the boundaries of our model, it seems clear that if prices are 'given' to upland farmers and the size of the upland labour force is endogenous, then any increase in upland productivity will simply promote further deforestation until some other constraint, such as managerial expertise or distance costs, binds to prevent further expansion.[17]

4.6   INTERSECTORAL EXTERNALITIES

Up to this point we have captured the idea that the social and private returns to upland agricultural decisions might diverge, simply by supposing that consumers derive utility from standing forest while upland producers' forest-clearing decisions are driven purely by the equality of private marginal costs and returns. This very simple and abstract construct is adequate for many purposes, since it captures the core idea that deforestation confers a negative externality, one that cannot easily be addressed at its source. It is also consistent with the majority of analytical constructs in the broader environmental economics literature (Baumol and Oates 1988; Cropper and Oates 1992; and see the discussion and references on this issue in Chapter 2). Empirically, however, this focus on the effects of agricultural *expansion* in uplands should properly be matched by concern about the costs of *intensification*, or the expansion of labour-intensive farming systems (in our story, food crops) as a fraction of the total upland farmed area. Intensification is associated with soil erosion and the consequent export of sediment (and, in some agricultural systems, fertilizer and pesticide residues) to downstream areas through rivers and drainage systems. The off-site effects of intensive upland agriculture are frequently the source of significant reductions in productivity in lowland agriculture unless abatement expenditures are incurred.

To model off-site externalities is potentially very complex, even if we put aside the issue of time lags and delivery rates. In the context of our current model with two lowland sectors, the most readily analysed form of off-site externality is the degradation of lowland agricultural infrastructure caused by upland erosion.

Addressing the intersectoral and interregional effects of an environmental externality introduces another complication. The total productivity loss in a sector that consumes pollution is unlikely in practice to be the result of uniform proportional reductions in the productivity of all inputs used. There are two sources of possible divergence in rates of factor productivity change: the sector-specificity of some inputs, and the input-specificity of some pollution effects. In agriculture, for example, land is conventionally regarded as sector-specific, while labour is not. *Ceteris paribus*, a downturn in lowland agricultural profitability will reduce returns to land by more than it will wages – and in fact, wages may be unaffected even as returns to land decline.[18] These factor price results are *indirect*, stemming from the derived-demand nature of factor employment. In addition, erosion-related damage affects land productivity *directly*, for instance through damage to irrigation and drainage works, but the productivity of labour is not normally affected in such direct fashion. Even at constant prices, therefore, pollution may alter relative factor productivity and rewards, with implications for production structure, welfare and the distribution of income.

In our two-region economy we can capture the physical impact of upland soil erosion, and its indirect factor market effects, by modelling its off-site impact as a form of factor-specific technical regress in the lowland region. This approach differs in a significant way from the conventional characterization of off-site impacts in which pollution appears as a separate (and separable) input in the production functions of polluted industries (see, for example, Cropper and Oates 1992). The latter study presents pollution damage in effect as equivalent to *factor-neutral* technical regress, whereas our approach allows for pollution to exert differential productivity impacts on factors. In doing so, it accounts for the overall productivity loss experienced in a sector in terms of productivity declines of individual factors employed. In general equilibrium, with factors exhibiting differing degrees of intersectoral mobility, the analogy of the physical effects of pollution with technical regress points to a convenient and intuitive way of modelling factor market effects of pollution-related shifts in relative sectoral profitability.

Generalizing the earlier analysis of technical progress in which attention was limited to factor-neutral changes, we model the lowland effects of upland erosion as a technical change affecting lowland land, the factor that is specific to lowland (irrigated) agriculture. At constant prices, erosion reduces the productivity of lowland land, both in absolute terms and relative to that of the mobile factor (labour) employed in the sector.[19] Define the *effective* quantity of lowland land as its physical quantity adjusted by a productivity parameter, B. Continuing to use subscript n for lowland agriculture, we write:

$$K_n = B\tilde{K}_n, \qquad (4.21)$$

where $\tilde{K}_n$ is the physical quantity, and K_n is the effective quantity, of irrigated land. To simplify, suppose that the off-site effects of erosion are generated only from land used for food crops in uplands; then the quantity of erosion produced is directly related to the quantity of upland land used for food. Ruling out other sources of productivity growth, we have $B = T_n^\beta$, $-1 < \beta < 0$, so:

$$K_n = T_n^\beta \tilde{K}_n; \; \frac{\partial K_n}{\partial T_n} = \beta \tilde{K}_n T_n^{\beta-1} < 0; \; \frac{\partial^2 K_n}{\partial T_n^2} = \beta(\beta-1)\tilde{K}_n T_n^{\beta-2} > 0, \quad (4.22)$$

where β measures the impact of erosion generated in the upland food sector on the productivity of lowlands, the specific factor in irrigated agriculture.[20] With this augmentation we can once again solve the model for the general equilibrium effects of changes in exogenous variables. This calculation must now include the value of lost (or regained) lowland productivity as the result of changes in erosion from upland food production. Accordingly, the lowland revenue function is redefined as:

$$S(K_m, K_n(\tilde{K}_n, T_n), L-L^U, p, q). \qquad (4.23)$$

A key component of the solution is to find an expression for the change in T_n, the quantity of upland land allocated to food production. This expression (equation (A4.8) in Appendix 4B) shows that the area of upland land devoted to food production is increasing in the food price, upland labour, the price of manufactures, and the capital stock (or land stock) of lowland agriculture. It is decreasing in the total area of cleared land (the Rybczinski result when non-food is land-intensive), the lowland labour force, and the capital stock in manufacturing. Accordingly, by (4.22), the productivity of lowland land is reduced by those factors that increase T_n and raised by the others.

So long as upland producers treat erosion-related losses in lowlands as purely external costs, the privately optimal forest-clearing decision will continue to be governed by (4.3); that is, cutting will occur until the marginal return on cleared land is just equal to the marginal clearing cost. When upland land use affects lowland productivity, however, the gap between the privately and socially optimal forest-cutting criteria will widen. The latter is obtained by using (4.23) to amend (4.1) and differentiating with respect to T:

$$R_T - E_T + S_{K_n} \beta \tilde{K}_n T_n^{\beta-1} \frac{\partial T_n}{\partial T} = \alpha R_L. \qquad (4.24)$$

Since $E_T < 0$, $S_{K_n} > 0$, $\beta < 0$, and $\partial T_n / \partial T < 0$, at the social optimum forest will be cut until the return on cleared land net of social costs – both the implicit cost of forest loss and the explicit off-site cost of soil erosion – is just equal to the clearing cost. As a result, less forest will be cleared in the socially optimal scenario.[21]

The foregoing results highlight a potential trade-off between the environmental outcomes associated with any given policy or exogenous shock. In general, shocks which reduce the rate of overall deforestation also increase the proportion of upland area devoted to relatively erosive food crop production. A policy which reduces one externality (say, deforestation) may need to be accompanied by another policy that inhibits the generation of greater quantities of the other (say, soil erosion from food production).

When pollution externalities affect large sectors of an economy, they trigger resource reallocation responses that may have significant effects on economic welfare. We have illustrated this in a variant of the model in which increased erosion caused by upland food production reduces lowland land productivity, bidding up food prices and thus stimulating allocation of more upland land to food crop production. These effects, which appear to be of considerable importance in some developing countries when self-sufficiency in food production is a policy priority, have until now been largely overlooked in the environmental economics literature, which concentrates on cases in which pollution has negligible differential effects in factor markets.

As the above analysis shows, an alternative specification of the nature of the environmental damage makes a difference to some of our results. On one hand, the analytical story is similar for aggregate variables such as welfare. On the other hand, changes in the structure of production, prices and factor payments are all contingent on the type of externality. This means, among other things, that we can expect to find that different specifications (and combinations) of environmental externalities will be associated with differences in the distribution of income. This distinction will potentially be important when poverty is a policy target, and also when the political economy of pollution and of pollution instruments is important.

4.7 POLICY DISTORTIONS AND REFORMS

We now turn to a new set of distortions, the effects of economic policy interventions on resource allocation, incomes, prices and welfare. As seen in Chapter 3, agriculture as a whole remains a prominent sector in most developing countries, whether measured in terms of its contribution to aggregate income, its share of household expenditures or its share in total trade and government budgets. Policies affecting agriculture can thus be expected to have economy-wide repercussions, just as national-level policies are likely to have direct and indirect impacts on resource allocation within agriculture. The analysis of policy reforms is complex since, with a combination of distortions (some environmental, some policy-driven), few unambiguous statements about comparative statics results are possible without assigning specific values to model parameters. In this section we presage empirical exercises in Chapters 6–8 with a highly simplified discussion of two selected policies: trade barriers for either manufactures or food, and the control of food pricing through domestic purchase, storage and release of excess grain supplies.[22]

Tariff Policy and Trade Liberalization

One of the most controversial questions in the debate over trade and the environment in developing countries concerns trade liberalization. As seen in Chapter 2, we can expect the reform of trade policy, like any other major economic change, to affect incomes, spending patterns and the structure of production through more than one channel. In this analysis we focus on the composition effects of a reform to an existing policy. Suppose that the manufactured good is import-competing as before, but that its initial price

q is now equal to the world price q^* (measured in domestic currency units) raised by a tariff t. To simplify further, suppose that $q^* = 1$, so $q = 1 + t$. What is the structure of the tariff-distorted economy, and how are resource allocation, real expenditures and aggregate welfare altered by tariff reform?

By comparison with free trade, a tariff results in higher rewards to factors used intensively in manufacturing. By itself, the imposition of a tariff must reduce lowland food production relative to the free trade case. At the same time the tariff creates excess demand for food through substitution effects in consumption. Both the factor market and the demand-side effects create excess demand for food, and so drive up its price. Other things equal, we can expect that this will result in a greater area of upland land allocated to food production. Whether the tariff on its own results in more land clearing or not is not answerable without more information, as some or all of the land switched to food production may come at the expense of non-food. We have noticed, however, that in general a short-run increase in the area devoted to food production in uplands is associated with a reduction in total upland area cultivated when food is the less land-intensive of two upland crops.

From section 4.4 we see that under these assumptions an increase in the relative price of manufactures reduces total demand for forest clearing in uplands through two distinct mechanisms: down-slope labour migration, and an induced food price increase that both increases land-clearing costs and reduces the returns to the land-intensive non-food crop in uplands. The extent to which either land-clearing response occurs at all, let alone in the direction indicated, depends on the assumptions of the model, such as the need for the food market to clear domestically and the ability of labour to migrate between upland and lowland regions. We address some of these issues analytically in later sections of this chapter, and others through the use of numerical simulation models in Chapters 6–8, although nowhere can we claim to present a completely general model encompassing all possible situations. Rather, our goal is to use simplifying assumptions to expose and understand economic mechanisms whose precise influence will of course vary widely according to circumstances. Thus the claim just made, that a tariff on manufactures causes reduced deforestation, is valid only for a specific variant of the model and should not be read as an empirical assertion.

What is interesting to explore is how a distorting policy, such as a tariff, interacts with other distortions, such as those resulting from the undervaluation of standing forest by upland farmers in an open-access property rights regime. This is our main focus in the analysis that follows. To avoid unnecessary complications, in this section we do not pursue the idea of intersectoral technological externalities. We assume, moreover, that the tariff revenues collected by the government are returned to consumers in lump-sum fashion. Given this, the aggregate budget constraint for the economy requires that the value of expenditure at distorted prices be equal to the value of aggregate net production plus tariff revenue.

Adapting (4.1) to the case of a tariff gives:

$$E(p, q, T, u) = R(T, L^U - \alpha T, p) + S(K, L - L^U, p, q) + tZ_q, \quad (4.25)$$

where $Z_q = E_q(p, q, T, u) - S_q(K, L - L^U, p, q)$ is excess demand for manufactures as before, so tZ_q is the value of tariff revenue earned on imports. If the initial tariff is non-zero, then a tariff reform will have first-order welfare effects through its impact on domestic prices, resource allocation and the production of environmental externalities. Since the direct price effect of the tariff is identical to that of an exogenous rise in the price of manufactures, any differences between the results we obtain for a tariff change and those for a terms of trade shock will be capable of being interpreted as due either to the distorting effect of the tariff on its own or to its interactions with environmental externalities.

In the tariff-affected economy, changes in distortions can be transmitted only through adjustments in the domestic food market. This is demonstrated by the case of a tariff increase when the food price is not endogenous – the tariff change counterpart to equation (4.6). With food freely traded at a constant price, a rise in t has no effect in uplands except indirectly, through the labour market. In this variant an equiproportionate rise in either q^* or t has the same impact on lowland labour productivity, so the effects in uplands are also identical: when upland food production is relatively labour-intensive, a manufacturing sector tariff increase will cause down-slope migration and reduce the amount of land cleared for upland cultivation, exactly as shown in (4.6a) and (4.6b). Since the relative price of food to upland non-food crops is unchanged, so too is the allocation of upland land to crops.

This result is consistent with that reached by Deacon (1995), whose model, with only labour mobile between sectors and no endogenously priced final goods, generates the outcome that any tax on import-competing manufactures is equivalent to a similar tax on resource sectors, and thus reduces deforestation. We have argued, however, that it is unrealistic to think of the labour market as the sole conduit between regional economies. In particular, we should think of the food market (or, more generally, the markets for non-traded goods produced in different regions) as alternative (or, more strictly, supplementary) conduits. With endogenously priced goods, the resource allocation impacts of a tariff are potentially very different.

To see the effect of the food market linkage, assume now that this market must clear as in (4.2), but that there is no interregional migration; that is, (4.4) does not hold. We can obtain the effects of a small change in the existing tariff on T, p, and aggregate real expenditures by taking the total differentials of (4.25), (4.2) and (4.3), holding other exogenous variables constant at their base values, so as to obtain a system of equations written in matrix form as:

$$\begin{bmatrix} \tau E_u & -tZ_{nq} & E_T \\ -\mu E_u & -Z_{nn} & (R_{nT} - \alpha R_{Ln}) \\ 0 & (R_{nT} - \alpha R_{Ln}) & R_{vv} \end{bmatrix} \begin{bmatrix} du \\ dp \\ dT \end{bmatrix} = \begin{bmatrix} tZ_{qq}dt \\ Z_{nq}dt \\ 0 \end{bmatrix}, \quad (4.26)$$

where $\tau = (1 - tc_M)$ is the tariff multiplier, and $0 < \tau < 1$ in stable models (Vousden 1990). The determinant of the coefficient matrix in this system is:

$$-E_u D^{p,t} = -E_u \{\tau Z_{nn} R_{vv} + \tau (R_{nT} - \alpha R_{Ln})^2 + \mu (E_T (R_{nT} - \alpha R_{Ln}) + tR_{vv} Z_{nq})\}$$
$$= -E_u (\tau D^p + (1 - \tau)\mu E_T (R_{nT} - \alpha R_{nL}) + \mu tR_{vv} Z_{nq}), \quad (4.27)$$

implying (since $R_{vv} < 0$) that $D^{p,t}$ is unlikely to be negative for small values of μ and t. (Indeed, as expected, the value of $D^{p,t}$ converges on τD^p as $t \to 0$.) We therefore assume the determinant to be negative.

A small increase in the rate of the tariff gives:

$$\frac{dp}{dt} = -\frac{(\tau Z_{nq} + \mu tZ_{qq})R_{vv}}{D^{p,t}} > 0 \text{ if } \mu = 0 \quad (4.28a)$$

$$\frac{dT}{dt} = -\left(\frac{R_{nT} - \alpha R_{Ln}}{R_{vv}}\right)\left(\frac{dp}{dt}\right) \quad (4.28b)$$

The tariff rise drives up the food price through substitution effects. In uplands, due to Stolper–Samuelson effects, this reduces total cultivated area *if food production is labour-intensive* as shown by the sign of $R_{nT} - \alpha R_{Ln}$. Conversely, if upland food production is land-intensive then the opposite result will be found. When upland production is diversified, a tariff that causes down-slope migration need not result in reduced pressures for deforestation.

Whatever the sign of dT/dt, if the income effect is non-zero (that is, if $\mu \neq 0$) both this and the induced relative price change will be reduced by the extent to which the tariff rise exacerbates the existing misallocation of resources to production of manufactures. If the initial tariff rate is sufficiently high, it is conceivable that the negative income effect of further trade policy tightening could dominate substitution effects, resulting in a *fall* in the relative food price. Under the assumption that upland food is labour-intensive, this would increase deforestation. Such a result is broadly indicative of the effects of failed ISI policies, that is, those which achieve only limited industrial growth at a very high cost in terms of resource misallocation. When protection is awarded to industries producing negative value-added, poverty will increase and the newly poor will presumably migrate to the frontier in search of a livelihood.

For the less extreme case of a tariff rise without such large initial distortions, interactions between the trade policy and the environmental externality affect overall welfare when the tariff rate is altered in the following ways. From (4.25):

$$E_u(1 - tc_M)\frac{\partial u}{\partial t} + E_T\frac{\partial T}{\partial t} = tZ_{qq} + tZ_{nq}\frac{\partial p}{\partial t},$$

or, using (4.28b) to eliminate $\partial p/\partial t$ and rearranging:

$$E_u(1 - tc_M)\frac{\partial u}{\partial t} = tZ_{qq} - \left(E_T + \frac{tZ_{nq}R_{vv}}{R_{nT} - \alpha R_{Ln}}\right)\frac{\partial T}{\partial t}. \qquad (4.29)$$

When labour is immobile (as assumed here), the overall welfare effect from *reducing* protection (that is, from lower t) has four components. The first is the change in utility from consumption of marketed goods, as shown on the left-hand side of (4.29), captured by the first term on the right-hand side of (4.29). This is equal to the sum of the conventional gain from increased economic efficiency as resource misallocation is reduced (the first term on the right-hand side), plus effects occurring through environmental changes. This consists of the effect of a change in T on the welfare of the consumer via the externality effect (the first term inside brackets) and a factor endowment effect, the result of any change in the endowment of upland land on the economy's production of marketable goods. When dT/dt is positive, this term raises utility, so the converse applies when the tariff is reduced.

This analysis yields two conclusions. First, definitive statements about the effects of general equilibrium instruments such as tariffs on deforestation or any other environmental variable are very difficult to support in all but the most simple models. Outcomes depend on the nature and number of links among regions or sectors, on the structure of production in each sector, on preferences, and on underlying institutions such as property rights. Second, whether or not a tariff change increases deforestation or agricultural intensification, it also affects consumers' capacity to purchase non-environmental goods, so the fundamental question that must be addressed is whether consumers are made better or worse off by a change, *inclusive* of environmental and market effects.

Food Policy

We now consider a different type of policy, one targeting either the price of basic foodstuffs or the quantity made available to domestic buyers. As we have seen (Chapter 3), many developing countries pursue development strategies in which self-sufficiency and price stabilization for basic products, especially food, feature prominently. In addition to their widely debated welfare and distributional effects, food policies based on price and trade restrictions may also accelerate land degradation and/or deforestation by promoting expansion of relatively erosive grain crops at the expense of other land uses that are less demanding of environmental services.

Food security policies typically involve interventions in international trade and domestic markets. If a domestic supply shock occurs in cereals while restrictions on international trade are binding, then either cereal prices must adjust to clear the domestic market, or the market may clear at a constant price through a quantity mechanism such as government purchases and releases from buffer stocks; this has been the mechanism highlighted by our assumption of non-traded food.

The basic effects of food policies can be discerned on the basis of insights acquired thus far from the model. First, policies that raise producer prices of food provide upland farmers with incentives to intensify production by switching from non-food to food crops. Whether these result in an expansion of upland land at the expense of forest will depend on relative factor intensities in uplands, as shown, as well as on the effect that the policy has on the regional distribution of labour. Of course, any policy that prevents food trade at world prices, and also supports domestic production at prices above their autarky level, can only be sustained if the government buys surplus production and either stores or otherwise disposes of it. The costs of doing so must be financed through taxes or reduced expenditures elsewhere in the economy, and constitute another source of welfare loss. At the same time, however, food policy will provide food producers with partial compensation for the intersectoral effects of tariffs on manufactured goods, thereby reducing another source of welfare loss.

Because food policies involve storage, their analysis requires an intertemporal dimension excluded from the model developed in this chapter. Moreover, some of the critical effects of food policy may be transmitted not through prices themselves, but through their variability. Risk-averse upland farmers will tend to devote more resources to production of a price-stabilized crop, other things equal, than one whose price is highly variable.

4.8   LIMITS AND LIMITATIONS OF THE MODEL

Our goal in this chapter has been to take formal analysis of economy–environment interactions beyond the very highly stylized insights of generic economy-wide models by incorporating specific characteristics that, while limiting the models in some ways, permit a deeper and more nuanced look at an important subset of issues.

It hardly needs to be pointed out that the model and comparative static exercises raise as many questions as they resolve. This is appropriate for this type of stylized analysis; the measure of its success will be if the questions that are raised are more prevalently empirical rather than analytical in nature, since they can then be addressed in larger, more complex numerical models. On the analytical front, however, the use of a model that limits intertemporal dynamics and ignores risk leaves open some obvious avenues for further research. Moreover, our assumptions about the structure of production in either region (that is, about the region- or sector-specificity of factors), while more general than in any previous model, nevertheless constrains the set of analytical results yielded by the model. The number and nature of interregional linkages similarly limit the variety of results that can in principle be obtained.

4.9   THE EFFECTS OF SHOCKS IN REPRESENTATIVE ECONOMIES

In this chapter we have constructed a formal model of a developing economy incorporating many of the characteristics identified in an empirical review as important departures from a standard, abstract model. These include spatial differentiation of production and technology, open access to forest resources, interregional labour migration, and food policies that impede market clearing through international trade. The model explains migration between lowland and upland regions, deforestation and agricultural intensification (the switching of land from extensive to intensive crops) in terms of their fundamental drivers: population growth and capital accumulation, technical progress, international price shocks, and domestic price shocks arising from policy changes. We examine the predictions of the model with regard to environmental variables and economic welfare under a range of alternative assumptions about the structure of production, as motivated by our distillation of several similar, but differentiated, 'representative' economies in Chapter 3.

Although we present a wide variety of comparative static results, their broad nature is reasonably straightforward to interpret in terms of the economic mechanisms at work. For a given environmental change (in our analysis, deforestation or agricultural intensification in uplands), we have a chain of causation that begins with an exogenous shock, then traces its effects on the relative prices of products and the returns to labour, and through these on the allocation of resources both across sectors and between upland and lowland regions. In this process, the three first-order conditions (4.2)–(4.4) play the critical role of ensuring that adjustment to a shock is such as to restore the equality, at the margin, of returns to the same factor in different uses.

The actual environmental effects of a given exogenous shock are determined by the sectoral and regional structure of production and the nature of the initial policy regime, as summarized in Figure 3.2, and on the relative technologies of upland agricultural production. Although the results of the analysis are in the main ambiguous (that is, they depend on actual parameter values), the model serves to highlight the economic mechanisms that relate the decisions of optimizing agents across sectors and regions. In so doing, it provides a set of 'base' solutions against which environmental results obtained with more complex, but structurally similar, numerical models may be evaluated.

Looking further, the model presents a means to approximate welfare changes when consumers derive utility both from the consumption of goods and from environmental services. The welfare measure, though crude, provides a reminder that consumers may be willing to trade environmental services for improvements in their material standard of living. Not surprisingly, we find that both welfare *and* environmental damage may be increased by some policy changes.

Finally, for a given set of assumptions about the relative factor intensity of upland sectors, the comparative static results give unambiguous answers in most cases of a change in some exogenous variable when either the food market or the labour market (but not both) dominates interregional adjustment to the shock. When adjustments in *both* these markets affect the outcome, there is less certainty in the predicted effects, as shown in the appendix to this chapter.

Whether a given shock generates down-slope or up-slope migration (and a corresponding reduction or increase in forest clearing) depends critically on the factor intensity of upland production except in the special case of no change in the price of food. As has been shown, a shock that increases (or reduces) labour productivity in lowlands but does not materially alter the food price causes down-slope (or up-slope) migration; higher (or lower) forest-clearing costs also reduce (or increase) T. However, in any case in which the food price changes (whether exogenously or as the endogenous result of some other shock), the labour intensity of food relative to non-food production in uplands helps determine the signs of upland responses. Moreover, some results further depend on whether the manufacturing sector produces a net export or an import-competing good. With these results in hand, we can now recast some earlier, more heuristic, statements about the likely implications of a set of possible exogenous shocks on migration, deforestation, the land use decisions of upland farmers, and economic welfare.

In one of our stylized economies, the 'jeepney' economy, the manufacturing sector produces an import-competing good, while in uplands, food production is both a more labour-intensive activity than non-food production and also occupies the greatest part of upland agricultural land. This has been the 'base' case for our analysis. In this economy, price, endowment or policy changes that increase factor productivity in lowlands will in general induce down-slope migration and can be expected to have large pro-forest effects. This set of results corresponds broadly with those presented in the model of Deacon (1995). In this economy, trade liberalization tends to increase pressures for deforestation (if not for agricultural intensification). However, our analysis has shown that these predictions depend on a particular set of assumptions about the structure of the economy.

In the 'becak' economy, the manufacturing sector produces an import-competing good but in uplands, food production is a *less* labour-intensive activity than non-food production. In this economy, shocks that increase lowland productivity will induce down-slope migration, as in the jeepney economy. Due to the labour intensity of upland non-food crops, however, food production will increase as a proportion of upland area. In both the becak and the jeepney economies, food sector policies that use price or quantity interventions to increase producer prices will promote agricultural intensification in uplands; in the becak economy this will be accompanied by a higher rate of deforestation.

In the 'proton' and 'tuk-tuk' economies, the manufacturing sector produces a net *export*. The tuk-tuk economy produces traded food, and this activity dominates upland land use, so the labour market is the only meaningful interregional link. An increase in labour demand in lowlands will result in reduced deforestation as labour migrates to the cities and the total area of upland agriculture diminishes. The proton economy offers a variant in which upland land use is dominated by relatively capital-intensive plantation crops. Upland–lowland linkages operate as in the other economies, and the effects of lowland productivity shocks are the same, but there is the additional possibility of investment, including foreign direct investment, in plantation sector activity. This will be associated with an expansion of upland areas at the expense of forests – the more so, the more elastic is the supply of labour. A new set of policies applies in this case.

To sum up, whether a given economic or policy shock increases or reduces migration to uplands, deforestation and the production of damaging off-site effects of soil erosion from upland food production depends very much on the structure of the economy. As far as the degradation of forest and land resources is concerned, no generalizations about the environmental consequences of policy, trade or investment shocks are possible except as qualified. This rather agnostic conclusion stands in sharp contrast to much stronger statements often made on the environmental effects of trade, investment and economic policy.

APPENDICES

4A Complete Comparative Static Results from Section 4.3

The following analysis provides expressions for the general equilibrium effects of changes in the exogenous elements of $\mathbf{P}$ and $\mathbf{V}$. Whereas in the text we conduct analyses holding one or other of the food and labour markets 'constant', here both markets are resolved simultaneously. Define the set of exogenous variables $\lambda = (q, L, K)$, and consider a change in some λ_j. Taking derivatives of (4.1)–(4.4) with respect to this variable and collecting terms gives:

$$E_u \frac{\partial u}{\partial \lambda_j} + E_T \frac{\partial T}{\partial \lambda_j} = \mathbf{X}_1$$

$$-\mu E_u \frac{\partial u}{\partial \lambda_j} - Z_{nn} \frac{\partial p}{\partial \lambda_j} + (R_{nT} - \alpha R_{nL}) \frac{\partial T}{\partial \lambda_j} + (R_{Ln} - S_{Ln}) \frac{\partial L^U}{\partial \lambda_j} = \mathbf{X}_2$$

$$(R_{nT} - \alpha R_{nL}) \frac{\partial p}{\partial \lambda_j} + (R_{TT} - 2\alpha R_{LT} + \alpha^2 R_{LL}) \frac{\partial T}{\partial \lambda_j} + (R_{LT} - \alpha R_{LL}) \frac{\partial L^U}{\partial \lambda_j} = \mathbf{X}_3 \quad (A4.1)$$

$$(R_{Ln} - S_{Ln}) \frac{\partial p}{\partial \lambda_j} + (R_{LT} - \alpha R_{LL}) \frac{\partial T}{\partial \lambda_j} + (R_{LL} + S_{LL}) \frac{\partial L^U}{\partial \lambda_j} = \mathbf{X}_4,$$

where a double subscript indicates a second derivative, $Z_{nn} = (E_{nn} - R_{nn} - S_{nn}) < 0$ is the derivative of excess demand for food with respect to its own price, and each $\mathbf{X}_i$ is a vector of exogenous changes, as defined in (4.7) below. The first equation in (A4.1) uses the first-order conditions (4.2)–(4.4) to eliminate terms in p, T, and L^U. The second equation makes use of the fact that $E_{nu}/E_u = \mu$, the marginal propensity to consume food out of income. To facilitate comparative static analysis, we rewrite (A4.1) in matrix form as:

$$\begin{bmatrix} E_u & 0 & E_T & 0 \\ -\mu E_u & -Z_{nn} & (R_{nT} - \alpha R_{nL}) & (R_{nL} - S_{nL}) \\ 0 & (R_{nT} - \alpha R_{nL}) & (R_{TT} - 2\alpha R_{LT} + \alpha^2 R_{LL}) & (R_{LT} - \alpha R_{LL}) \\ 0 & (R_{nL} - S_{nL}) & (R_{LT} - \alpha R_{LL}) & (R_{LL} + S_{LL}) \end{bmatrix} \begin{bmatrix} \partial u/\partial \lambda_j \\ \partial p/\partial \lambda_j \\ \partial T/\partial \lambda_j \\ \partial L^U/\partial \lambda_j \end{bmatrix}$$

$$= \begin{bmatrix} \mathbf{X}_1 \\ \mathbf{X}_2 \\ \mathbf{X}_3 \\ \mathbf{X}_4 \end{bmatrix}. \tag{A4.2}$$

The changes in exogenous variables are:

$$\begin{bmatrix} -Z_q & S_L & S_K \\ Z_{nq} & -S_{nL} & -S_{nK} \\ 0 & 0 & 0 \\ S_{LQ} & S_{LL} & S_{LK} \end{bmatrix} \begin{bmatrix} \partial q/\partial\lambda_j \\ \partial L/\partial\lambda_j \\ \partial K/\partial\lambda_j \end{bmatrix} = \begin{bmatrix} \mathbf{X}_1 \\ \mathbf{X}_2 \\ \mathbf{X}_3 \\ \mathbf{X}_4 \end{bmatrix}, \tag{A4.3}$$

where $Z_q = (E_q - S_q)$ is domestic excess demand for the manufactured good (and is thus positive for an import-competing good, negative for a net export); $Z_{nq} = (E_{nq} - S_{nq}) > 0$; and

$$\frac{\partial\lambda_i}{\partial\lambda_j} = \begin{cases} 1 \text{ if } i=j \\ 0 \text{ otherwise,} \end{cases} \text{ for all } i, j \in (q, L, K).$$

Thus, for example, if we are interested in the effect of a change in L holding q and K constant, only the coefficients in the second column of the left-hand matrix in (A4.3) apply. Taking each column of this matrix in turn, we can find the comparative static effects of a change in the relative price of the manufactured good, in the size of the labour force, or in either or both of the lowland-specific factors on aggregate welfare, the price of non-traded food, upland land area, and the regional distribution of labour. We can subsequently use these solutions to solve for changes in land and labour allocation within uplands, as well as for the degree to which private incomes and social welfare diverge as the result of the deforestation externality.

By Young's theorem we have $R_{ij} = R_{ji}$ and $S_{ij} = S_{ji}$ for all prices and quantities i, j. By the concavity of the revenue function in factor endowments we have $R_{LL} < 0$, $R_{TT} < 0$, and $S_{LL} < 0$, and by the assumption that factors are substitutes we have $R_{LT} > 0$. Production in each lowland sector uses one mobile factor (labour) and one specific factor; it follows that an expansion of the sector induced by an own-price increase causes labour demand to increase, so $S_{nL} > 0$. The expenditure function is increasing in p, q and u, so $E_u > 0$, $E_n > 0$, and $E_q > 0$. Deforestation reduces forest benefits so $E_T < 0$; food and manufactures are normal goods so $\mu > 0$ and $Z_{nn} < 0$, $Z_{qq} < 0$.

In the calculations that follow, it is convenient to replace the compound terms in the lower-right 3×3 symmetric sub-matrix in (A4.2) with abbreviations. Let $a = -Z_{NN}$; $b = (R_{NT} - \alpha R_{LT})$, and so on, and rewrite it as:

$$\Delta = \begin{vmatrix} E_u & 0 & E_T & 0 \\ -\mu E_u & a & b & c \\ 0 & b & d & e \\ 0 & c & e & f \end{vmatrix}. \tag{A4.4}$$

Now with the information provided so far, we can assert $a > 0$, $d < 0$, $e > 0$, and $f < 0$. The signs of b and c depend, respectively, on the relative labour intensity of food production in the upland region and the relative responsiveness of labour demand to food price in each region. For the analysis in most of the chapter we impose the following:

> *Assumption 4.1 (factor-intensity of upland production)* In the region of equilibrium, food production in the upland region is labour-intensive relative to tree crop production, such that $R_{nT} \leq \alpha R_{nL}$. Then $b \leq 0$ in (A4.2).

To study interactions between the food and labour markets we also need:

> *Assumption 4.2 (regional price responsiveness of food sector labour demand)* In the region of equilibrium, labour demand for food production in the upland region is no more elastic with respect to food price than is labour demand in the lowland region, or $R_{nL} - S_{nL} \leq 0$, so $c \leq 0$ in (A4.2).

In each case we use weak inequalities: the values of both b and c could be close to or equal to zero.

With the above assumptions, $\Delta > 0$. To see this, expand down the first column of (A4.2):

$$\Delta = E_u(C_{11} - \mu C_{21}),$$

where C_{ij} is the signed cofactor of the ijth element. Expanding each cofactor:

$$C_{11} = -aR_{VV} + 2bce - b^2f - c^2d > 0,$$

where $R_{VV} = df - e^2 > 0$ by strict concavity of the revenue function in $\mathbf{V}$, and:

$$C_{21} = E_T(bf - ce) < 0$$

so long as $E_T < 0$; that is, the marginal willingness to pay for forest is positive.

Signs of comparative static effects

When the manufacturing sector produces a net import, then an increase in Q is a negative terms -of -trade shock for the economy as a whole. It also turns the domestic regional terms of trade against the uplands, since manufactures are produced only in the lowland region, and thus increases the marginal value product of labour used in the lowland economy. Labour market and food market responses to a rise in q are captured in the comparative static expressions:

$$\frac{\partial L^U}{\partial q} = \{(Z_{nq} - \mu Z_q)(be - cd) + S_{Lq}(ad - b^2 - \mu bE_T)\}/D \qquad \text{(A4.5a)}$$

$$\frac{\partial p}{\partial q} = \{(Z_{nq} - \mu Z_q)R_{VV} + S_{Lq}(be - cd + \mu eE_T)\}/D. \qquad \text{(A4.5b)}$$

Expressions (A4.5a) and (A4.5b) correspond to those in the text for each market separately, but also include interactions between the food and labour markets. Each has two parts, one associated with each of the two markets that link upland and lowland regions. The first conveys the effect of the terms of trade shock on the food market, and consists of a substitution effect (Z_{nq}) and an income effect (μZ_q). The second conveys the impact of the shock in manufacturing to other sectors through the labour market. To examine these in isolation, suppose that no labour is used in the manufacturing sector, so $S_{Lq} = 0$. With positive excess demand for manufactures (that is, more is produced than is consumed domestically), $Z_q > 0$. The terms of trade shock lowers total income, which lowers the demand for food, and also raises the price of manufactures relative to food. Thus the change in p in (A4.5b) is positive if substitution effects dominate income effects, and negative otherwise. Note that for a positive terms -of -trade shock ($Z_q > 0$), both effects would reinforce one another and $dp/dq > 0$.

Supposing the substitution effect to dominate, the upland region has now experienced a terms of trade decline relative to the lowland region: the prices of food and manufactures have both risen in terms of the tree crop price. By assumptions (A4.1) and (A4.2), the term ($be - cd$) in (A4.5a) is non-positive, so some upland labour moves to the lowland region. There is down-slope migration, that is, the change in L^U is negative.[23]

We now focus on the labour market in isolation. To do this, suppose that $S_{Lq} > 0$, but there are no income or substitution effects in the market for food, that is, $Z_{nq} = \mu = 0$. The terms in parentheses following S_{Lq} in each expression govern the labour market effect of a rise in manufacturing- sector labour demand. To begin, abstract from the forest valuation effect by supposing that its virtual price E_T is zero. A higher q raises the value marginal product of labour in manufacturing, and so draws labour from other sectors, including uplands; in (A4.5a) this movement is governed by the coefficients ($ad - b^2$) < 0. As with the food price effect, the wage rise causes down-slope migration. Paradoxically, however, manufacturing labour demand growth on its own exerts a *downward* effect on the food price (the second term in (A4.5b) is negative). The economy-wide wage increase raises costs fastest in the most labour-intensive sectors – the uplands – and the resulting migration is equivalent to an increase in the lowland labour endowment, which reduces costs, *ceteris paribus*, in both lowland sectors (see Dixit and Norman 1980). The negative migration effect offsets somewhat the substitution effects on food prices; however, since the former is induced by the latter, the relative food price must rise.

Finally, consider the effects associated with E_T. Consumers derive utility from both forest and food. If the forest has value to consumers, $E_T < 0$, and as income rises, consumers are willing to pay a higher price for food in order to preserve the forest. In (A4.5a), when food production is land-intensive ($b < 0$), the income effect of the price change accelerates down-slope migration, by an amount that is increasing in the absolute value of E_T.

Thus in a model with a non-traded good, a terms of trade decline engenders a 'second-round' expansion in demand for food through substitution effects; if these dominate income effects, the food price will rise. A disproportionate share of the supply response is met by the expansion of lowland food. This must be so, since the upland region, by assumption the most labour-intensive part of the economy, and within it the food sector, by assumption the more labour-intensive upland sector, suffers the greatest cost increase when the expansion of manufacturing drives up the economy-wide wage. Down-slope migration – an increase in the lowland region's labour endowment – then somewhat offsets increased labour costs in *both* lowland sectors.

We have now established that $\partial L^U/\partial q \leq 0$ and $\partial p/\partial q \geq 0$ under reasonable assumptions about the relative magnitudes of income and substitution effects and the factor market effects of the shock. When the price of the manufactured good increases, there is down-slope migration, and the price of food relative to tree crops is likely to rise. Because there are contradictory effects on the food price, however, it is reasonable to suppose that the *overall* effect of an exogenous shock on p could be small, whatever its impacts on resource allocation in each sector and region.

How is deforestation affected by an increase in q? The land conversion decision is made by upland producers on the basis only of the private profitability condition (4.3), which says that, in equilibrium, the value of the marginal product of converted land (R_T, or the marginal return to land) is just equal to the conversion cost (αR_L, the value of the unit labour requirement for clearing forest). A change in q, or in any other exogenous variable, alters land returns relative to wages; this then stimulates an increase or reduction in deforestation so as to restore the equality of marginal costs and returns.

Examining the general equilibrium solution for $\partial T / \partial q$ obtained by Cramer's Rule from (A4.1), we find, after collecting terms:

$$\frac{\partial T}{\partial q} = \{(Z_{nq} - \mu Z_q)(ce - bf) + S_{Lq}(bc - ae)\}/D \tag{A4.6}$$

Under assumptions (4.1) and (4.2), the pure food market effect of the terms of trade shock (assuming the substitution effect to be dominant) diminishes the demand for upland land. The labour market effect is ambiguous since, on one hand, labour (forest-clearing) costs have risen, and, on the other, labour is drawn from uplands to lowlands.

The labour market effect is scaled by the impact on the economy-wide wage of an increase in manufacturing- sector labour demand, S_{Lq}. When this is positive, the expansion of manufacturing raises labour costs in all sectors; when labour costs rise, the costs of land clearing rise faster than returns, and this has a negative effect on T. The indirect effect is secondary: there may be additional wage changes as labour is reallocated among sectors and regions according to their capacity to respond to the cost increase. If all agricultural sector responses were equal ($b = c = 0$), there would be only the direct wage effect. With lowland food production more responsive to a wage increase than upland, the wage rise shifts the distribution of food production towards uplands. The reallocation of food production thus has a *positive* effect on T, although clearly this indirect effect, being a consequence of the wage rise, must be dominated by the direct; the net labour market effect on T (the sum of direct and indirect effects) is therefore negative.

The indirect labour market effect is a consequence of the requirement that the food market clear domestically rather than through trade at an exogenous world price. The second term in (4.8) captures food market effects deriving from non-tradability. Assume for a moment that the demand for food is perfectly inelastic with respect to prices and income: in other words, that domestic food demand is a fixed quantity. Under this assumption, the terms of trade shock leaves food demand unchanged. However, the shock also raises the wage, and at constant product prices this causes the supply of food to fall. Under the assumption of a vertical food demand curve, the price of food must then rise to restore equilibrium. If the additional food supply needed to clear the market is sourced from uplands, there is pressure to increase forest clearance.

What effects do demand-side responses have on deforestation, independent of the labour market effects? Under assumption (4.1), the upland food sector is less labour-intensive than the lowland food sector, so $(bf - ce) > 0$ and the effect of a change in food demand is to reduce deforestation. Recall that with a fixed total labour supply, the equilibrium regional distribution of the labour force is that which equates labour's value marginal product between uplands and lowlands. Any change that disrupts this equilibrium results in a movement of labour either up-slope or down-slope. When the agricultural labour force contracts (because manufacturing has expanded) and aggregate food demand increases, the value of labour's marginal product rises faster in the region whose output supply is more responsive to a change in the labour endowment.[24] Because there has been no increase in the total labour supply, the output of the other region must therefore contract. If a contraction takes place in uplands, the deforestation rate also falls. Less formally, we may think of the economy as consisting of manufacturing and two kinds of agriculture, lowland and upland. An exogenous shock occurs that results in an increase in the manufacturing labour force as well as a change in the relative price of food. Some labour moves into manufacturing; the remaining agricultural labour then moves among agricultural enterprises (which are themselves expanding or contracting in response to the relative food price change) until the benefits from further moves are zero.

4B   Derivation of Changes in Upland Land Use

Consider the demand for land used in upland food production. We may obtain the change in demand for a factor from the solution to the cost minimization problem. As in any two-factor production technology, a constant elasticity of substitution (CES) functional form is completely general; assuming constant returns and totally differentiating the first-order conditions of the cost function yields:

$$dx_{ij} = \frac{\theta_{ij}}{w_i}(p_j dy_y + \sigma x_{kj} dw_k) \quad i \neq k,$$

where x_{ij} and w_i are factor quantities and prices, p_j and y_j are output price and quantity, θ_{ij} is the cost share of factor i, and σ is the elasticity of substitution. In the notation of our model, a change in the demand for land used in upland food production is:

$$dT_n = \frac{\theta_{Tn}}{w_T}(pdY_n + \sigma(1-\alpha)L^U dw_L), \tag{A4.7}$$

in which we know that $Y_n = R_n(T, L^U - \alpha T, p)$ and $w_L = S_L(K, L - L^U, p, q)$. In general equilibrium, we have:

$$\frac{dT_n}{d\lambda} = \frac{\theta_{Tn}}{w_T}\left\{p(R_{nT} - \alpha R_{nL})\frac{dT}{d\lambda} + (pR_{nL} - \gamma S_{LL})\frac{dL^U}{d\lambda} + (pR_{nn} + \gamma S_{Ln})\frac{dp}{d\lambda}\right.$$

$$\left. + \gamma\left[S_{LK}\frac{dK}{d\lambda} + S_{LL}\frac{dL}{d\lambda} + S_{Lq}\frac{dq}{d\lambda}\right]\right\} \tag{A4.8}$$

where $\gamma = \sigma\theta_{Ln}(1-\alpha)L^U > 0$ for $\alpha < 1$, that is, when it requires less than one unit of labour to clear a unit of forest, and $\lambda = \{K, L, p, q\}$ as before. From (A4.8) it is easy to see that:

$$\frac{\partial T_n}{\partial T} < 0, \frac{\partial T_n}{\partial p} > 0, \frac{\partial T_n}{\partial L^U} > 0, \frac{\partial T_n}{\partial L} < 0, \frac{\partial T_n}{\partial q} > 0, \frac{\partial T_n}{\partial K} > 0.$$

Other things equal, and for a given quantity of upland land in cultivation, *intensification* (an increase in the proportion of upland used for labour-intensive crops) increases with the upland labour force, the price of food relative to non-food, and with other changes that draw resources out of lowland food production. Conversely, *extensification* (a drop in the food crop share of upland land) occurs when lowland food production capacity is increased, *ceteris paribus*, or when deforestation occurs but upland food production remains static. Equation (A4.8) becomes the basis for general equilibrium calculations of the change in total land area used for upland food production.

NOTES

1. In some countries it is customary to distinguish subsets of what we have called 'uplands'. In Thailand, for example, this term is used only to describe mid-altitude areas with settled, relatively highly commercialized agricultural systems inhabited predominantly by members of the ethnic majority. Thais contrast this with 'highlands', which, although not necessarily high-altitude, are areas inhabited primarily by tribal minority groups whose economic and cultural systems have traditionally been reflected in distinct patterns of land use and forest exploitation. The economic and cultural basis of the distinction, although historically important, has become somewhat blurred over time with economic modernization, the spread of market and technological information, migration and changes in the political status of Thailand's ethnic minorities. In developing the model in this chapter we refer to all such areas as uplands.

2. In practice, there are sometimes large-scale conversions of forest to agriculture making use of more capital-intensive ('modern') methods, as in land -clearing carried out by the state or by large plantation corporations.

3. The usual operational definition of a country's real exchange rate is an index of the wholesale prices of its traded goods relative to those of its trading partners, adjusted by nominal exchange rates. The authoritative J.P. Morgan real exchange rate series (www.jpmorgan.com) is calculated in this way; the only goods excluded from each country's wholesale price index (WPI) series for this purpose are food prices.

4. Stocks and other forms of intertemporal arbitrage are ruled out by this assumption, even though these are frequently important in the short run (Williams and Wright 1991). In section 4.8, however, we sketch a simplified version in which the government engages in marketing and storage to clear the food market at a fixed price.

5. In a multiperiod model, this construction requires that *every* unit of land be cleared in *each* period. It can be defended as representing a single clearing cost spread over several crops within a single period (Lopez and Niklitschek 1991). Some related partial equilibrium analyses model clearing costs as being incurred only when land area is increased, but not when it remains constant or decreases (Coxhead *et al.* 2002).

6. The specification of a single set of preferences for a representative consumer is a major simplification in a model of this kind. For analytical purposes it may be desirable to specify at least as many distinct consumers as there are regions, given the sources of regional heterogeneity and their empirical motivation (see section 4.2.1 p. 82). The reduction to a single representative consumer diminishes the complexity of the model, however; intuitive stories about the effects of heterogeneous preferences are possible (see Chapter 8 for an elaboration), and so is the extrapolation of distributional results, as shown in empirical work reported in Chapters 6 and 7.

7. If the forest-clearing decision took account of social costs, the optimal clearing rate would be that which satisfied $R_T - \alpha R_L = E_T$, and the decision to cut trees would be socially optimal only if $R_T - E_T > \alpha R_L$; that is, the return on cleared land *net of the loss of forest amenities* should be greater than the cost of clearing.

8. These properties are analogous to the Stolper–Samuelson effect in a standard Heckscher–Ohlin model. Note that due to the endogeneity of agricultural land supply,

these properties depend on some further restrictions on the properties of the sectoral production functions. We assume these properties to be satisfied, and this assumption is critical to many of our comparative static results.

9. As we shall be considering solutions to several structural variants of the model, as a notational convention we shall write the determinant of a particular variant with a superscript identifying the key assumptions that characterize it. Hence D^L is the determinant of the variant in which only the labour market links regions; D^p will be used when only the domestic food market does so, and so on.

10. Alternatively, if upland food is land-intensive relative to non-food, then a rise in p can increase both up-slope migration and forest clearing for agriculture.

11. Conversely, if the change in q represented a positive terms of trade shock (that is, if manufactures were net exports), then each of the two components of the welfare change would be positive.

12. If q was the price of an exportable (so $Z_q < 0$), the income and substitution effects would reinforce one another; the price of food would unambiguously rise, and deforestation unambiguously decline. Again, the outcome occurs even with no interregional movement of labour.

13. Empirically, it is often the case that income effects are dominated by substitution effects; this is likely to be particularly true for staple food grains.

14. The model of technical progress in this section is an extension of one presented in our earlier work (Coxhead and Jayasuriya 1994), which explored the implications of technical progress in a two-region economy for upland *intensification*, that is, the area planted to labour-intensive food crops.

15. The assumption of a factor-neutral technical change is made purely for expositional convenience. For analyses incorporating non-neutral technical change in a general equilibrium context, see Warr and Coxhead (1993).

16. However, this does not necessarily imply that the aggregate environmental effect would be positive. Upland environmental gains must be set against the degradation of lowland environments due to increased water use, nutrient export from the flushing and leaching of inorganic fertilizers, and the harmful effects of uncontrolled pesticide use, which rose significantly with the adoption of Green Revolution technologies (IRRI 1978; Rola and Pingali 1993).

17. For corroborating empirical studies on prices, land use decisions and upland labour market responses from a common time-series data base, see Coxhead et al. (2001, 2002); and Rola and Coxhead (2001).

18. This insight is a specific variant of a more general observation by Jones (1971) that, under constant returns to scale, the change in returns to factors that are specific to a sector are always magnified versions of changes in the sector overall. Intuitively, the value marginal product of an intersectorally mobile factor (say, labour) is a weighted average of its productivity in all the sectors in which it is employed. Thus a downturn in one sector (in our example it is due to technical *regress* in lowland agriculture) has less effect on the return to labour than it does on the return to land, which is intersectorally immobile.

19. The assumption used here – that erosion has *direct* effects only on fixed factors – has intuitive appeal as well as simplifying the algebra. That mobile factor productivity should not be directly affected can be seen by considering the case of erosion affecting a sector that is a price taker in labour markets. Labour's value marginal product in the sector will remain unaffected by erosion (some labour will move out to other sectors), while that of land will decline. Accordingly, a change in the productivity of land represents, at constant prices, a change *relative to* the productivity of labour.

20. We have simplified by assuming that non-food cultivation generates no off-site erosion effect. It is a simple task to construct a more general model in which there are non-zero β_i for each upland crop i, thus making it possible to measure the effects of both upland expansion and intensification in terms of lowland damages. There are few new analytical insights to be gained by this, however. For recent empirical modelling of off-site damages by source, see Shively (2000).

21. Using (4.23) and (A4.8) in (4.24) gives the complete expression for the forest-clearing equilibrium when all externalities are taken into account. Recalling that:

$$\theta_{Tn} = w_T T_n / p R_n$$

and rearranging:

$$R_T - E_T + p\theta_{K_n}\beta B\frac{S_n}{R_n}(R_{nT} - \alpha R_{nL}) = \alpha R_L.$$

The social value of losses due to soil erosion is increasing in the food price, the land intensity of lowland food production, the productivity impact of erosion on lowland land, the ratio of lowland to upland food production, and the extent of factor intensity differences between upland sectors.

22. The food price control scenario is of particular interest; as noted in Chapter 3, most countries in developing Asia now engage in agricultural protection to some degree.

23. The labour result is sensitive to our assumptions on factor intensity and the responsiveness of labour demand. If $b = 0$, implying that factor intensity differences between upland sectors are very small, a rise in the price of food has a correspondingly smaller differential effect on upland food supply, and this reduces the extent to which labour is released by the upland food sector. Similarly, if $c \geq 0$, additional food demand caused by the shock would be met by expanded supply from uplands rather than lowlands; this could result in reverse migration.

24. The output supply response with respect to labour endowment, R_{nL} or S_{nL}, is equal to the response of labour's value marginal product to an increase in the corresponding product price, R_{Ln} or S_{Ln}, by Young's theorem.

5. Applied general equilibrium models and methods

5.1 INTRODUCTION

The magnitudes of natural resource and environmental degradation values in relation to developing economy GDP have frequently been estimated to be quite large (Chapter 1). These relative magnitudes are due to the importance of the sectors using environmental and natural resource (ENR) assets intensively, particularly agriculture, in relation to the total size of the economy. We have argued that these magnitudes, along with the factor and product market links that connect resource sectors to the overall economy, merit a general equilibrium approach to the measurement of the economic implications of environmental change. In general equilibrium, all prices are assumed to vary endogenously; in general equilibrium, given competitive markets, prices vary until all markets clear. Thus 'general equilibrium takes account of all of the interactions among markets, as well as the functioning of the individual markets' (Varian 1992: 313).

In practice, computational and information constraints limit the 'generality' of the general equilibrium approach. Economists concerned to capture general equilibrium processes face a trade-off between analytical clarity, which requires very highly simplified models, and meaningful numerical results, which require large, very detailed computational models. In Chapters 2–4 we presented the former type of model, to identify and understand fundamental intersectoral and interregional linkages and the mechanisms through which economic 'shocks' are transmitted. In the following chapters we present three examples of the latter approach: relatively large, numerical applied general equilibrium (AGE) models, from which we can obtain simulation results that stand up to empirical scrutiny and provide detailed quantitative information to inform policy formulation. While the match between analytical and numerical models is not exact, the insights obtained from study of analytical models help us to understand, interpret and verify the results of numerical simulations.[1]

In the following sections we first set out a basic AGE model, review methods and empirical approaches to the incorporation of environmental and natural resource phenomena, then briefly describe ways in which the basic model is adapted to incorporate environmental phenomena.

5.2 AGE BASICS

Applied general equilibrium models, for the most part, describe a Walrasian equilibrium in a manner sufficiently detailed to support the claim that they are realistic representations of actual economies. This typically means that they are too large and complex to be solved analytically (as with the models in previous chapters); instead, they take advantage of the power of computers to generate simultaneous numerical solutions for a large number of variables. The numerical solutions cannot be subjected to hypothesis testing in the way that econometric models can. Nevertheless, AGE models are founded upon the same body of economic theory as are the smaller analytical models, and their numerical results must therefore be consistent with theoretical predictions. This provides one kind of check on the veracity of their results.[2]

The advantages of AGE models derive from their size. Unlike analytical models, they permit the representation of an economy in which many products are produced using many factors; they can accommodate many households with diverse sources of income and patterns of expenditure, making distributional comparisons possible; they can also be used for highly disaggregated analysis of trade, government revenues and expenditures, and other microeconomic phenomena. They can be used with the very detailed data on sectoral production and input use, trade and the sources and disposition of incomes that are available from input–output tables and the national accounts; moreover, these 'base' data can be used in combination with econometric estimates of the parameters that govern marginal rates of factor and product substitution and marginal propensities to consume and save, so as to reproduce the behaviour of optimizing producers and consumers.

The standard approach to AGE modelling is to construct a database representing a benchmark (or initial) equilibrium, then to apply hypothetical shocks resulting in a new, counterfactual equilibrium. In this book we use AGE models which, although they originate in different projects and have different features, are all solved by the 'Johansen' method, meaning that the equations of the model are linear in proportional changes of variables and the whole system is solved by inversion of a matrix of coefficients. Solutions are likewise expressed in proportional or percentage changes from their base values. Because the solutions are linear in proportional changes, they are subject to the errors of linearization associated with all first-order approximations; however, these are small for small changes in exogenous variables, and methods to minimize them exist (Dixon *et al.* 1992). The linearization approach has the advantage that the effects of individual shocks can be combined, or decomposed, simply by adding or subtracting individual results. By this means, for example, a simulation result can be decomposed into separate contributions from adjustments in factor markets, product markets and so on.

The main technological and behavioural relationships of a basic model are derived from the first-order conditions of revenue, cost and utility functions. For an economy consisting of N products and F primary factors, define the following variables and vectors (vectors in bold; set size in parentheses):

$\mathbf{P}$	commodity prices (N)	$\mathbf{W}$	mobile factor prices (F)
$\mathbf{R}$	sector-specific factor prices (N)	$\mathbf{Y}$	domestic commodity supplies (N)
$\mathbf{X}$	mobile factor demands ($N \times F$)	$\mathbf{D}$	domestic final demands (N)
$\mathbf{S}$	net imports (N)	$\mathbf{V}$	factor endowments (F)
U	aggregate utility (1)	ϕ	foreign currency exchange rate (1)

Suppose factor endowments and commodity prices to be given, and let $\phi = 1$ be the numéraire price. Aggregate revenue (that is, GNP) is given by $G(\mathbf{P}, \mathbf{V}) = \max\{\mathbf{P} \cdot \mathbf{Y} \mid \mathbf{V}\}$; from the first-order conditions of this problem we obtain, using the envelope theorem, the sectoral supply functions:

$$Y_j = Y_j(\mathbf{P}, \mathbf{V}) \qquad (j = 1, ..., N), \tag{5.1}$$

and the prices of mobile and specific factors:

$$W_i = W_i(\mathbf{P}, \mathbf{V}) \qquad (i = 1, ..., F), \tag{5.2}$$

$$R_j = R_j(\mathbf{P}, \mathbf{V}) \qquad (j = 1, ..., N). \tag{5.3}$$

Each sector is assumed to be a price taker in factor markets. Therefore, the output level that maximizes revenue is also the cost-minimizing level, and from the first-order conditions of the sectoral cost-minimization problem $C_j(\mathbf{W}, Y_j) = \min\{\mathbf{W} \cdot \mathbf{X} \mid Y_j\}$, we obtain demands for intersectorally mobile factors:

$$X_{ij} = X_{ij}(\mathbf{W}, Y_j) \qquad (i = 1, ..., F; j = 1, ..., N). \tag{5.4}$$

Domestic final demands for each commodity are found by the envelope theorem from the first-order conditions of the consumer's expenditure minimization problem $E(\mathbf{P}, U) = \min\{\mathbf{P} \cdot \mathbf{D} \mid U\}$:

$$D_j = D_j(\mathbf{P}, U) \qquad (j=1, ..., N). \tag{5.5}$$

Net commodity trade volumes are determined by market-clearing conditions:

$$S_j = D_j - Y_j \qquad (j=1, ..., N), \tag{5.6}$$

where $S_j > (<) \, 0$ indicates a net import (export) good. Import prices are set in world markets, while for M exportables $(M \leq N)$, prices are set by inverse foreign demand functions:

$$P_k = P_k(S_k) \qquad (k=1, ..., M). \tag{5.7}$$

Finally, the model is closed by an aggregate budget constraint:

$$E(\mathbf{P}, U) = G(\mathbf{P}, \mathbf{V}) \tag{5.8}$$

The system (5.1)–(5.8) contains $4N + F + FN + M + 1$ equations, but the model contains $5N + 2F + FN + 2$ variables. A solution requires that the number of endogenous variables be just equal to the number of equations. The choice of a *closure*, technically speaking, is the choice of a subset of $(N - M + F + 1)$ variables to be exogenous, such that the condition for a solution is satisfied. In a short-run neoclassical closure, $\mathbf{V}$ is declared exogenous, and so is a subset $(N - M)$ of the vector $\mathbf{P}$. The exchange rate ϕ is selected as numéraire price. The number of equations is thus made equal to the number of endogenous variables, and (5.1)–(5.8) solve for $\mathbf{Y}$, $\mathbf{W}$, $\mathbf{R}$, $\mathbf{X}$, $\mathbf{D}$, $\mathbf{S}$, U, and the M endogenous elements of $\mathbf{P}$.

Alternative closures may be specified by selecting different combinations of variables to be exogenous. In some economies, for example, the assumption of a fixed wage with 'slack' (unemployment) in the labour market may be judged to be more empirically robust than that of a flexible nominal wage and full employment. The closure reflecting this would require fixing W_L exogenously, and allowing the value of the corresponding factor endowment, V^L (interpreted as total employment), to be solved within the model.

In an economy with complete and competitive markets and constant returns to scale, it is a condition of equilibrium that factor and product markets clear, aggregate expenditure is equal to income, and trade is in balance. In the basic model just sketched, factor-market clearing is implied by the conditions for revenue maximization, and the markets for non-traded commodities (for which $S_j = 0$) clear by (5.6). Aggregate expenditures are set equal to income in (5.8). By Walras' law, when these conditions are all met the balance of trade is also zero, thus satisfying the conditions for general equilibrium.

Our simulation models add considerable complexity, but do not alter this basic framework. They allow for intermediate inputs and for inputs and products distinguished by source (domestic or foreign), and they distinguish different kinds of labour input, for example skilled, rural and urban, which can be combined to create a composite labour input. The productivity of primary factors and intermediate inputs can be altered to represent input-specific technical progress in each sector. Final demands for domestic and imported commodities are also distinguished by use category: households, government, net trade and capital creation. Government commodity demands and the demands for capital creation are exogenous. Markets are assumed to be perfectly competitive and, with constant returns to scale, there are zero pure profits in production, trade and capital creation. Trade and transport margins are possible in each sector and, where they are non-zero, are proportional to the relevant commodity flows. Domestic and foreign goods within the same commodity category are differentiated by origin, so domestic and foreign prices may differ. We also allow for taxes, tariffs and subsidies to drive wedges between domestic and foreign prices, and between producer and consumer prices. In production, we assume that intermediate inputs are combined with an aggregate primary factor in fixed proportions. However, this assumption of fixed proportions does not apply to the individual primary factors. Rather, where data permit, production technology for primary factors is specified as a flexible functional form with econometrically estimated parameters; otherwise, we assume constant elasticity of substitution (CES) technology. This specification ensures that producers can respond to changing relative factor prices by altering the input mix, even if the final 'aggregate' primary factor must then be combined with intermediate inputs in fixed proportions.

In addition to solving for price and quantity responses, we are interested in a variety of aggregate economic magnitudes, such as employment, GDP, government revenues and expenditures, income distribution and approximations to measures of economic welfare. These are computed in the AGE models by means of appropriate addition and aggregation rules. The models are solved in linearized form using Gempack software (Harrison and Pearson 1996). Additional details of the individual AGE models are provided in Chapters 6–8.

5.3   AGE ANALYSIS OF ENVIRONMENTAL ISSUES

Incorporating Environment and Natural Resource Depletion in AGE Models

The use of AGE models with explicit environmental features is a very recent innovation. Most existing models were built for some other purpose, typically the analysis of tax and/or trade policies, and have subsequently had environmental features added. The environmental components of such models are usually specified through some interaction between production processes and environmental characteristics, such as emissions of air or water pollution, or demands for natural resources. Most models focus exclusively on domestic environmental implications, ignoring international spillovers or externalities. As changes occur in the real economy (for example, as the result of terms of trade shocks or policy reforms), the model captures environmental changes through the responses of optimizing agents in production sectors.

There have been several previous efforts to apply AGE methods to the study of environmental problems, including some addressing issues in developing Asia (Burniaux *et al.* 1992; Goulder *et al.* 1998; Bergmen 1995; Vennemo 1997; Jorgenson 1998; Abler *et al.* 1999; Babiker 2001; Alavalapati A. *et al.* 1996; Anderson and Strutt 2000; and many more cited in a recent survey by Angelsen and Kaimowitz 1998). Many of these models emerge from broader, interdisciplinary efforts to understand and measure environmental processes in a developing economy context. A common feature is that they typically embody significant amendments to standard representations of economic structure in order to capture environmental processes. They may, for example, include explicit quantifications of the consequences of the depletion of a natural resource stock, or the productivity effects of emissions from one sector that affect production in another. One methodology for this is given in the following subsection.

Other AGE models, by contrast, being built for the analysis of more narrowly defined sets of economic questions, generate environmental information through interpretation and extrapolation of results using data on known environmental processes. In such models the environmental results are obtained as a 'side calculation' from the simulation results, using data external to the model. As an example, an AGE model may be used to simulate the effects of a policy change, with the implications of that change for environmental variables then computed from a separate database on emissions by sector or activity. Because sectors have different propensities to pollute, a policy change that alters relative profitability will affect pollution and natural resource degradation.

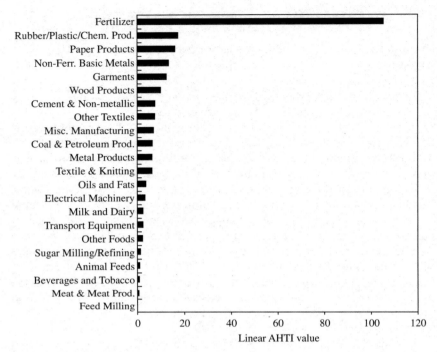

Source: Hettige *et al.* (1995)

Figure 5.1   Acute human toxicity indices for manufacturing industries

Figure 5.1 provides an indication of the ways in which changes in the structure of production contribute to changes in the output of emissions. It shows summary sectoral data from a widely used measure of industrial emissions, the Acute Human Toxicity Index (AHTI), for manufacturing industries.[3] Clearly, any change that induces a change in the output mix by altering relative sectoral profitability has predictable implications for emissions.

Where forests, soils and water are concerned, there is less information overall, and it is less reliable at the level of any country, region or sector. It is rare to be able to use econometric or other statistical methods to test hypotheses about the influences of economic variables on natural resource use, even at the level of a single developing country. Simulations using an AGE model enable modellers to anchor numerical analyses on explicit and internally consistent frameworks, even where the true values of underlying technological parameters are not well established.

Modelling Agricultural Land Degradation

An important feature of the Philippine and Sri Lankan models of Chapters 6 and 7 is the allocation of agricultural land to different crops, each of which has a unique propensity to contribute to soil erosion. To the structure of the basic model summarized in section 5.2, therefore, we add relationships governing land mobility among some agricultural sectors as well as accounting equations for quantities of land degradation. The methodology is as follows. To measure on-site effects of soil erosion, we define total erosion (Q, measured as total tons of soil lost per year) as the sum over sectors $i = 1..., N$ of per hectare erosion rates, H_i, multiplied by land area, Z_i:

$$Q = \sum Z_i H_i \tag{5.9}$$

We express the above equation in percentage change form (percentage changes of variables are defined by lower-case characters, for example, $x = dX/X$ for each variable X) to obtain an expression for the change in total erosion as the weighted sum of sectoral area and erosion rate changes, the weights being each sector's base year contribution to total erosion:

$$q = \sum \alpha_i (z_i + h_i), \tag{5.10}$$

where $\alpha_i = Z_i H_i / Q$. Each crop grown in each region (for example, 'upland', 'midland' or 'lowland') is associated with a specific erosion rate. We assume that in percentage change form, erosion in sector i is linearly related to land use in that sector – that is, we abstract from the possibility that land quality differences, management practices, or investments in soil-conserving technology might alter the erosion rate associated with each crop and each ecosystem. Thus $h_i = 0$, and we have:

$$q = \sum \alpha_i z_i. \tag{5.11}$$

Land use changes (z_i) are endogenously related to changes in prices, production and technology through CES agricultural input demand functions derived from the cost-minimizing behaviour of firms. Let Y_j denote the output of sector j, W_k the price of input k, and T_j and T_{kj} respectively be sector-wide and input-specific rates of technological progress. We then write the demand for land in sector j, Z_j, with price w_{zj}, in percentage change form as:

$$z_j = y_j - \sigma_j (w_{zj} - \sum_k w_{kj} \delta_{kj}) - \sigma_j (t_{zj} - \sum_k t_{kj} \delta_{kj}) - t_j, \tag{5.12}$$

where σ_j is the elasticity of substitution among inputs in sector j and $\delta_{kj} = W_i X_{ij}/\sum_k W_k X_{kj}$ is the value of payments to factor i as a fraction of total costs in sector j. Equation (5.12) states that if relative factor prices and technology remain unchanged, land use in the sector will increase or decline in direct proportion to output. If factor prices or technology also change, land use in the sector will be modified accordingly, and thus, by (5.11), the production of aggregate erosion will also change. In our models, values of Y_j, W_{ij}, and Z_j are endogenous and the T_{ij}s are exogenous. For the most part we assume that aggregate land supply is fixed, to maintain the medium-run focus on resource allocation among sectors and subsectors in the economy. Further, land in each region is mobile (that is, can be reallocated) among crops. The market-clearing condition for land in each region, therefore, is:

$$\sum_i S_i^r z_i^r = 0, \qquad (5.13)$$

for all $r = \{\text{regions}\}$ and $i = \{\text{crops}\}$, where $S_i^r = Z_i^r/\sum_i Z_i^r$ are initial shares of each subsector in total use of land type r. With land mobility among sectors in each region, a change that alters the relative profitability of subsectors will induce reallocation of land, thus altering aggregate erosion levels.

If there is no change in land use in a particular sector in a particular region, then its soil erosion level will remain at the base level. The changes in land use may occur either through changes in the derived demand for land as sectoral output levels rise or fall, or through changes in relative factor prices and hence substitution of land for other factors, or through factor-biased technical progress. In this regard, equations (5.12) and (5.13) deal with estimating on-site changes in soil erosion, taking into account shifting patterns of land use due to profit-maximizing behaviour in each sector-specific crop-industry. A limitation of this procedure is that the level of erosion is governed solely by exogenously given technology and land allocated to specific crops; output of erosion per unit of land for a given crop is not a choice variable for the producers.[4]

The major off-site effect of soil erosion is the reduction of productive capacity in downstream electric power generation and irrigated agriculture. These effects can be considered as equivalent to non-neutral technological regress in the affected sectors, since sector-specific capital is directly affected, while the factor productivity of mobile factors may be altered by a smaller amount or not at all. We follow Coxhead (1994) in modelling this relationship and consider the following production function (for simplicity, sectoral subscripts are suppressed):

$$Y = Y(L, K(V, Q)), \qquad (5.14)$$

where L is the (vector of) effective quantities of labour, K is the effective quantity of capital, V is the physical endowment of capital, and Q is the overall rate of erosion. The percentage change form of the above equation is:

$$y = \epsilon_L l + \epsilon_K v + \epsilon_V \gamma_E q, \qquad (5.15)$$

where $\varepsilon_L = (\partial Y/\partial L)(L/Y) > 0$; $\varepsilon_K = (\partial Y/\partial K)(K/Y) > 0$; $\varepsilon_V = (\partial K/\partial V)(V/K) = 1$ by the assumption of sector specificity of K; and $\gamma_Q = (\partial Y/\partial Q)(Q/K)$ is the change in specific capital productivity attributed to the effects of soil erosion – the 'productivity impact parameter', or PIP.

At constant prices and for a given capital endowment, (5.15) states that an increase in soil erosion reduces the lowland sectors' output by reducing their effective specific capital endowment. The extent of this output decline is determined by the initial contribution of the specific factor to total value-added in the sector concerned, and the degree of substitutability of other inputs for the specific factor.

5.4 DATA AND SOLUTION ALGORITHMS

The fundamental database for any AGE model is an input–output (I–O) table, showing the disposition of each industry's output and its expenditures on intermediate goods and primary factors. These data are used to compute base year sales and costs as well as household income from factors. The I–O data are augmented with information from the national accounts to form a social accounting matrix (SAM), which records the breakdown of final demands (sales to households, government, investment goods production and net trade). These permit the computation of revenue shares by industry as well as the distribution of demand by each final demand category. In equilibrium, the SAM is balanced in the sense that the total value of sales by each industry, summed across all categories of intermediate and final demand, is equal to that industry's expenditures on primary and intermediate inputs and net taxes; the government's revenues from net taxes are equal to its expenditures net of savings; households' incomes from factors and transfers are equal to their expenditures for consumption net of taxes and savings; and the value of imports equals that of imports net of international capital flows.[5]

While the SAM provides the data needed to 'account' for economic activity in the initial equilibrium, describing the behaviour of optimizing firms and consumers requires an additional parameter set. This contains elasticities that quantify marginal rates of substitution in production and consumption; namely marginal rates of transformation among jointly produced goods, export demands, and the substitutability of goods from imported and domestic sources. In most AGE models these elasticity values are acquired through literature surveys or informed guesswork. Two of the models we use, those for the Philippines and Thailand, make use instead of elasticity data sets based on econometric estimation (see Chapters 6 and 8 for detailed references).

When a parameter is obtained through econometric estimation, standard errors of the estimates provide an indication of the degree to which we may suppose the estimate to approximate the true value of the parameter. When, on the other hand, elasticity values are obtained by means of literature searches or 'guesstimation', it is appropriate to analyse the sensitivity of AGE simulation results with respect to parameter values. Source papers for each of the models reported in Chapters 6–8 report such analyses; we refer to these only as necessary.

5.5   CLOSURE

The macroeconomic closure of a general equilibrium model reflects assumptions about economic structure. Alternative closures can thus be used to conduct what might be called 'structural sensitivity analysis'; that is, to examine the robustness of simulation results with respect to the specification of macroeconomic relationships.

Closures adopted in the models of Chapters 6–8 are typically neoclassical for small open economies. World prices of tradables are exogenously fixed (there are a few exceptions, such as that of tea in Sri Lanka, as noted in individual chapters), and so is the nominal exchange rate, providing a numéraire for domestic prices. In general, we assume that the domestic prices of goods and services adjust to eliminate excess demand. There are some exceptions to this general rule, however. In labour markets it may be thought more empirically reasonable to assume initial slack accompanied by nominal wage rigidity; this is the assumption adopted in the Sri Lanka model in Chapter 7. Similarly, the market for agricultural land may be supposed to clear through adjustments in quantity rather than price, to replicate the addition or removal of fallow from the land use pattern at the margin. This assumption is applied in Chapter 6. In any such case of a non-neoclassical closure, care must be taken to ensure that measures of welfare based on the real expenditures of households take account of income changes due to increases or reductions in the employment level of factors.

Finally, macroeconomic aspects of the model closure are also important. In the following chapters the current account, budget deficit and real savings of households are all fixed, ensuring that the effects of exogenous shocks are fully absorbed by current-period changes in real household expenditures. The requirements of fiscal neutrality and current account balance are artefacts of the static nature of this class of AGE model. In the real world, governments can run budget deficits or surpluses over the short term, financing deficits by recourse to intertemporal instruments such as bonds and foreign borrowing in the anticipation of increased future tax revenues. Similarly, economies can run persistent current account deficits so long as a zero balance of payments is maintained by accommodating capital inflows. The closure in a one-period model cannot accommodate intertemporal transfers of this kind. Unless fiscal and current account balance is imposed, an excess of domestic expenditure over income would simply result in borrowing without limit, and the usual measures of real income and welfare would be meaningless. Instead, a one-period model must mimic the intertemporal solution by forcing the government to finance a deficit (or expend a surplus) by means of an endogenous tax or expenditure instrument imposed on the current generation of households and firms. Similarly, unless endogenous foreign capital inflows are specifically permitted, the current account of the balance of payments must remain in balance.

5.6 CONCLUSION

Applied general equilibrium models are dauntingly complex, as attested to by the frequency with which even economists are tempted to malign them as 'black boxes'. We prefer to think of them as analogous to topographical maps. The optimal scale of a map depends on the use to which it is put. AGE models must be 'drawn' at a scale that is useful for empirical and policy analysis; this requires that they are highly complex, but does not of itself render them incomprehensible, any more than is a highly detailed map to a reader with the requisite skills. This chapter has provided a very brief overview of the basic characteristics of AGE models, with heavy emphasis on the ways in which standard models can and have been adapted for the analysis of environmental phenomena arising from economic stimuli. We have stressed the underlying common elements of AGE models in order to provide readers with the 'map-reading' skills needed to interpret the simulation results presented in the next three chapters. Each of the models to be presented builds on essentially the same platform, even though each differs from the others in important ways, as will be described in more detail as the need arises.

NOTES

1. Uncertainty about the true values of parameters used in a model can be addressed through sensitivity analysis, accomplished by systematically varying the parameter values in question and recomputing the solutions.
2. See Shoven and Whalley (1984) for an excellent survey of the characteristics and methodologies of AGE models.
3. AHTI is an aggregate emissions score developed for developing countries by Hettige *et al.* (1995). The score is measured in risk-weighted pounds of Toxic Release Inventory (TRI) emissions per $1,000 of shipment value (the TRI aggregates 322 chemicals in an index developed by the US Environmental Protection Agency). Higher AHTI scores indicate greater emissions intensity. These emissions measures are not based on developing country-specific data due to unavailability; however, 'the present version [of the AHTI data] can be useful as a guide to probable pollution problems [in developing countries], even if exact estimates are not possible' (ibid.: 7). The web site of the World Bank's project on New Ideas in Pollution Regulation (http://www.worldbank.org/nipr) provides additional details of the AHTI database and lists many developing country studies that make use of it.
4. For partial equilibrium models of land use in which soil erosion is a choice variable, see Burt (1981); Clarke (1992); McConnell (1983); and Shively (1997).
5. King (1981) provides a succinct and clear overview of the concept and construction of a SAM.

6. Protection, food policy and the environment in the Philippines

6.1 INTRODUCTION

In this chapter we study interactions between policies, economic growth and the environment in the Philippines. We focus on deforestation and land degradation issues, and also on the causes and consequences of inter-regional migration and the relative price movements that help to drive natural resource allocation decisions. We also consider some urban/industrial pollution issues. In the following sections, we first review recent economic and environmental trends (section 6.2). Next, in section 6.3 we examine specific recent economic trends and policy initiatives that have a bearing on environment and development, in particular the effects of partial trade liberalization, and those of the Green Revolution in a policy-distorted economy. Using an AGE model of the Philippine economy (section 64), we present some simulation results indicating likely trends in economic and environmental variables given trade liberalization or technical progress in agriculture. Section 6.5 presents a brief conclusion.

6.2 THE STATE OF THE PHILIPPINE ENVIRONMENT[1]

The Philippines' environment and natural resource sector is generally classified as comprising five major interlinked, and sometimes overlapping, ecosystems:

1. forest and upland;
2. agriculture/cropland;
3. fresh water;
4. coastal and marine; and
5. urban/industrial.[2]

Some of these ecosystems include significant mineral and other natural resources; others also host a rich variety of flora and fauna. The country is home to 5 per cent of the world's flora, 6 per cent of the birds, and 4 per cent of the mammals; 67 per cent of the species in the major groups of animals and plants are not found anywhere else in the world. Its coral reefs are second only to those of Australia's Great Barrier Reef in terms of the diversity of coral and fish species, and the country has the second highest number of seagrass species in the world. However, each of the Philippine ecosystems faces significant, often severe, problems of environmental degradation, both from the depletion of resource stocks and from the production of polluting emissions.

Forests and Uplands

The forest and upland ecosystem covers around 45 per cent of total land area, and its resources directly support about 30 per cent of the population, including some of the poorest in the country. It is experiencing severe pressures of a variety of kinds, of which the most prominent is rapid deforestation.

Between 1900 and 1950 national forest cover fell from around 70 per cent of total land to 50 per cent, and by the end of the 1980s had fallen further to less than 25 per cent (Kummer 1992); by the close of the twentieth century forest cover was less than 19 per cent.[3] In a regional perspective, the Philippine deforestation rate is well in excess of rates in neighbouring countries – even those which, like Vietnam, do not have especially large initial forest stocks. A large proportion of the uplands, most of which are classified as forest, are steeply sloped and have soils which are prone to severe degradation and erosion once cleared of their permanent cover.

The two main causes of deforestation are land clearance for agriculture and commercial exploitation of forests for logs, lumber, fuel (including charcoal) and pulpwood. The relative importance of these two activities is a matter of dispute, but commercial logging, both legal and illegal, appears to be primarily responsible for depletion of old-growth *dipterocarp* forests with valuable timber, with conversion to agricultural uses accounting for much of the deforestation of secondary or residual forest lands.[4] During the 1980s, total cultivated area increased by about 230,000 ha per year, a rate of over 2 per cent (FAO 2001).

In upland areas, increases in agricultural production have traditionally come to a great extent from expansion at the cultivated margin rather than by improving the efficiency with which existing land resources are utilized. Between 1960 and 1987, the upland population more than doubled to an estimated 18 million, and the area devoted to upland agriculture increased sixfold, coinciding with a rapid decline in forest cover (Bee 1987; World Bank 1989; WRI 1999a). In upland agriculture, the highest fraction of land is planted to rice and corn, with lesser amounts planted to vegetables, tree crops and pasture, among other uses. During the 1990s the national planted area of cereal crops declined somewhat, but this was due to the conversion of lowland land to other crops and non-agricultural uses rather than to a contraction in uplands and at the land frontier.

Deforestation in the Philippines has had quite direct and tangible economic effects, as well as environmental impacts whose economic costs are less immediately visible. In the recent past, Philippine timber and processed wood products were major sources of foreign exchange, accounting for as much as a third of all exports during the late 1960s. They now account for only 0.2 per cent of export revenues (NSCB 1995). Similarly, gross value-added in forestry and wood products fell in absolute terms throughout the 1970s and 1980s. In relative terms, the GDP share of forestry and wood industries fell from 2.5 per cent in 1975 to only 0.3 per cent by 1994. A large part of the population, particularly in rural areas, depends on fuelwood for household energy, and deforestation threatens future fuelwood supplies. The potential for irreversible changes in the stock of biodiversity, although more difficult to quantify, has recently risen to the forefront of environmental concerns (Republic of the Philippines 1998).[5]

Watershed degradation as a consequence of deforestation has emerged as perhaps the most important environmental problem of the Philippines, and its impacts are felt in lowlands as well as in uplands. By 1993, 17 per cent of the total land area was estimated to be badly eroded, 28 per cent moderately eroded, and a further 29 per cent slightly eroded. Nearly 60 per cent of the total cropland area is considered to be degraded to varying degrees (Republic of the Philippines 1998); the annual value of on-site damage from erosion *only* has been estimated to be about 0.25 per cent of GDP. Deforestation and the associated conversion of forested uplands to agriculture has degraded the hydrological functions of watersheds, and in watersheds where water retention capacity has been lost along with forest cover and biomass, annual fluctuations in stream flow are exaggerated, making such systems more prone to the effects of drought and flash flooding (Deutsch *et al.* 2001). Deforestation and the conversion of land to agriculture have exacerbated soil erosion. Shifting cultivation (*kaingin*) systems traditionally practised by indigenous upland communities may have been environmentally sustainable in the past, but increased population pressure in uplands has reduced fallow periods, and the more intensive farming practices of new immigrants to uplands are more land degrading (Table 6.1; and see David 1988; Cruz *et al.* 1988). Soil runoff has raised the total suspended sediment (TSS) loadings of rivers, and silt deposits in dams and canals have diminished the capacity and efficiency of irrigation systems and hydroelectric power facilities. In areas where commercial agricultural

Table 6.1   Erosion rates by land use: the Philippines

Land use	Erosion rate (tonnes/ha/yr)
Undisturbed forest	0.1–0.4
Second-growth forests	1–7
Rice paddies	0.2–10
Plantations (depending on age and species)	2.4–75
Grasslands	1.5–3
Overgrazed lands	90–270
Shifting cultivation (no conservation measures)	90–240
Annual cash crops (uplands)	30–180

Source of basic data: NRAP (1991)

production is intensively pursued, pesticide runoff is also a problem (Deutsch *et al.* 2001).

Agriculture and Croplands

Agriculture remains the largest single sector and employer in the Philippine economy. Well over half the population depends either directly or indirectly on income generated through agricultural production. Although investments in irrigation and periods of technical progress have increased the productivity of some land and the yields of some crops, Philippine agriculture has experienced relatively low overall rates of productivity growth. Cereal and root crop yields and fertilizer use rates are among the lowest in tropical Asia (WRI 2000).

Thus, though expansion of agricultural land area was almost certainly an appropriate strategy in earlier decades when land was abundant, in recent decades the conversion of forests and upper watershed areas to agriculture (and especially to production of annual crops) has become a significant source of environmental problems. Evidence on long-term trends in the productivity of lowlands is equally disturbing. Staple grains (mainly rice and corn) account for most lowland land use. Intensive monoculture of any of these crops is known to be associated with long-term land productivity decline, a phenomenon sometimes disguised in recent years by technological progress (Cassman and Pingali 1995). Moreover, the productivity of lowland agriculture is directly dependent on the quality of irrigation services. Deforestation and watershed degradation have clearly diminished the quality of irrigation services in many areas of the country. The cost of restoring and maintaining such services appears to be rapidly rising. With the upland frontier virtually closed, and emerging signs of productivity growth slowdown – or even reversal – in the 'best' lowland irrigated areas, the degradation of the Philippine agricultural land base is a source of serious concern.

In cereal crops, agricultural development has been associated with intensive use of inorganic fertilizers and pesticides. Although 'environment-friendly' techniques such as integrated pest management (IPM) are increasingly popular, chemical control of pests remains the norm. Rice cultivation accounts for a large fraction of total agricultural chemical demand in the Philippines: in 1987, 47 per cent of all insecticides and 82 per cent of herbicides sold were for use in rice (Rola and Pingali 1993). Uncontrolled pesticide use and inappropriate application methods account for many deaths as well as eye, skin, respiratory, cardiovascular and neurological illnesses among farmers and their families. Such health problems have been documented by Rola and Pingali, who noted that, on average, the pesticide-related health cost to a sample of Central Luzon rice farmers far exceeded its benefits in terms of improved crop yields. Off-site, inorganic fertilizers and agricultural chemicals further contribute to water pollution, loss of biological function in lakes, streams and estuaries, and downstream health and abatement costs.

Coastal and Marine Ecosystems

The Philippines has 7,107 islands and a total coastline of 17,460 km; its marine territorial waters cover more than 2,000,000 sq. km of oceanic and coastal waters. The coastal and marine ecosystems are clearly major components of the country's environmental resources, performing critical ecological functions, hosting important resources such as mangroves, coral reefs and seagrass beds, and providing facilities for recreation and tourism. As with other environmental resources of the country, these too have been significantly degraded. With more than half the population residing in coastal areas, and most big cities located on the coast, these areas are subject to most of the environmental pressures emanating from population growth and the full range of human activities.

The most tangible and direct economic impact of environmental degradation of marine ecosystems is reflected in the depletion of fish stocks (due primarily to over-fishing, often with destructive methods such as bottom trawling, explosives and harmful chemicals), the destruction of mangrove areas and corals, and pollution of coastal waterways. Fish production levels have been maintained and even increased through greater fishing effort, further diminishing the future reproductive capacity of fish (Republic of the Philippines 1998).

Mangrove swamps play a key role in the coastal ecosystems, forming the foundation of the coastal fisheries food chain and the breeding ground for many species of fish and crustaceans. They also provide timber and charcoal for coastal households. Of approximately 450,000 ha of mangroves that existed in 1918, more than two-thirds had been destroyed by 1987–88. With continuing conversion of mangrove land to fishponds and other forms of aquaculture, tourism development, and exploitation for wood and charcoal, mangrove area declined further to only 120,500 ha by 1994, with most located in isolated regions. There is less quantitative information available on seagrass beds, whose importance in sustaining viable marine ecosystems is considered to be under-appreciated. However, they too are known to have experienced ongoing rapid degradation brought about by various forms of human activities such as coastal land development, mining, blast fishing and runoff induced by deforestation.

The Philippines' coral reefs not only provide a habitat for fish and other forms of marine life, contributing some 10–15 per cent of total fish production, but are also a major tourist attraction. Most (nearly 95 per cent) of the reefs have suffered some degree of degradation, with nearly a third being in poor condition. Direct human activities, though they make a major contribution, are not solely responsible for coral reef degradation; sediment deposit due to deforestation is considered a major source of coral damage, along with other factors such as mine tailings, destructive fishing methods and coastal developments.

Urban/Industrial Ecosystems

Rapid population growth and urbanization have contributed to urban population growth rates far in excess either of national or of regional averages in recent decades (Table 1.1). Industrial growth has also been highly concentrated in and around urban areas. As a consequence, air and water pollution problems are most acute in urban regions, and especially in Metro Manila, which has the largest concentration of population and industry.

Air pollution in Metro Manila is quite serious.[6] In 1992, in locations in Metro Manila where 80 per cent of the people lived, annual average total suspended particulates (TSP) concentrations were found to be frequently more than five times higher than the World Health Organization Air Quality Guidelines (WHO AQG). Measures of PM_{10} (particulate matter of less than 10 microns) were also two to three times higher than WHO AQG, and long-term measured lead levels exceeded both national and WHO guidelines.[7] Although these emissions levels are not very high by the standards of Southeast Asian cities (Table 1.2), their impact on health is nevertheless large. It has been estimated that in 1995, PM_{10} alone may have caused 1,300 deaths and respiratory diseases costing 4,594 million pesos (equivalent to 0.3 per cent of 1995 GDP) per year. According to some official sources, TSP emissions are on an upward trend.[8] The primary source of air pollution has been increased fuel consumption, both by motor vehicles and for power generation. Bunker oil combustion in small to medium-sized industrial and commercial enterprises was the major contributor to high TSP, followed by vehicle exhausts from diesel trucks, buses and jeepneys; vehicle exhausts contributed a greater share to PM_{10}. Gasoline contributed most lead, and the introduction of low lead gasoline in the early 1990s appears to have reduced ambient lead levels in air.

Rapid growth of urban centres has not been matched by infrastructure development to provide clean water, traffic control and mass transit systems, and problems of urban decay are mounting. The country's large cities do not have adequate sewage and waste disposal facilities. Only 13 per cent of households in Metro Manila are linked to a sewage system, and 40 per cent of solid household waste is dumped illegally, part being burnt, thereby adding to air pollution. Reporting these data, the 1998 Philippine National Development Plan (Republic of Philippines 1998) summed up conditions in urban areas as follows:

> The absence of far reaching comprehensive land use and human settlement plans has resulted in the deterioration of the country's cities as human habitats beset with interrelated problems like inadequate mass transportation and road systems; pollution and inadequate and inappropriate waste disposal systems; flooding; water shortage; deterioration and lack of basic social services; and proliferation of crime and other social evils. (pp. 4–9)

Freshwater Systems

The freshwater ecosystem, comprising 384 major river systems and 54 lakes and covering an area of about 569,600 ha, faces severe problems due to pollution and watershed degradation. Many of the major rivers and lakes, particularly those passing through or close to urban centres, are heavily polluted. The main river systems in Metro Manila are biologically dead,[9] and siltation and chemical residues are a serious problem for major lakes.

Urban water pollution is caused primarily by inappropriate disposal of household waste. Much of the remainder is contributed by industrial enterprises, the majority of which do not comply with existing water pollution standards. As mentioned earlier, inadequate sewage and other failings of waste disposal systems lead to much illegal dumping; a considerable proportion of daily household waste ends up in waterways. Elsewhere, with few river or lake system management schemes in place and little effective control over effluent discharges or runoff, agricultural chemical residues and, in some locations, effluents from mining operations also contribute to water pollution. The case of Laguna Lake illustrates many of these problems (Malayang 1993; World Bank 2000b).

This review, though brief and necessarily somewhat cursory, vividly illustrates the scope and severity of the challenges that human interventions pose for the integrity of Philippine ecosystems. Postwar population growth and economic expansion have been associated with decades of damage, both transitory and permanent, to these ecosystems. Considering that Philippine economic growth has been rather slow by regional standards, the extent of environmental damage incurred appears to have been very high.

Spatial Dimensions of Environmental Problems

The Philippines is geographically diverse, and poverty, growth and development are strongly spatially differentiated. The three major island groups (Luzon, Visayas and Mindanao) differ markedly in key demographic and socio-economic characteristics as well as in climate, topography, terrain and other biophysical attributes that influence natural resource endowments, including mineral deposits, land types and crop productivity. Urban–rural contrasts are also stark. By 2000, almost 60 per cent of the population lived in urban areas (of which a third were in Metro Manila); in contrast, in 1948, only 30 per cent lived in urban areas. Metro Manila produces a third of the country's GDP and, in general, average family incomes in urban areas are more than twice as high as in rural areas.

Within rural areas, population density and general indicators of household welfare are correlated with land quality, with irrigated lowlands supporting the wealthiest rural populations. Irrigated lowland rice cultivation is concentrated in the Manila hinterland as well as in several smaller areas in northern Luzon, the western Visayas and southern Mindanao. The largest numbers of rural poor are found in other parts of Mindanao and in the resource-poor, typhoon-prone eastern Visayas. In these areas, beyond relatively small pockets of irrigated rice land, the major crops are corn (grown both for feed and for human consumption), and coconut, the latter grown mainly in coastal and low-altitude areas.

In the postwar era there has been a geographic bifurcation of population growth rates. Natural increase and internal migration have both resulted in faster increases in urban populations and populations in upland/forest ecosystems. The reasons for this unusual pattern have largely to do with development policies, as discussed below.

The effects of various types of environmental and resource degradation similarly have differential spatial impacts. In general, industrial emissions are concentrated in and around urban agglomerations. Similarly, deforestation and the associated degradation of soils and watersheds in upland eco-systems affect rural (and within rural, upland) populations most directly. The extent of land degradation, too, varies quite substantially by region. The spatial distribution of environmental damages, like that of natural resources, becomes important when considering possible trade-offs between environmental conservation, poverty alleviation and the reduction of disparities in the real incomes of households.

6.3 DEVELOPMENT STRATEGY AND THE ENVIRONMENT

As we saw in Chapter 2, in decomposing the relationship between economy and environment it is important to separate, where possible, the effects of economic policies from those attributable to secular processes of growth and economic change. This is especially important in the Philippines, because development strategies and the institutions that support them have had a significant impact on the pace and nature of economic development. A case can be made that inappropriate land use, involving large-scale deforestation and land degradation affecting fragile uplands and water-sheds as well as coastal and marine ecosystems, and the associated migra-tion patterns observed in the Philippines, are not merely the inevitable consequences of rapid population growth and resulting pressures on the land frontier, but are at least partly attributable to the effects of policy.

Industrial and Agricultural Policies

The development strategy pursued by the Philippines from the early post-independence period was based on protectionist ISI policies. In this respect the Philippines was not very different from many other developing coun-tries. But unlike many of its neighbours in East and Southeast Asia, it failed to make an early transition to an export-oriented strategy. Significant trade reforms were initiated only in the late 1980s, and the country really started to shake free of its strong protectionist regime only in the 1990s.[10] Protectionist policies, together with highly centralized and heavily corrupt administrations, resulted in a boom–bust economic growth pattern that had both direct and indirect effects on resource use patterns and the growth of emissions. Industrial growth behind protective trade barriers discrimi-nated against the labour-intensive export-oriented activities in which the Philippines enjoyed comparative advantage; the structure of effective pro-tection was such that industries that were least internationally competitive had the highest protection. Not surprisingly, following the early phase of 'easy' import substitution industrialization, manufacturing sector growth slowed, despite large net transfers from other sectors, principally export agriculture.

The agricultural sector, which was indirectly penalized by the ISI strategy, was itself the target for a number of policies. Imports of rice and corn, the principal cereal crops and consumer staples, were heavily regulated in pursuit of 'food security' – in practice defined as self-sufficiency (Coxhead 2000). The state exerted a monopoly over international trade in these products and their substitutes. This in effect meant that rice and corn were converted into non-tradables and their domestic prices insulated from international prices. Domestic market interventions by the National Food Authority were aimed at stabilizing supply and prices. Cereals, principally lowland irrigated rice, also benefited from some direct and indirect subsidies in the form of state-funded irrigation investments, research and extension, and chemical inputs.

Corn gained increasingly high effective protection through trade policy, rising from near zero in the late 1960s to above 70 per cent in the early 1990s (Pagaluyang 1998). Corn is grown very widely in uplands (with upland rice, it accounted for about 45 per cent of cultivated land on slopes of above 18 per cent in the late 1980s). The land area devoted to corn has expanded significantly, often at the expense of forests, in uplands. Thus protection that raised the profitability of domestic corn production had a direct and negative environmental impact, as corn cultivation on steeply sloping lands is highly erosive under the land and crop management regimes practised by the majority of Philippine upland farmers.

Though agricultural sectors such as rice and corn benefited from some government policies, the overall impact of the policy regime on the agriculture sector was strongly negative (Bautista 1984; Intal and Power 1990). These policies generated periodic economic crises and related political upheavals, further blurred the rate of return 'signals', and eroded both domestic and foreign investor confidence. As a consequence, despite high tariff barriers, the manufacturing sector's share of GDP and total employment failed to increase, and the Philippines' overall growth performance was the worst among the ASEAN countries from the 1970s until the 1997 Asian economic crisis.

Policies that diminished profitability and dampened employment growth in agriculture and traditional, rural-based industries impacted on the spatial and sectoral distribution of increments to the Philippine population. Philippine urbanization, and especially the growth of Manila relative to other urban centres, was in part a consequence of the ISI strategy.[11] With few new employment opportunities in traditional, lowland-based agriculture and rural industry, and a high rate of natural increase, Philippine population growth was fastest in urban centres (principally Metro Manila) and at the forest frontier. Migrants from depressed rural areas created a boom in upland populations (Cruz and Francisco 1993). Land colonization, deforestation and agricultural intensification on sloping and marginally arable lands ensued.[12]

Clearly, the distribution of incentives within agriculture was skewed by policy, with import-competing crops like rice and corn gaining relative to export crops. Technological progress, generated by research conducted in national research institutes as well as at the International Rice Research Institute located outside Manila, also conferred benefits on producers of cereals. The Green Revolution in rice, associated with modern technology and large irrigation and other supplementary investments, had a major impact on rice productivity in the Philippines, but was primarily confined to lowland irrigated regions (David and Otsuka 1994). It was responsible for a significant decline in the real rice price during a period of rising demand (David and Huang 1996).

Forest and Forestry Policies

Policies that had a direct impact on the forestry sector fall into three groups. First, there were government programmes that encouraged the conversion of forests to agricultural land, including state-sponsored settlement schemes.[13] Second, the state did not always enforce regulations limiting forest conversion. This was the case with respect not only to the activities of large commercial interests, but also to those of small farmers, often new immigrants to uplands. Third, there was both legal and illegal logging, with logging concessions being disbursed as part of patronage politics to politically powerful groups, and a considerable proportion of 'illegal' logging being carried out with the sanction and often the complicity of government officials at all levels. In practice both legal and illegal logging facilitated land conversion to agriculture and hence played a critical role in this process even though selective logging, in principle, need not cause deforestation.[14]

Government programmes that encouraged conversion of forests to agriculture were not unique to the Philippines; indeed they were ubiquitous throughout developing Asia and globally. With hindsight, the basic thrust of those programmes can be criticized on both economic and environmental grounds, but it cannot be denied that they reflected the mainstream development policy thinking of the time. In general, their environmental costs were poorly understood, and in any case were assumed to be much lower than the expected benefits. In both economic and political terms the sponsorship of internal migration to the forest frontier was an attractive policy: it eased population pressures in the more densely populated regions, increased agricultural output and exports, and ameliorated the political pressures for land reform that fuel left-wing insurgencies. But when it came to logging, central to the rapid deforestation process, government activities were driven much more directly by the priorities and interests of privileged elites who controlled the state rather than by any concerns about national development. Discussing the role of the state in the logging-induced deforestation process, Kummer (1992: 154–5) concluded that population growth was not the primary cause of deforestation in recent times; in reality:

> the Philippine government had a large control over this process and turned this control over to a small group of people. The process did not just happen; rather it served the financial interests of the wealthy and well connected.

As in many other areas of Philippine economic life, national interests were made subservient to the narrow private interests of the politically powerful, who used the state as a tool for the exploitation of national resources. Not only did the country lose potential economic rents from timber extraction, but logging also served as a conduit for capital outflows: with judicious undervaluation of export receipts, it provided a mechanism for circumventing exchange controls to repatriate funds overseas.

This review of the actions of the government makes clear that deforestation and associated agricultural land degradation problems in the Philippines cannot be attributed to population growth and/or 'market forces' alone. Development strategy and the institutional and legal context have been very important. As we have argued throughout this book, therefore, environmental outcomes depend not only on direct environment-specific measures, but also on the indirect impacts of many other policies as well as exogenous developments in the economy. Many legislative and policy changes, even when they do not specifically target environmental variables, can have potentially large environmental effects. The modern history of the Philippine economy underlines this point.

During the 1990s the Philippines implemented significant economic policy reforms aimed at opening the economy and creating a more liberal environment for trade and investment. Manufacturing sector tariffs (and other import restrictions) were substantially reduced. Food and agriculture sector policies were also liberalized somewhat, notably by the abolition of long-standing quantitative restrictions (QRs) on rice and corn importation, a step required under the terms of the country's accession to the World Trade Organization. However, QRs in agriculture were replaced by tariffs set at high rates, with the ironic result that, after decades in which trade policy discriminated against agriculture, rice and corn are now among the most heavily protected industries in the economy (WTO 1999a).

Given the strength of factor and product market linkages, the environmental implications of major economic reforms may be at least as significant as those of any single environmental protection measure. It is similarly interesting to ask what difference the exclusion of rice and corn from the liberalization agenda makes to changes in the demands on environmental and natural resource assets.

6.4 THE APEX MODEL OF THE PHILIPPINE ECONOMY

The rigorous analysis of questions about the fundamental determinants of environmental change is exceptionally difficult. While the broad nature of the economic forces that operate can be gleaned from stylized models (as discussed in earlier chapters), actual outcomes depend on complex general equilibrium relationships. In the remainder of this chapter we present the results of simulations using the APEX AGE model of the Philippine economy.

APEX (Agricultural Policy Experiments) is an applied general equilibrium model of the Philippine economy developed under a collaborative venture by researchers at the Australian National University and the Philippine Department of Agriculture (Clarete and Warr 1992). APEX is a conventional, real, micro-theoretic general equilibrium model designed to address microeconomic policy issues for the Philippines. It belongs to the class of models (sometimes known as Johansen models) that are linear in proportional changes of variables, as described in Chapter 5. APEX shares many features with the well-known ORANI model of the Australian economy (Dixon *et al.* 1982), although these features have been adapted to fit the realities of the Philippine economy. Input–output data in APEX are drawn from the Philippine social accounting matrix. Unlike most other AGE models of comparable size, however, in APEX all parameters describing technology and preferences are constructed from original econometric estimates.[15]

The model contains 50 producer goods and services produced in 41 industries. There are 38 manufacturing and services sectors and 12 agricultural sectors, with spatially distinct agricultural production, as described below. Producer goods are aggregated into seven consumer goods. There are five households, each representing a quintile of the income distribution and having unique income and consumption characteristics.

Consumer demands are all described by flexible functional forms.

Similarly, factor demands and the aggregation of factors of different types all depend on flexible functional forms, allowing for substitution in response to changing relative prices. In agricultural production, primary factors and fertilizer are aggregated, using a flexible functional form with econometrically estimated parameters, into a composite 'primary factor' input which is assumed to be used with intermediate goods (other than fertilizer) in fixed proportions. This structure is thus flexible enough to permit primary factor substitution in response to changes in the relative prices of primary factors and fertilizer. Finally, imports and their domestically produced substitutes are aggregated using CES forms with econometrically estimated Armington elasticities. Other details of the model structure can be found in Clarete and Warr (1992), and some illustrative experiments and associated discussion in Warr and Coxhead (1993).

Agriculture produces a vector of intermediate and final consumption goods using land, capital, unskilled labour and fertilizer as well as intermediate inputs. Production takes place in three regions, Luzon, Visayas and Mindanao, which are distinguished by their economic, geographic and climatic characteristics. Each of the three regions has endowments of land and capital that are specific to agricultural uses, while labour and variable capital are intersectorally mobile. Agricultural inputs are non-allocable due to data constraints, so the model cannot directly identify the quantity of each input used in the production of any individual agricultural output. Rather, the model operates as though farmers in each region purchase a production possibilities frontier, then choose their location on the frontier – that is, the product mix – in response to relative output prices.

Within this structure, some groups of agricultural products are presumed to be jointly produced. One such group is the category 'rainfed crops', which consists of rainfed rice, corn and root crops. We identify this sub-aggregate as the set of agricultural crops in which the potential for measurable soil fertility reduction through erosion can take place. Value-added in the rainfed crops sector is dominated by corn (60 per cent of total value-added); root crops account for 28 per cent, and rainfed rice 12 per cent. Empirically, these crops (especially corn and rainfed rice) account for the greatest part of land use in Philippine uplands. Erosion in uplands comes mainly from their production, particularly that of corn (Coxhead and Shively 1998). Thus changes in the area of corn and rainfed rice determine erosion outcomes in the model.

The joint production function for rainfed crops is nested within that for agriculture as a whole in each region. The composition of production within the rainfed crops sector is altered by changing relative prices of the three crops or by crop-specific technical progress. Similarly, the share of rainfed crops in total agricultural production depends on prices and rates of technical progress of the sub-aggregate relative to those of other agricultural sectors. Each of the three rainfed crops is classed as an importable in APEX, although in practice the shares of imports in total domestic availability are very small due to long-standing trade restrictions.

Tables 6.2 and 6.3 show, for the 50 APEX sectors, some basic information from the model database on sectoral size and labour intensity, and approximate protection levels. Table 6.3 also shows the AHTI emissions intensity data and rankings for Philippine manufacturing industries.

In its base form, APEX contains no explicit environmental information. However, for a given policy reform simulation it does provide detailed predictions of input and output changes at the industry level, as just described. These results can be used in conjunction with external information on the sectoral distribution of emissions, estimates of soil erosion rates under different crops, and estimates of changes in the returns to land to calculate the likely effects of a given change on industrial pollution, deforestation and agricultural expansion.

6.5   POLICY EXPERIMENTS

Trade Policy Reform

To illustrate the possible environmental effects of a broad-based policy reform, we use APEX to examine the predicted outcomes of two counterfactuals: a 25 per cent reduction in tariffs on all non-agricultural sectors (in practice, on manufactures), and a reduction of the same amount for *all* sectors. By asking what would happen if protection policies were relaxed, we obtain insights into the effects of past protection policies on economic activity and, by extrapolation using additional information, on environmental phenomena such as the allocation of agricultural land to crops, pressures for agricultural expansion, and the production of industrial emissions.[16]

The model closure chosen for the trade reform simulations embodies numerous assumptions about the nature of the Philippine economy. External trade and the government budget are assumed to be in balance initially, and the economy must adjust following a 'shock' (such as the exogenous revision of tariff rates) to restore these balances. Supplies of non-land primary factors (unskilled labour, skilled labour and capital) are assumed to be fixed; the markets for these inputs clear through factor price adjustments.[17] For agricultural land, however, we assume that acreage can be altered in the short to medium run, in effect creating a flexible supply of land at a constant nominal price per hectare. In other words, at the margin

Table 6.2   Agricultural, natural resource and service sectors

	GDP share	Labour cost share (%)	Implicit tariff 1994
Agricultural commodities	0.14		
Irrigated rice	0.24	0.54	50.0
Rainfed rice	0.02	0.54	50.0
Corn	0.12	0.56	115.0
Coconut	0.08	0.37	0.0
Sugar	0.05	0.57	—
Fruits	0.11	0.51	40.0
Vegetables	0.06	0.54	21.66
Rootcrops	0.02	0.55	—
Other comm'l crops	0.10	0.56	4.34
Hogs	0.16	0.38	—
Chicken and poultry	0.03	0.49	—
Other livestock	0.00	0.58	10.95
Natural resources	0.08		
Marine fisheries	0.47	0.47	19.14
Inland fisheries	0.15	0.38	—
Forestry	0.16	0.28	11.84
Crude oil & nat. gas	0.03	0.22	29.16
Other mining	0.19	0.44	9.14
Services	0.57		
Agricultural	0.07	0.46	
Construction	0.08	0.59	
Elect. gas and water	0.04	0.22	
Trans. & comm.	0.08	0.48	
Transpt/storage/w'sale	0.37	0.36	
Banks	0.02	0.65	
Insurance	0.09	0.17	
Government services	0.14	0.98	
Other	0.11	0.56	

Notes:
Value-added shares shown for each sector are within-group shares.
— = not available.

Source: Calculated from 1989 data in APEX database

Table 6.3   Agricultural processing and manufacturing

Sector	GDP share	Lab. cost share (%)	Implicit tariff 1994	AHTI score	AHTI rank
Agricultural processing	0.07				
Rice and corn milling	0.35	0.47	51.58	—	—
Sugar milling/refining	0.07	0.31	59.21	1.121	18
Milk and dairy	0.06	0.28	29.23	2.251	15
Oils and fats	0.22	0.39	16.12	3.721	13
Meat & meat products	0.21	0.36	82.21	0.431	21
Feed milling	0.02	0.37	26.49	0.281	22
Animal feeds	0.05	0.44	72.69	0.701	19
Other foods	0.03	0.40	29.52	2.021	17
Manufacturing	0.15				
Beverages and tobacco	0.07	0.37	41.99	0.5921 *0.272	20
Textile & knitting	0.08	0.49	14.5	6.071 *1.312	12
Other textiles	0.02	0.47	19.69	7.21 *6.042	8
Garments*	0.16	0.65	24.69	12.351 *12.762	5
Wood products	0.05	0.53	13.31	9.91 *0.642	6
Paper products	0.05	0.46	19.97	16.111 *4.232	3
Fertilizer	0.01	0.38	4.07	105.31	1
Rubber/plastic/chem. prod.	0.11	0.42	28.59	17.41 *15.692	2
Coal & petroleum prod.	0.04	0.12	28.88	6.231 *1.442	10
Non-ferr. basic metals	0.09	0.19	6.19	13.231	4
Cement & non-metallic	0.10	0.28	16.51	7.31 *4.172	7
Semiconductors	0.06	0.55	7.70	n.a.	
Metal products	0.07	0.49	17.24	6.081 *3.382	11
Electrical machinery	0.05	0.47	18.78	3.291 *1.252	14
Transport equipment	0.01	0.54	23.75	2.181 *0.96	16
Misc. manufacturing	0.04	0.56	18.83	6.71 *2.962	9

Notes:
Value-added shares shown for each sector are within-group shares.
* CV of AHTI scores, when calculated as weighted average from several subsector values.

Source: As for Table 6.2

there is fallow land that can be brought into production, or planted land that can be fallowed. This permits the model to capture pressures for agricultural expansion in response to economy-wide shocks. The remaining details of the macroeconomic closure are chosen to ensure that the burden of adjustment to a shock falls entirely on household expenditures.[18] The model thus yields a measure of welfare change based on increases or declines in real household consumption expenditures.

Changes in major macroeconomic variables occurring as the result of the trade policy reform experiments are shown in Table 6.4. Sectoral output and price changes are found in Table 6.5. Table 6.4 shows that trade policy reforms have a very small effect on aggregate welfare, measured as the sum of real household consumption expenditures. Because the supply of land is elastic, and with the economy distorted by a number of taxes, of which tariffs are only one form, there is neither any expectation nor any assurance that the tariff reduction by itself will raise welfare. In the real world, of course, the Philippine tariff reform programme was implemented along with many other types of reform; our experiment captures only one element of the entire package. The observed small negative effect on aggregate real consumption may well be due to rounding errors, reflecting basically unchanged overall welfare. Trade liberalization – whether applied only to manufacturing or to all sectors – has a pro-labour impact, and real wages of both skilled and unskilled labour increase, with the latter increase being greater. While returns to variable capital also rise, those to specific capital in formerly protected sectors decline.[19] Intersectoral variations in returns to specific capital indicate pressures for investment or disinvestment in the next period, although of course the model itself, being static, does not quantify actual investment responses.

It can be seen from the sectoral results in Table 6.5 that, as expected, trade liberalization generally reduces output in the import-competing manufacturing sectors, which receive the highest initial protection, and increases it in the labour-intensive electronics sector ('semiconductors'), food processing, and in several primary industries, including forestry and mining. At the same time, most agricultural sectors also contract, even when trade liberalization is restricted to non-agricultural sectors. The agricultural contraction can readily be understood in terms of two factor-market effects. First, profitability in the sector is reduced by the significant labour cost increase, which is only partially offset by output price increases. Second, the flexibility of total land area means that the sector can shed even more labour by allowing some land to become fallow.

Turning to the environmental impact of trade liberalization, it can be seen that within manufacturing there is a general correspondence between capital intensity, protection rates and emissions intensity. As some heavily

Table 6.4   Macroeconomic effects of trade liberalization (% change)

	Manufacturing tariff reduction	Across-the-board tariff reduction
Overall economy		
Gross domestic product		
Nominal (local currency)	−0.18	−0.24
Real	−0.04	−0.02
Consumer price index	0.00	−0.10
GDP deflator	−0.14	−0.23
External sector		
Export revenue (foreign currency)	0.42	0.51
Import bill (foreign currency)	0.40	0.49
Trade deficit (in levels, foreign currency)	0.00*	0.00*
Government budget		
Revenue		
Tariff revenue	−22.14	−24.00
Aggregate revenue		
Nominal, local currency	0.56	0.41
Real	0.57	0.51
Expenditures		
Nominal (local currency)	0.35	0.34
Real	0.36	0.44
Budget deficit (in levels, local currency)	0.00*	0.00*
Household sector		
Consumption		
Nominal (local currency)	−0.06	−0.14
Real	−0.06	−0.04
Factor returns		
Wages: unskilled labour	0.66	0.56
Wages: skilled labour	1.26	1.36
Return to variable capital	1.14	1.19

Note: 0* indicates figure is identically zero.

Source: APEX simulation results

emissions-intensive sectors contract, industrial pollution will tend to decrease. Declines in the prices of competing imports reduce domestic producer prices, although by less, since domestic and imported goods are imperfect substitutes. Conversely, many labour-intensive export-oriented industries, which expand as a result of liberalization, are not especially emissions-intensive; the net result, although mixed, is arguably a composition effect that is positive for manufacturing.

Table 6.5   Sectoral effects of trade liberalization (% change)

	Manufacturing tariff reduction		Across-the-board tariff reduction	
	Price	Output	Price	Output
Agriculture				
Irrigated rice	0.37	−0.16	−0.38	−0.75
Rainfed rice	0.37	−0.18	−0.38	−0.61
Corn	0.11	−0.45	0.00	−0.44
Coconut	0.45	−0.21	0.33	−0.04
Sugar	0.22	−0.22	0.22	−0.17
Fruits	0.17	−0.38	0.11	−0.31
Vegetables	0.51	−0.01	0.56	0.11
Rootcrops	0.59	−0.01	0.54	0.10
Other commercial crops	0.25	−0.15	0.24	−0.14
Hogs	0.48	−0.06	0.40	−0.10
Poultry	0.35	−0.13	0.15	−0.15
Other livestock	0.37	−0.12	0.19	−0.19
Natural resource & agricultural processing				
Marine fisheries	0.21	−0.29	0.21	−0.22
Inland fisheries	0.33	−0.06	0.30	−0.07
Forestry	0.90	0.84	0.90	0.87
Crude oil	−0.49	−0.02	−0.55	−0.07
Other mining	−0.19	0.67	−0.20	0.71
Rice & corn milling	0.53	−0.12	0.15	−0.01
Sugar milling	0.11	−0.24	0.11	−0.18
Dairy	−1.52	−0.15	−1.60	−0.14
Oils	−0.06	0.20	−0.08	0.33
Meat	0.44	−0.06	0.35	−0.08
Feed milling	0.24	−0.08	−1.80	0.17
Animal feeds	−0.17	−1.74	−0.50	−1.74
Other foods	−0.48	0.79	−0.60	1.05
Manufacturing				
Beverages & tobacco	−0.83	0.08	−1.10	0.17
Textile	−0.58	−1.01	−0.67	−0.97
Other textile	−0.06	0.11	−0.07	0.12
Garments	0.10	−0.73	0.09	−0.68
Wood products	*−0.34*	*2.08*	*−0.36*	*2.19*
Paper products	*−0.48*	*−0.53*	*−0.52*	*−0.52*
Fertilizer	*−0.05*	*0.18*	*−0.08*	*0.07*
Other rubber products	*−0.95*	*−0.07*	*−0.99*	*−0.10*
Coal & petroleum	*−0.17*	*−0.12*	*−0.20*	*−0.15*
Basic/non-ferrous metals	*0.06*	*−0.43*	*0.06*	*−0.44*

Table 6.5 (cont.)

	Manufacturing tariff reduction		Across-the-board tariff reduction	
	Price	Output	Price	Output
Cement	−0.81	−0.48	−0.86	−0.47
Semiconductors	−0.31	1.95	−0.31	1.97
Metal products	*−2.51*	*−0.36*	*−2.68*	*−0.31*
Elect. machinery	−0.96	−0.41	−1.00	−0.42
Transport equipt	−1.15	−0.47	−1.21	−0.47
Misc. mfg	−0.71	−0.88	−0.72	−0.87
Services				
Agricultural	0.18	−0.16	0.10	−0.35
Construction	−0.56	0.21	−0.61	0.22
Elect., gas & water	0.13	−0.01	0.13	−0.02
Trans. and comm.	0.41	0.12	0.40	0.07
Transport & storage	0.52	−0.05	0.52	−0.03
Banks	0.47	−0.10	0.49	−0.13
Insurance	0.50	0.00	0.50	−0.04
Gov't services	0.98	0.03	1.05	0.02
Other	0.01	−0.22	−0.06	−0.22

Note: Sector name in italics denotes manufacturing sectors with highest emissions intensity scores (see Table 6.3).

Source: APEX simulation results

The net environmental effects in land-using industries depend on the environmental effects arising from the expansion in output of the 'commercial forestry' sector (whose output is the value of marketed timber) and the contraction in most agricultural industries. In the 'forestry' sector, trade reforms bring about a rise in the producer price, and output (timber production) expands. What happens to the commercial timber sector in the long run as a result of trade reforms depends on the question of property rights. If property rights in forestry were well defined and enforced – an implicit assumption of the model – then an increase in the relative price of forestry would promote a sustained expansion of timber output, which in an intertemporal context would imply increased investment in timber tree stocks. On the other hand, if property rights were not well defined or not enforced, then, by raising the stumpage value of existing trees, trade liberalization that increases profits in timber extraction would instead lead to increased cutting of existing forests. In this case trade liberalization would promote accelerated deforestation.

Finally, the trade reforms raise the domestic prices of most exportable agricultural products, and reduce those of rice and corn, which are import-competing crops. Rice and corn prices fall modestly in nominal terms, but by greater amounts relative to the producer prices of other agricultural goods with which they compete for land. The structure of agricultural production thus shifts in the direction of exportables, especially tree crops such as coconut and fruit. Corn and upland rice, the two crops that account for virtually all agriculture-related soil erosion in uplands, both contract in area (Table 6.6), especially when the tariff reform extends to these industries. With rising labour costs, incentives to use labour to clear additional upland land for agriculture must diminish; indeed, the area of fallowed land increases in all regions, especially when trade reforms include agricul-

Table 6.6   Agricultural land use changes due to trade liberalization in non-agricultural sectors

Industry	Luzon		Visayas		Mindanao	
	Manuf. tariffs	All tariffs	Manuf. tariffs	All tariffs	Manuf. tariffs	All tariffs
Irrigated rice	0.08	−0.60	−0.09	−0.64	−0.18	−0.71
Rainfed rice	0.06	−0.49	−0.01	−0.34	−0.27	−0.61
Corn	−0.04	−0.31	−0.16	−0.12	−0.44	−0.37
Coconut	0.14	0.11	0.02	0.00	−0.25	0.08
Sugar	−0.03	−0.03	−0.19	−0.14	−0.28	−0.15
Fruits	−0.06	−0.10	−0.24	−0.25	−0.32	−0.24
Vegetables	−0.17	0.23	0.05	0.19	−0.06	0.14
Root crops	−0.89	0.46	−0.08	0.05	0.90	−3.41
Fallow land	−0.04	0.26	0.08	0.17	0.29	0.33
Erosion	−0.03	−0.30	−0.14	−0.13	−0.42	−0.38

Note: For definitions of 'fallow' and 'erosion' see text.

Source: APEX simulation results

tural sectors. As a consequence of these shifts in land use, erosion in uplands diminishes, particularly in Luzon. Overall, we may conclude that trade policy reform induces composition effects that are consistent with (or which at least do not run counter to) increased environmental protection in the lowland and upland/forestry ecosystems, provided institutional failures (such as open access in commercial forestry) are not severe.

That some agricultural sectors and some exportable manufacturing sectors should contract as the result of trade liberalization requires further explanation, given that these, along with traditional exportables such as forestry and mining, are normally assumed to be the industries most negatively affected by an ISI regime. In the simple models of Chapter 4, there was only one exportable and one importable, and the impact of liberalization was clear-cut. But when there are many goods in each category, each using many inputs and with differing factor intensities, the net impact on a particular sector reflects not only the change in its output price but also the complex set of changes in input prices that affect the cost of production. Sometimes, the change in output price may be more than offset by changes in input prices and overall costs of production, so that supply increases (decreases) may take place even when output prices fall (rise).

It should also be noted that rice and corn are both import-competing crops in APEX. Initial trade shares are very low, and estimated Armington elasticities (of substitution between imported and domestically supplied goods) are not high for these commodities. The trade policy reforms reduce the prices of imported grains substantially, and their domestic producer prices fall somewhat as a result. Moreover, the trade reforms promote activity in some highly labour-intensive sectors. Unskilled labour demand rises in semiconductors, wood products, 'other foods' processing, mining, forestry and construction. Labour-intensive agricultural sectors must compete with these additional demands.

The trade policy reform simulations provide predictions about composition effects and, in a comparative static sense, scale effects. Of course, longer-run growth outcomes are beyond the scope of the model. In the longer run, if trade policy reform leads to faster overall growth, then production of some kinds of environmental 'bads' could increase in spite of the changes in industry structure towards less pollution-intensive industries. A mix of economic policy reforms and environmental protection measures is implied, to ensure that the scale effect is not the dominant influence on the trajectory of environmental quality.

The Green Revolution[20]

In Chapter 4, we discussed the potential effects of technical change in lowland agriculture in the context of our analytical model. This issue is of particular interest in the Philippines because it hosts the International Rice Research Institute (IRRI), which led the breeding and dissemination of high-yielding Green Revolution rice varieties in tropical Asia. In the mid-1970s, the Philippines implemented the 'Masagana 99' programme, aimed at intensifying rice production through adoption of the new rice varieties. The new varieties were best suited for and most productive in the irrigated lowlands, and their adoption proceeded quite rapidly in such areas.

Lowland yield growth rates accelerated, while those in upland and rainfed areas hardly changed. Thus the Green Revolution, at least in its early stages, bypassed the unirrigated areas of cereal production.

This bias in the new rice technology towards a specific land type in turn imparted a profound regional asymmetry to its productivity impact. Those regions that had the largest endowments of well-irrigated lowlands (or were able to attract funds to develop them through new irrigation investments) experienced the highest rates of technical progress in rice production. With inelastic domestic demand, rice production in less-favoured regions (and areas within regions) diminished as lowland intensification advanced.

In the second simulation experiment with the APEX model, we replicate the effects of the Green Revolution. The 'shock' applied to the model, based on econometric estimates of the actual effects of productivity growth in Philippine agriculture, increases the productivity of primary factors and fertilizer in irrigated rice production. The increases are not equal across factors (Table 6.7), reflecting the land-saving, fertilizer-using bias of the new rice technology. Tables 6.8 to 6.10 report the main results of this simulation experiment.

Table 6.7   Estimated short-run productivity growth in Philippine agriculture by input and land type (% change)

Land type	Overall rate of technical change	Factoral rates of technical change[a]		
		Land	Labour	Fertilizer
Irrigated	7.645	14.826	6.265	−1.911
Non-irrigated	0.267	1.031	−1.164	−0.019

Note: [a] Figures represent short-run (approximately annual) rates. Negative numbers indicate a decline in productivity.

Source: Calculated from estimates in Coxhead (1992)

Technical progress in irrigated rice raises real GDP and real household incomes, when the government deficit and trade deficit are held constant (Table 6.8). Because of the structure of trade protection (as well, perhaps, as intrinsic differences between domestically produced rice and imports), the price of rice is driven sharply lower by the change (Table 6.9), even as production in irrigated areas expands. The expansion, however, is insufficient to prevent a decline in employment in the sector; the rate of output growth is less than the rate at which the productivity of labour increases.

The Green Revolution thus has two important intersectoral effects. Wages decline, boosting labour-intensive industries in other sectors (especially

Table 6.8   Macroeconomic effects of the Green Revolution

	Per cent change
Overall economy	
Gross domestic product	
Nominal (local currency)	0.10
Real	0.20
Consumer price index	−0.15
GDP deflator	−0.10
External sector	
Export revenue (foreign currency)	0.02
Import bill (foreign currency)	0.02
Trade deficit (in levels, foreign currency)	0.00*
Government budget	
Revenue	
Aggregate revenue	
(nominal, local currency)	−1.01
Real	
Expenditures	
Nominal (local currency)	0.11
Real	0.26
Budget deficit (in levels, local currency)	0.00*
Household sector	
Consumption	
Nominal (local currency)	0.09
Real	0.24
Savings (in levels, local currency)	0.01
Factor returns	
Wages: unskilled labour	−0.61
Wages: skilled labour	0.67
Return to variable capital	0.23

Note: 0* indicates a figure is identically zero.

Source: APEX simulation results

agriculture), and the falling price of rice reduces returns to upland (rainfed) rice production, which contracts very severely. While the effects on industrial emissions are presumably low since the supply responses of polluting industries are small, the effects of the Green Revolution on land allocation within agriculture, and on overall land area, are dramatic (Table 6.10). Fallow area increases – especially in Luzon, the region with the greatest proportional area of irrigated rice – and erosion falls as both the total area planted in uplands and its allocation to cereals and root crops diminish.

Table 6.9 Sectoral effects of the Green Revolution

	Producer price	Dom. output		Producer price	Dom. output
Agricultural commodities			**Manufacturing**		
Irrigated rice	−4.21	0.96	Bev. & tobacco	0.07	0.18
Rainfed rice	−4.21	−2.30	Textile	0.08	0.51
Corn	−0.25	0.08	Other textile	−0.02	0.00
Coconut	−0.42	0.40	Garments	0.04	0.16
Sugar	−0.40	0.25	Wood products	0.01	−0.04
Fruits	−0.07	0.36	Paper products	0.10	0.26
Vegetables	−0.51	0.40	Fertilizer	−0.06	−0.69
Rootcrops	−0.25	0.34	Other rubber products	0.06	0.08
Other commercial crops	−0.06	−0.05	Coal & petroleum	0.05	0.01
Hogs	−0.71	−0.03	Basic/non-ferrous metals	0.02	−0.08
Poultry	−0.32	0.18	Cement	0.07	0.05
Other livestock	−0.41	0.11	Semiconductors	0.02	−0.16
			Metal products	0.01	0.08
Natural resources			Elect. machinery	0.04	0.01
Marine fisheries	−0.04	0.23	Transport equipt	0.03	−0.08
Inland fisheries	−0.02	0.04	Misc. manufg	0.06	0.16
Forestry	−0.02	0.00			
Crude oil	0.04	−0.06	**Services**		
Other mining	0.01	−0.09	Agricultural	−0.27	−0.67
			Construction	0.02	0.02

Agricultural processing		Elect., gas & water	0.12	0.07
Rice & corn milling	-2.11	0.37	Trans. & comms	0.06	-0.12
Sugar milling	-0.06	0.29	Trans./store/w'sale	0.03	0.12
Dairy	0.04	0.07	Banks	0.21	0.19
Oils	0.00	0.12	Insurance	0.24	0.10
Meat	-0.30	0.03	Gov't services	0.35	-0.03
Feed milling	-0.02	0.37	Other	0.00	0.29
Animal feeds	-0.76	-0.17			
Other foods	-0.08	0.32			

Note: Sector name in italics denotes manufacturing sectors with highest emissions intensity scores (see Table 6.3).

Source: APEX simulation results

167

Table 6.10   Agricultural land use changes due to the Green Revolution

Industry	Luzon	Visayas	Mindanao
Irrigated rice	−0.86	−2.76	−1.97
Rainfed rice	−2.62	−2.43	−2.34
Corn	−0.92	−0.19	0.16
Coconut	0.05	−0.58	0.59
Sugar	0.15	−0.66	−0.15
Fruits	0.61	−0.48	0.11
Vegetables	0.23	−0.54	−0.05
Root crops	−17.04	−1.95	−2.34
Fallow	1.38	1.02	0.67
Erosion	−1.13	−0.35	0.03

Source: APEX simulation results

There is both agricultural contraction and de-intensification. These results indicate clearly the indirect environmental benefits, in terms of reduced pressures on forests and upland watersheds, of productivity growth in lowland agriculture. The implied value of these environmental gains must be added to the overall welfare gain shown in Table 6.8. On the other side of the ledger, of course, is the increased environmental damage associated with lowland agricultural growth, as noted in Chapters 3 and 4.

6.5   CONCLUSIONS

The general equilibrium analysis of Philippine environmental problems provides an empirical illustration of the ways in which widely implemented economic policies can influence environmental outcomes. The direct and indirect impacts of past Philippine development strategies have aggravated environmental and natural resource depletion rates, quite severely in some cases. These particular development strategies have more than just constrained economic growth. By perpetuating poverty in rural areas they encouraged population movement to crowded cities and to ecologically fragile uplands. By distorting agricultural incentives they encouraged cultivation of more soil-erosive crops. The blatant use of state power to allow favoured elite groups to exploit national resources and flout all controls on emissions and effluents worsened environmental outcomes. In particular, by undermining respect for property rights in nationally owned natural resources, they promoted deforestation. These legacies now weigh heavily on the Philippines.

The 1990s saw the partial dismantling of trade protection and the liberalization of domestic markets. Future environmental trends will reflect this more open policy context, along with such specific environmental policy and investment initiatives as might be adopted in response to national and international environmental concerns. In previous analytical chapters and through the analysis in this chapter, we have outlined the structural impacts that seem likely in an open policy regime. Liberalization tends to improve overall export performance, while previously highly protected import-competing sectors contract. The environmental impact is not necessarily negative; indeed, there are some indications that land degradation and deforestation, and the intensity (if not the volume) of industrial emissions, may be lower under a more liberal trade regime. Though scale effects associated with growth may tend to increase environmental degradation, they may be at least partly offset by benign composition effects, shifting the country on to a cleaner growth path.

But free trade is not a panacea; indeed, the Philippine case demonstrates the need to combine liberalized trade with appropriate government action to address market failures that produce harmful environmental outcomes. Some legislative steps in this direction have already been taken. Bills have been passed addressing property rights in forests and uplands, and others have been formulated to protect forests, fisheries and other natural resources. Conversion of mangrove lands has been banned. Low-leaded and unleaded gasoline were introduced in 1993 and 1994 respectively, and it was planned that leaded gasoline would be completely phased out by 2001. The 1999 Clean Air Act set out guidelines for the control and reduction of emissions into air, and additional bills for the protection of freshwater resources and watersheds are being prepared.

Applied general equilibrium analysis, in this case with the APEX model, is a powerful tool for quantifying the complex relationships described in highly stylized form in lower-dimensional models. In the Philippine case, this mode of analysis permits a deeper exploration of the indirect environmental implications of development policies unrelated (in direct fashion) to the environment. In particular, these results clarify the multi-stranded composition effects of policy changes which affect prices throughout an open developing economy. Moreover, the model permits a more detailed disaggregation of spatial phenomena: not only upland and lowland, but also across major geographic regions within the country.

Some of the limitations imposed by our simplifying assumptions in this kind of model should be noted. The geography of the Philippines, and the underdeveloped nature of roads and communications infrastructure linking remote regions to other regions and the urban centres, mean that transactions and trade costs are non-trivial. These drive wedges between the prices faced by different agents even for the same goods or factors, weaken the degree of market integration, and dampen the extent to which changes in the patterns of market signals produce the assumed producer and consumer responses. The importance of such transactions costs is an empirical issue. There are several studies of commodity market integration in the Philippines which suggest that, over the medium term, market integration is quite high (Silvapulle and Jayasuriya 1994; Mendoza and Rosegrant 1995; Coxhead *et al.* 2001). Empirical evidence on internal labour migration and occupational labour mobility also indicates that the assumption maintained in the model, that labour moves both interregionally and intersectorally, is reasonable for the medium term. The outcomes generated by the APEX model in these policy experiments therefore seem acceptable as reflecting at least orders of magnitude of the effects and their general direction.

NOTES

1. This and the following section draw heavily on Coxhead and Jayasuriya (2002).
2. This classification is based on Chapter 4 of *The Philippine National Development Plan: Directions for the 21st Century* (Republic of the Philippines 1998), *Philippine Agenda 21: A National Agenda for Sustainable Development for the 21ˢᵗ Century* (Philippine Council for Sustainable Development 1997), and *Philippines: Environment and Natural Resource Management Study* (World Bank 1989). The latter, though published in 1989, remains a very useful source of material on several environmental issues facing the Philippines.
3. The 2.9 per cent rate for the 1990–95 period is given in Republic of Philippines (1998). According to the World Bank's *World Development Report 1999/2000*, the annual average rate of deforestation during this period was 3.5 per cent. Kummer (1992), in his study of the deforestation problem in the Philippines, has a detailed discussion of data issues in the forestry sector. Fujisaka *et al.* (1986) also provide a useful overview of the nature and evolution of the upland ecosystem.
4. Commercial logging facilitates subsequent conversion of logged forests to agriculture.
5. Of the endemic Philippine flora, 60 per cent is considered already to be extinct, and a great many other species are endangered.
6. Data cited in this paragraph come from Shah and Nagpal (1997).
7. SO_2 levels appear not to be very serious in Metro Manila.
8. See Republic of Philippines (1998). The figure given for 1995, however, is lower than the 1992 average.
9. The dissolved oxygen content is below the 5 mg/litre needed to sustain aquatic life.
10. For discussions of the nature and consequences of trade policy in the Philippines, see Baldwin (1975), Bautista *et al.* (1979), and Medalla *et al.* (1995). The following discussion draws on their analysis of the impact on industry structure and growth.
11. This does not imply that ISI policies alone are responsible for the urban bias in Philippine industrialization, particularly the Metro Manila bias. While ISI policies clearly contributed to this phenomenon, powerful economic forces of agglomeration tend to generate an urban bias in growth, and that would have occurred even under a more open trade regime (see Fujita *et al.* 1999).
12. Irrigation investments and the Green Revolution, by raising productivity in lowland agriculture, helped somewhat to offset these trends. However, the rapid increase in rice

yields did not last for much more than a decade, and the derived labour demand effect was itself diminished by implicit and explicit subsidies for capital-intensive agricultural techniques (Jayasuriya and Shand 1985; Coxhead and Jayasuriya 1986).

13. See Paderanga (1986) for a historical review of land settlement policies in the Philippines.
14. Government policies in many other developing Asian countries have also had important negative effects on forests (see Repetto and Gillis 1988).
15. The PARA model of the Thai economy, described in Chapter 8, is another.
16. Strictly speaking, changes in the prices of goods and services, and in the production and valuation of pollution, cause optimizing agents to respond by adjusting their abatement expenditures. These effects are not captured in the model.
17. Empirically, the Philippine labour market is characterized by considerable unemployment and under-employment, and labour supply is quite elastic at the going wage rate. Coxhead and Jayasuriya (2002) report the analysis of trade liberalization under the assumption of a 'slack' labour market with fixed nominal wages.
18. Specifically, any shortfall or surplus in the government budget is made up by a lump-sum tax on household incomes, while nominal household savings remain fixed.
19. The latter figures, although not shown in the tables, are available from the authors as part of the complete set of simulation results.
20. This section draws on results and analysis in Coxhead and Shively (1998).

7. Development policy and the environment in Sri Lanka

7.1 INTRODUCTION[1]

This chapter presents the second of the three case studies applying the general methodological approach of Chapter 4 to specific environmental issues. Our focus in this chapter is on land degradation in the hilly regions of Sri Lanka. In recent years the implementation of wide-ranging policy reforms and institutional changes designed to move Sri Lanka towards a liberal, outward-oriented, market economy – argued to be essential to economic growth – has intensified concerns about environmental degradation and the sustainability of the country's natural resource base. These have been accompanied by debates about the environmental consequences for Sri Lanka of policy reforms in the broader context of Sri Lanka's obligations under the World Trade Organization (WTO).

Sri Lanka's environmental problems are both serious and multidimensional (ADB 1990). Among these, the issues of deforestation and land degradation have a long and prominent history, recognized as far back as the 1870s and discussed regularly since the 1920s. In addition, the degradation of coastal eco-resources and environmental pollution in urban industrial zones have been identified as areas requiring urgent remedial action. There is also a general consensus that past policies, which relied almost solely on regulatory mechanisms, have been ineffective in practice, and that concrete and effective policies to address environmental concerns are urgently needed. There is now a far greater appreciation of the costs of environmental degradation within the general community, and government policy statements almost invariably make specific reference to environmental issues.

The wide-ranging nature of the policy reforms made it impossible to ignore the potentially economy-wide repercussions of various sector-specific policies. Environmental concerns therefore needed to be addressed using a general equilibrium framework, and this chapter describes how this was implemented to analyse a key environmental issue in Sri Lanka: the problem of land degradation. The analysis combined an explicitly general equilibrium analysis with partial equilibrium analysis as appropriate. The main empirical results of general interest can be summarized as follows. First, the economic losses from soil erosion in Sri Lanka are quite substantial even under quite conservative assumptions. Second, in circumstances such as those of the Sri Lankan economy – that is, where there are significant initial policy-induced distortions – trade liberalization may increase both national income and environmental quality. Third, while trade liberalization has a positive environmental impact by reducing soil erosion, its effects are relatively small, and additional policies that directly target soil erosion are required to reduce losses significantly. Fourth, policy options to target erosion often involve significant trade-offs in terms of developmental goals.

7.2   BACKGROUND

The topography of Sri Lanka consists of coastal plains surrounding a central massif. The country may be subdivided into a dry zone, a wet zone, and an intermediate zone on the basis of rainfall, and into low-country, mid-country and up-country on the basis of elevation.[2] Up-country and much of mid-country correspond roughly to the notion of 'upland' as used in earlier chapters. Rivers originating in the central hills supply hydro-electric power, which is the main source of electricity, and feed a complex irrigation system which enables cultivation of irrigated rice (paddy) and other food crops in the drier parts of the coastal plains.

Land use in Sri Lanka has undergone major changes since the nineteenth century, when extensive forests covered the hilly regions as well as large tracts in the plains. Forests covered over 80 per cent of the land area until the 1880s, but only 44 per cent in 1956 and about 22 per cent at present (Gamage 1999). The emergence of land degradation as an issue of significant concern can be traced to the deforestation that accompanied the establishment of commercial plantations in the hilly regions during the mid-nineteenth century. The British colonial administration implemented a policy of alienating 'Crown land' – which included almost all forested land – to plantation companies, and subsequent clearing for plantation crop cultivation led to widespread soil erosion. This was recognized as a serious problem as far back as the 1870s. In 1876, following representations that indiscriminate clearing of forests was leading to land degradation and jeopardizing water supplies, the Colonial Secretary issued a directive that land above 5,000 ft (1,500 m) in elevation was not to be alienated and should be kept in its natural state. Nevertheless, as both large-scale commercial plantations and smallholdings spread rapidly through most of the country's wet and intermediate zones, considerable tracts of highly erodible land continued to be converted to agriculture in subsequent years. The present-day land use pattern reflects the culmination of this process. The agricultural sector now comprises plantation crops (mainly tea and rubber) and a large domestic food production sector. Rice is the main food crop while coconut is a major food and cash crop (see Table 7.1).

The plantation sector is not homogeneous; large modern 'estates' co-exist with thousands of smallholdings. Tea dominates the wet zone up-country, though it is also grown in parts of the intermediate zone and in some coastal regions (Table 7.2). Rubber is grown in the wet zone low-country and in the mid-country at elevations of up to 500 m. Food production is overwhelmingly a smallholder activity. Low-lying areas in the plains are typically devoted to rice, while other crops are grown in rainfed areas. Most of the rice is produced in the dry zone with irrigation, and large areas of previously forested land have been brought under irrigation in recent decades. Shifting cultivation continues in parts of the up-country – around 0.2 million ha is planted annually – but has been declining. Temperate climate vegetables are grown in parts of the cooler hilly regions, as are tobacco and potatoes. The remaining forest cover, including that in ecologically crucial watersheds, is under serious threat. In the hilly regions, during 1983–92 forested areas declined by nearly 5 per cent (Jewell and Legg 1994).

Among land use changes, both deforestation and shifts from perennial tree crops to annuals have impacted strongly on land degradation. The tea and rubber areas (and, more generally, the area under permanent crops) have contracted sharply in recent decades. Between 1962 and 1982 the area under tea fell by 10 per cent while that under rubber fell by 25 per cent. Between 1956 and 1992, the tea area in the Upper Mahaweli catchment,[3] the most important watershed in the country, declined dramatically. Its land use share fell by one-third, from 38 per cent to 25 per cent, while the area under annual crops, as well as that under more relatively stable forest plantations, home gardens and grasslands, expanded (Manthritilleke 1999a). Overall, the total land area under permanent crops has been falling both absolutely and relatively, with the share of plantation crops declining from 58 per cent to just over 46 per cent between 1962 and 1982. Excluding the increase in area devoted to paddy, which is grown almost entirely in low-country, land under temporary crops (almost all of which are annual food crops) increased from 4.3 per cent to 11.3 per cent.[4] As the Report of the Land Commission (1987) pointed out, these changes aggravated land degradation problems, as a sizeable number of local residents who had previously found casual employment on plantations turned instead to cultivation of food crops. The resulting intensification of up-country agricultural land use further accelerated land degradation, deforestation, stream siltation and other forms of environmental degradation and natural resource depletion.

Table 7.1 Agricultural crop area by elevation zone

Sector	High-country		Mid-country		Low-country		Total	
	ha.	%	ha.	%	ha.	%	ha.	%
Tea	73,110	33	84,062	38	64,938	29	222,110	100
Rubber	0	0	97,416	49	102,232	51	199,648	100
Coconut	0	0	55,529	13	360,894	87	416,423	100
Paddy	25,601	6	68,898	15	352,635	79	447,134	100
Other export agriculture	3,692	5	35,956	50	32,569	45	72,217	100
Other agriculture	26,788	15	28,500	16	124,937	69	180,225	100
Forestry	120,444	5	160,669	7	2,030,669	88	2,311,782	100
Total	249,635	6	531,030	14	3,068,874	80	3,849,539	100

Sources: Department of Census and Statistics (1993); Ministry of Plantation Industries (1994)

Table 7.2   Land use by crop and elevation zone (%)

	High-country	Mid-country	Low-country	All
Tea	29	16	2	6
Rubber	0	18	3	5
Coconut	0	10	12	11
Paddy	10	13	11	12
Other export agriculture	1	7	1	2
Other agriculture	11	5	4	5
Forestry	48	30	66	60
Total	100	100	100	100

Source: Computed from Table 7.1

These land use changes must be understood in the context of the prevailing policy regime and incentive structures. Plantation crops have historically been subjected to severe direct and indirect taxation, and have experienced a long period of stagnant or declining real prices in world markets. Taxes on international trade and, in particular, heavy taxes on tea and rubber, the principal export crops grown in hilly regions, were the main source of government revenue.[5] As in many other developing countries, the then-dominant development strategy of import substitution protected manufacturing industry and indirectly taxed agriculture. But the negative impact of this strategy on the agricultural sector was not uniform. Some crops, in particular rice, enjoyed a host of countervailing subsidies. Although a tradable commodity in principle, rice was effectively converted into a non-tradable through extensive government interventions that limited its international trade. Rice producers further enjoyed subsidies on water, material inputs such as fertilizer, and research and extension services. Similarly, under a dual exchange rate system in force from 1968 to 1977, so-called 'non-traditional' export crops such as spices[6] were given the benefit of a substantially higher exchange rate. Finally, import bans conferred protection on a range of other food crops, such as potatoes. Thus the structure of relative protection was strongly biased against tea and rubber, not only in relation to manufacturing but (perhaps even more importantly) in relation to other agricultural crops.[7] In addition, the nationalization of large plantations in 1975 inaugurated a period during which large tracts of tea land were subjected to poor management, resulting in severe land degradation. As a consequence, many plantations were deemed totally uneconomic and beyond rehabilitation by the mid-1990s.

A new political regime in 1977 initiated a period of fundamental change in development strategy. Policy shifted from an inward and state-reliant orientation to an outward oriented, pro-market stance. Policy changes in 1977–78 included an extensive programme of trade liberalization, a shift to a more flexible exchange rate regime, and greater incentives for foreign investment. Trade and exchange rate policies were further liberalized in a second wave of policy reforms initiated in 1989.[8] In agriculture, prominent features of policy reforms in the 1990s included the de-nationalization of large tea and rubber estates, reduction of export taxes on tea and rubber, and relaxation of some import restrictions on food crops such as potatoes. However, agricultural trade liberalization has lagged well behind the pace of reform in other sectors, and many agricultural commodities remain subject to non-tariff barriers. At the national level, reform-driven changes in prices and institutions can be expected to alter land use and management, with potentially important environmental implications.

7.3 LAND USE PRACTICES AND ENVIRONMENTAL EFFECTS

The direct – 'on-site' – effects of soil erosion in Sri Lanka's agricultural lands have been substantial, as indicated by the large areas of land that have become uneconomic for agriculture. For example, over 22 per cent of the Upper Mahaweli catchment area is considered to be badly degraded, and another 8 per cent to be degrading rapidly.[9] But adverse effects are not confined to upper catchment areas. Off-site damages are significant: silting of rivers, reservoirs and canals has become a serious threat to irrigation and hydroelectric power (HEP) generation, as well as a cause of unwelcome floods and considerable damage to the road network.[10]

Productivity loss in HEP generation is a particularly important issue, as the country relies on it for over 80 per cent of its electricity supply. These problems are compounded by other adverse ecological changes associated with land degradation, such as those affecting rainfall and drainage as forest cover is removed. There is considerable controversy over the relationship between land use changes and rainfall, but several studies in Sri Lanka suggest that rainfall has been declining in recent times; according to some analysts average rainfall declined by 20 per cent in the century to 1980, while meteorological records indicate that average rainfall during 1961–90 was 7 per cent lower than during 1931–60 (see Manthritilleke 1999b). Thus, although the incidence of soil erosion is most severe in the hilly regions, its impact is by no means confined to them.

Present rates of soil erosion in Sri Lanka are widely considered to be socially suboptimal. Though this is not based on a rigorous and systematic analysis, it is clear that many of the factors that lead private decision makers to adopt suboptimal land management practices (imperfect information about the productivity effects of soil erosion; absence of well-defined and enforced property rights; divergence between social and private time preference rates in the context of imperfect capital markets; and uncompensated off-site productivity effects) are present in Sri Lanka. It thus makes sense to ask what policies might mitigate the social cost of land degradation, and at what cost in terms of other activities, employment and national income.

Economic analysis of such a question, requires data on the relationships between crop and cultivation practices, rates of soil erosion, and the on-site and off-site impacts on productivity of affected industries and sectors. Such data are seldom readily available. The study on which we base this chapter devoted a considerable effort to obtaining reliable data on key biophysical parameters of environmental phenomena, through collaboration with leading natural science specialists. Critical data gaps were identified and specific research studies designed and implemented to address them. As a result, despite the fact that important data gaps remain, the study was able to draw on a body of scientific data of higher quality than has typically been available to economic analysts of developing country land degradation.[11]

Table 7.3 provides some data on average soil erosion rates associated with the cultivation of particular crops, and estimates of the value of soil loss.

Table 7.3   Sectoral erosion contributions and value of soil erosion in Sri Lanka

Crop	Erosion rate (av. tons/ha/yr) (1)	High-country (ha)	Mid-country (ha)	Total (ha) (2)	Annual value of soil loss (US$) (3[a])	Share (%)
Tea	17.5	73,110	84,062	157,172	4,257,311	27.7
Rubber	10.0	0	97,416	97,416	1,507,830	9.8
Coconut	10.0	0	55,529	55,529	859,492	5.6
Export Ag.	10.0	3,692	35,956	39,648	613,682	4.0
Other Ag.	85.0	26,788	28,500	55,288	7,273,978	47.2
Forestry	2.0	120,444	160,669	281,113	870,228	5.7
Total	14.5[b]	224,034	462,132	686,166	15,382,521	100.0

Notes:
[a] (3)=(1)×(2)×1.55, where nutrient loss is valued at US$ 1.55/ton/yr (Clark 1994).
[b] Weighted average.

Source: (1) Based on Somaratne (1998)

These estimates, being averages, mask substantial variation in erosion rates even in lands cultivated with the same crop. A range of factors, such as topography, soil type, pattern and intensity of rainfall, management quality and the extent to which soil conservation measures are adopted, influence the magnitude of soil losses. Nevertheless the estimates are indicative of the large intercrop variation in soil erosion rates, subject to some important management factors. For example, the level of management is critical for soil loss in lands cultivated with tea. Well-managed tea, particularly vegetatively propagated (VP) tea, which provides a dense cover protecting the topsoil from erosion, is one of the least soil-erosive land use systems for sloping hilly lands. On the other hand, poorly managed 'seedling' tea[12] is associated with erosion rates similar to those of highly erosive annuals. Estimates of annual erosion rates in sloping uplands culti-vated to annual crops such as vegetables, potatoes and tobacco and various forms of shifting cultivation, at 70–100 tons per ha, are four to five times higher than those for uplands under well-managed tea, but comparable to those under poorly managed tea.

In principle, the on-site cost of soil erosion is the discounted present value of the future stream of net revenue lost due to soil erosion.[13] The two most widely used methods for valuing on-site soil losses are the nutrient replacement cost method (NRCM) and the value of loss of productivity method (VLPM). The NRCM values erosion cost as being the cost of restoring the damaged soil to its previous state, while the VLPM values it as the output loss valued at market prices. Estimates of the value of soil losses are sensitive to the method of valuation. NRCM can overestimate the productivity impact of losses, particularly when the remaining stock of topsoil is relatively deep, as it can take several years for the on-site effects of erosion to impact on crop yields; on the other hand, VLPM may under-estimate the losses when the remaining stock is close to exhaustion. Further, replacement of nutrients addresses only one aspect of erosion-related productivity losses, as many other attributes of topsoil have a bearing on soil productivity. The value can also be sensitive to the discount rate used to discount the future losses to obtain their present value. Accordingly, any set of estimates must be regarded as approximate.

Estimating off-site losses is similarly difficult. Few carefully conducted studies are available.[14] There may be long lags between the occurrence of erosion in uplands and its downstream impacts: with the exception of 'spike' events such as storms and flash floods, the full off-site effects of topsoil loss from uplands may be felt over decades rather than years. Several studies were undertaken to address information gaps in this area. In particular, rela-tionships between yield profiles over time and erosion were estimated for tea and rubber (Coomaraswamy *et al.* 1999; Samarappuli *et al.* 1999). These enabled quantification of economic losses from erosion for the major forms of land use in the hilly regions. The results indicate an average value of annual losses in the range 0.75–1.00 per cent of GDP (Somaratne 1998).

In the next section we describe how key environmental parameters were incorporated in an AGE model of the Sri Lankan economy and present the results of some policy experiments. We then go on to discuss some of the complementary partial equilibrium analyses that provide a richer perspective on issues that are difficult to address at the level of aggregation of an AGE model.

7.4   AGE ANALYSIS OF TRADE AND ENVIRONMENTAL POLICY REFORMS

The economic component of the AGE model used in this study builds on two previous models (Bandara 1989; CIE 1992). These models specify household and other final demands for commodities, industry production and input demand, price determination, and macroeconomic identities, all as described in Chapter 5.

The basic model, as documented in Bandara *et al.* (1995) and Bandara and Coxhead (1999), has been modified and extended for the purpose of addressing erosion-related issues in greater detail (Somaratne 1998). Tea and other agricultural sectors are disaggregated to allow for different soil erosion levels in different agro-climatic regions, namely up-country, mid-country and low-country.[15] The up-country zone contains three industries: upland tea, potatoes and 'other agriculture' (which includes vegetables and tobacco). Land in this zone is mobile between these three crops. Within this zone, upland tea is less erosive than the other two land uses. The mid-country zone contains two sectors, 'mid-country tea' and 'mid-country other agriculture', and land is mobile between these two crops. Finally, the low-country zone contains 'low-country tea' and 'low-country other agriculture'.

Two sectors, paddy rice and electricity generation, are identified as being affected by the off-site effects of soil erosion. Soil erosion affects these sectors through the productivity impact parameter (PIP), defined as γ_Q in Chapter 5. The PIP is the only parameter described in equations (5.1)–(5.7) that cannot be calculated from the Sri Lanka AGE model database. A study by Bandusena (1995) suggests that the off-site effects captured by the PIP are empirically important, but does not provide precise numerical estimates at the sectoral level. For this exercise we adopted a non-zero value for the PIP in the paddy and HEP sectors only (where we assumed $\gamma_Q = -0.3$), and set it equal to zero in all other sectors.

The model used in the simulations has 27 sectors and specifies three types of labour: rural, unskilled and skilled. The latter two types are mobile among all sectors, while the former is employed in agriculture only. The model utilizes the 1989 input–output database and incorporates elasticity values from previous Sri Lankan AGE models. Data on sectoral soil erosion rates come from several sources (Krishnarajah 1985; Stocking 1992; Bandarathilake 1999). The model is closed using the small-country assumption for all tradables except tea exports. Sectoral capital stocks are fixed. Land is fixed in agricultural sectors, other than in the up-country, mid-country and low-country regions where it is mobile between crops, as just described. Forestry, though important in terms of land use issues, is not explicitly modelled in the Sri Lanka model; this is because the major episodes of deforestation in recent periods have been driven by policy decisions to expand land allocated to agricultural and settlement uses, rather than by encroachment.[16]

In the simulations reported below, we assume that wages are rigid and aggregate employment is determined endogenously, indicating that there is initial slack in the labour market. The foreign exchange rate is adopted as a numéraire price; any change in domestic prices can thus be interpreted as a change relative to world prices. Finally, government demands and the rates of all taxes and subsidies are also assumed to be exogenous. Note that because the non-marketed benefits and costs of land use changes, particularly those of deforestation, are not incorporated in the model, changes in real GDP and real consumption ('measured GDP' and 'measured real consumption') do not fully capture the benefits and costs of changes in soil erosion.

7.5 TRADE, TAX AND ENVIRONMENTAL POLICY EXPERIMENTS

In this section we use the model to examine the impacts of specific trade and tax/subsidy measures on environmental damages caused by soil erosion. We evaluate five possible policy options:

1. trade liberalization (a 25 per cent uniform tariff cut);
2. a production tax on erosive crops, coupled with a subsidy on less erosive crops;
3. a land tax on erosive crops, with a subsidy on less erosive crops;
4. an export subsidy on less erosive agricultural exports with a production tax on more erosive crops; and
5. an export subsidy on less erosive agricultural exports with a land tax on more erosive crops.

Table 7.4   Macroeconomic effects of five policy packages

	Trade liberaliza-tion	Production tax/subsidy package	Land tax/ subsidy package	Export subsidy & production tax	Export subsidy & land tax
Real GDP	1.81	−0.44	−0.61	0.01	0.01
Nominal GDP	−7.39	1.48	0.78	3.89	1.60
Agg. employment	4.11	−0.08	−0.26	0.59	0.37
Rural employment	6.30	2.23	2.41	2.05	1.65
Skilled employment	3.64	−0.57	−0.81	0.14	0.03
Unskilled employment	3.55	−0.67	−0.97	0.40	0.12
Real consumption	2.35	−0.50	−0.69	0.68	0.24
GDP deflator	−9.19	1.92	1.39	3.80	1.58
Consumer price index	−7.26	2.08	1.54	3.37	1.42
Import costs	6.32	0.10	−0.15	0.89	0.37
Export earnings	7.19	0.11	−0.17	1.01	0.42
Erosion total	−0.61	−2.98	−2.42	−0.62	−0.63

The main results of these five experiments are shown in summary form in Tables 7.4 and 7.5.

Trade liberalization, as simulated, causes real consumption of goods and services to rise by 2.35 per cent and aggregate employment by 4.1 per cent. All three types of labour demand increase. Trade reform also has predictable effects on production structure and macroeconomic aggregates. The tariff reduction changes the relative profitability of industries and reduces discrimination against export-oriented industries. As a result, resources are reallocated away from import-competing to export industries; the latter generally expand while the former contract. In agriculture, trade liberalization thus causes land to shift from previously highly protected, more erosive crops (for example, potatoes) to relatively less erosive export crops such as tea. This has a direct impact on the rate and intersectoral consequences of soil erosion. The paddy and electricity sectors both expand, in part because they experience reduced rates of erosion-related technical regress.

Using the simulation results, we can estimate the value of reduced soil erosion damage associated with the trade policy reform in comparison with base case values developed by Somaratne (1998). The last line in Table 7.4 summarizes these estimated values for all five policy packages. For trade liberalization, the results indicate a positive though small environmental impact in terms of reduced erosion. Thus the insights of the stylized models in Chapter 4 carry over to this empirically richer AGE exercise. The central

Table 7.5   Effects of policy packages on industry outputs

	Trade liberalization	Production tax/subsidy package	Land tax/ subsidy package	Export subsidy & production tax	Export subsidy & land tax
1. Up-country tea	4.33	18.25	4.36	3.38	2.17
2. Mid-country tea	4.12	17.43	3.55	3.18	1.82
3. Low-country tea	8.37	−19.53	−5.53	5.77	1.52
4. Rubber	6.01	−1.42	−0.99	−2.58	−1.08
5. Coconut	3.13	−0.66	−0.55	−0.78	−0.33
6. Paddy	1.36	−0.02	−0.16	0.36	0.16
7. Other export ag.	3.96	−1.00	−0.70	−1.82	−0.76
8. Up-country other agriculture	−0.40	−7.43	−5.00	−2.28	−1.05
9. Mid-country other agriculture	−0.43	−7.53	−5.11	−2.31	−1.10
10. Low-country other agriculture	0.15	1.20	0.04	−0.19	−0.03
11. Potato	−2.40	−10.59	−8.62	−3.67	−3.26
12. Plantation development	0.00	0.00	0.00	0.00	0.00
13. Mining, fishing & forestry	0.20	−0.28	−0.33	0.12	0.04
14. Tea processing	5.90	2.94	0.21	4.29	1.83
15. Coconut processing	9.92	−1.94	−1.14	−4.59	−1.88
16. Rice products	5.58	−0.42	−0.37	−0.40	−0.18
17. Other food products	−2.88	−1.02	−0.92	−0.87	−0.40
18. Textiles & clothing	9.25	−0.81	−0.48	−1.94	−0.78
19. Wood & rubber products	1.70	−0.29	−0.43	0.45	0.17
20. Fertilizer & chemicals	−0.33	−0.31	−0.41	0.15	0.05
21. Petroleum	0.25	−0.34	−0.42	0.02	−0.01
22. Rubber products	7.87	−0.41	−0.17	−1.48	−0.58
23. Other manufacturing	−3.24	−0.31	−0.27	−0.41	−0.16
24. Elect., gas & water	0.74	0.47	0.32	0.11	0.12
25. Construction	0.32	−0.06	−0.09	0.09	0.03
26. Trade & transport	2.46	−0.49	−0.62	0.22	0.06
27. Other services	1.97	−0.41	−0.57	0.59	0.21

message is simple: when a pre-existing distortion due to tariffs exacerbates environmental problems by switching resources away from less erosive export crops, trade liberalization can improve environmental outcomes as well as raising measured real consumption.

Although the trade liberalization experiment indicates environmental gains, they are small in magnitude, and additional policies directly targeting the land degradation problem deserve consideration. Pigovian production taxes (subsidies) on polluting (pollution-reducing) activities are commonly advocated for pollution abatement. Such options must be evaluated with fiscal neutrality, however, in order to obtain true measures of their welfare costs. Because of this, in the Sri Lanka model we choose a tax or subsidy package such that the additional revenues (expenditures) associated with the change in one policy instrument are exactly offset by additional expenditures (revenues) from another. In experiments 2–5 we examine several policy reform packages that combine taxes on highly erosive up-country producers with subsidies to competing (less erosive) sectors in a revenue-neutral manner. These experiments do not enable us to determine strictly whether a given policy package produces an *optimal* outcome in terms of maximizing social welfare, but they do allow quantification of the impact on measured GDP, real consumption, environmental effects (erosion) and sectoral incomes. In turn they can help policy formulation by showing the potential trade-offs between GDP and environmental gains and/or compensation for adversely affected groups. In practice, the availability of a menu of policy reform packages, whose environmental benefits and costs (in terms of reduced values of marketed benefits) are known, permits more informed choices to be made with due regard for administrative efficiency and political feasibility.

In policy experiment 2, we introduce a 10 per cent tax on production of 'other agriculture' in up-country and mid-country regions and on potatoes. We then calculate the value of the revenue raised by the tax on the basis of the model's base year production value of those three sectors, and distribute it among the up-country and mid-country tea sectors as subsidies proportionate to the base year production of these two sectors. The results of this simulation are given in the second columns of Tables 7.4 and 7.5. From Table 7.4 we see that the production tax and subsidy package reduces aggregate soil erosion by about 3 per cent. The environmental policies are thus more effective in reducing soil erosion than the trade liberalization, principally because they act directly on production of the environmentally harmful erosive crops.[17] However, the overall impact on real consumption is actually negative (−0.50 per cent), and the tax–subsidy package has no effect on net employment; the demand for rural labour rises, but that for skilled and unskilled labour contracts. The measured benefits of reduced erosion (using the base value in Table 7.3) are less than the value of reduced GDP. Unless the non-marketed benefits from reduced erosion are high enough to compensate for the lower value of measured consumption, this policy will therefore reduce overall welfare – a possibility shown theoretically in Chapter 4, equation (4.29).

Policy experiment 3 introduces a land tax on more erosive crops to discourage their production, and uses the revenues so obtained to subsidize less erosive crops. We introduce a 10 per cent tax on land used to grow 'other agriculture' and potatoes in up-country and mid-country zones, and use revenue to subsidize land used in tea production. The results are shown in column 3 of Tables 7.4 and 7.5. They show that this policy package does reduce soil erosion, although by less than policy package 2. Moreover, the reduction in GDP is larger and (other than for rural labour) the negative employment effects are larger. Therefore, policy package 2 unambiguously dominates policy 3.

In the fourth policy package, we introduce a tea export subsidy combined with a 10 per cent production tax on erosive crops. The rate of the subsidy depends on the revenue earned by the tax. These results are shown in column 4 of Tables 7.4 and 7.5. This policy both reduces soil erosion – by about the same magnitude as trade liberalization – and (in contrast to the previous two packages) does not reduce measured real consumption. This is because the export subsidy compensates for the negative intersectoral effects of the protection of import-competing industries.

The fifth policy package consists of a subsidy on tea exports financed by a 10 per cent tax on land used for more erosive crops. The results, summarized in column 5 of Tables 7.4 and 7.5, are very similar to those of the previous experiment with only a relatively small impact on erosion, though some of the sectoral impacts vary. The export subsidy combined with a land tax reduces soil erosion without lowering measured real income. Like the export subsidy–production tax package, the effects on employment of each kind of labour are modestly positive.

As noted earlier, we lack a precise estimate of the value of the PIP parameter. It is therefore appropriate to explore the robustness of our results with respect for the PIP. The results of repeating policy experiment 1 (trade liberalization) using three alternative values for the PIP ($\gamma_Q = \{0.0, -0.1, -0.6\}$) are shown in Tables 7.6 and 7.7. These indicate that different values for the PIP produce only minor changes in the macroeconomic results, although, as might be expected, changes in the output of the paddy and HEP sectors in each experiment are more sensitive to the value of this parameter.

The foregoing set of experiments shows that alternative policies directed at reducing soil erosion damage can have quite different impacts in other

*Table 7.6   Sensitivity analysis for value of PIP: trade liberalization
experiment (macro results)*

Macroeconomic results	$\gamma_Q = 0.0$	$\gamma_Q = -0.1$	$\gamma_Q = -0.3$	$\gamma_Q = -0.6$
Real GDP	1.78	1.79	1.81	1.84
Nominal GDP	−7.38	−7.38	−7.39	−7.39
Aggregate employment	4.07	4.08	4.11	4.16
Rural employment	6.26	6.27	6.30	6.34
Skilled employment	3.60	3.61	3.65	3.69
Unskilled employment	3.51	3.52	3.55	3.60
Real consumption	2.31	2.33	2.35	2.38
GDP deflator	−9.16	−9.17	−9.19	−9.23
Consumer price index	−7.22	−7.24	−7.26	−7.29
Import costs	6.70	6.30	6.32	6.34
Export earnings	7.17	7.17	7.19	7.21
Erosion total	−0.61	−0.61	−0.61	−0.61

Note: $\gamma_Q = -0.3$ in base case.

sectors and on macroeconomic aggregates. What happens to other forms of environmental damage is a question we do not explicitly address in the model. However, some inferences can be drawn from the experimental results about other environmental variables, such as industrial emissions. Table 7.5 shows changes in some industries known to be pollution-intensive, especially the fertilizer and chemicals sector and the rubber products sector (see Figure 5.1). Trade liberalization causes the fertilizer sector to contract somewhat, while substantially expanding the output of the rubber products sector. Assuming that emissions change in proportion to industry output, these results convey information about changes in industrial emissions.

Similarly, we can consider the impact of policy packages on incentives for deforestation by running the model with a different closure (with real rather than nominal wages, being endogenous), or by interpreting current results in an intuitive way. The higher employment effect shown in the table indicates that labour demand increases with trade liberalization, suggesting that there would be upward wage pressure if wages were flexible. Higher wages, as discussed in Chapter 4, tend to reduce deforestation. Thus, policies that stimulate employment and wage growth are more likely, other things being equal, to confer further environmental benefits through reduced deforestation. Indeed, this broader impact may be even more significant than that on erosion *per se*.

A more complete assessment of the environmental consequences of

Table 7.7 Sensitivity analysis for value of PIP: trade liberalization experiment (sectoral results)

Sectoral results	$\gamma_E = 0.0$	$\gamma_E = -0.1$	$\gamma_E = -0.3$	$\gamma_E = -0.6$
1. Up-country tea	4.31	4.32	4.34	4.36
2. Mid-country tea	4.09	4.10	4.12	4.15
3. Low-country tea	8.33	8.35	8.37	8.42
4. Rubber	5.98	5.99	6.01	6.05
5. Coconut	3.10	3.11	3.13	3.15
6. Paddy	1.29	1.32	1.36	1.43
7. Other export agriculture	3.94	3.94	3.96	3.98
8. Up-country other agriculture	−0.42	−0.41	−0.40	−0.39
9. Mid-country other agriculture	−0.45	−0.44	−0.43	−0.41
10. Low-country other agriculture	0.13	0.14	0.15	0.17
11. Potato	−2.42	−2.41	−2.40	−2.38
12. Plantation development	0.00	0.00	0.00	0.00
13. Mining, fishing & forestry	0.17	0.18	0.20	0.22
14. Tea processing	5.87	5.88	5.90	5.93
15. Coconut processing	9.86	9.88	9.92	9.97
16. Rice products	5.56	5.57	5.58	5.60
17. Other food products	−2.90	−2.90	−2.88	−2.86
18. Textiles & clothing	9.20	9.22	9.26	9.31
19. Wood & rubber products	1.67	1.68	1.71	1.74
20. Fertilizer & chemicals	−0.37	−0.36	−0.33	−0.30
21. Petroleum	0.23	0.24	0.25	0.28
22. Rubber products	7.81	7.83	7.87	7.94
23. Other manufacturing	−3.29	−3.27	−3.24	−3.19
24. Elect., gas & water	0.60	0.64	0.74	0.88
25. Construction	0.32	0.32	0.32	0.33
26. Trade & transport	2.44	2.45	2.46	2.49
27. Other services	1.94	1.95	1.97	2.00

Note: $\gamma_Q = -0.3$ in base case.

trade liberalization would take account of such information, in addition to that on the costs of soil erosion and measured national income. Looking beyond the model results, we can also get some insight into the possibilities for technological changes that may influence environmental damages. For instance, higher profits in the rubber sector might be expected to stimulate new investment, bringing with them newer, possibly greener, technologies.[18]

To summarize, the net effects of trade liberalization in Sri Lanka need not be environmentally harmful. At least as far as soil erosion is concerned, freer trade is environment-friendly rather than environmentally harmful as often conjectured. However, the magnitude of this positive impact is small, suggesting that other policies directly targeting soil erosion are required if a higher rate of abatement is desired. In other words, our results are consistent with the conjecture that trade policy is a very blunt instrument of environmental policy. Trade liberalization together with targeted tax–subsidy packages appears to be a combination that may better meet the goals of erosion reduction along with growth of income and employment. Nevertheless, considering the relatively small magnitudes of the erosion impacts of these policy packages, larger reductions in erosion seem to require the availability of economically attractive land conservation technologies.

7.6   TEA SECTOR REHABILITATION STRATEGIES AND SOIL EROSION

A static general equilibrium analysis necessarily operates at a high level of aggregation and ignores both the details and the dynamics of the operation of markets and the actions of agents. But in policy-relevant research such real-world complexities cannot be ignored. Given the central importance of the tea sector, both in the national economy and in terms of agricultural land degradation, the general equilibrium analysis has been supplemented by several other analyses specific to this sector. These analyse tea sector issues in more detail, albeit at the cost of adopting a partial equilibrium approach, and focus on interactions between environmental variables and the adoption of new tea production technologies.[19]

As noted earlier in this chapter, vegetatively propagated (VP) tea is both more productive and less erosive in Sri Lanka than is the traditional tea propagated by means of seedlings. The de-nationalization of large plantations in the 1990s resulted in substantial changes in tea management practices; it is likely that these changes were reinforced by higher profitability in tea arising from trade liberalization, as suggested in the first of the policy experiments reported in section 7.5. Both changes should have increased the rate at which low-yielding seedling tea was replaced with higher-yielding VP tea. In the presence of erosion externalities, tea replacement raises additional questions about the differences between private and social optima in tea production, and in the timing of replanting.

The replacement of low-yielding tea, when both on-site and off-site soil erosion are explicitly taken into account, can be thought of as being part of a more general problem of asset replacement in the presence of externalities. This has been analysed in the Sri Lanka case by Samaratunga (1996), who shows that accounting for such costs unambiguously shortens the privately and socially optimal replacement age of tea. This is so because net revenues per year decline more quickly once erosion costs are taken into account. When a superior asset, such as VP tea, is available, the optimal policy is to bring forward replacement. The longer the existing asset is kept, the higher the marginal cost, as there is a cumulative loss due to the greater depletion of soil as well as the forgone earnings from a more productive asset. Using specific erosion-related parameter values for Sri Lanka tea, the optimal replacement analysis indicates that immediate replacement of most of the existing seedling tea in the up-country and mid-country regions by VP tea is both privately and socially preferred.

This finding begs the question of why producers do not, in fact, upgrade tea technologies at the rate indicated by the analysis. Part of the answer relates to information: when it comes to understanding the full long-term implications of soil erosion for tea productivity, there are major knowledge gaps, not only among smallholders but even among senior managers of large tea plantations and among senior tea scientists; in fact, it was only as a result of the research cited in footnote / that the first scientific analysis of the soil loss–long-term productivity relationship was implemented.[20] Moreover, even if there is awareness of the impact of erosion, capital market imperfections – particularly liquidity constraints – may constrain producers' actions. Both actions may lead to choosing a suboptimal replacement date; the latter is particularly likely to be relevant in the case of smallholders.

In a related study, Jayasuriya (1998) quantified total factor productivity (TFP) growth in the tea sector since 1960. The results highlighted the contribution of technological change, in particular the adoption of VP tea, to the overall performance of the sector. Despite a steady decline in real tea prices and the productivity-reducing effects of land degradation, TFP grew at an estimated annual rate of 1.8 per cent during 1960/61–1994/95. This came almost wholly from a decline in total input use, with both capital and capital inputs declining significantly. This rate of TFP growth was such as to outweigh productivity losses due to land degradation, but the findings merely underline the costs of soil mining: the full benefits of technological change could not be reaped and it only helped maintain productivity in the face of land degradation. Indirectly, continuing land degradation reduces the potential returns to R&D expenditures. Indeed, if returns to research were evaluated without recognition of its role in counteracting the underlying decline of land quality, its full impact would be grossly underestimated and could lead to the misleading conclusion that public expenditures on tea research are wasteful. On the contrary, the tea research effort has been very fruitful in terms of shielding the sector (and the national economy) from the full impact of the extensive degradation of tea lands.

7.8   CONCLUSIONS

The ongoing process of policy and institutional reform in a country like Sri Lanka means that the economic importance of land degradation is constantly changing. Research outlined in this chapter indicates that land degradation, in the form of soil erosion, imposes significant economic costs on the economy, both by diminishing the on-site productivity of tea and rubber – two major export crops – in particular, and by contributing to off-site damages in the economically important paddy and electricity generation industries. From the AGE model we find that trade policy reforms reduce land degradation by reducing incentives to cultivate erosive crops while increasing national income and employment. Supplementary microeconomic analysis of tea sector issues suggests that increased profitability in tea production may itself lead to erosion-reducing investments in new technologies and raise the rate of return to future R&D investments in tea. Nevertheless, the impacts of trade and investment policies alone are likely to be minor, though still significant, and there is a clear need to address land degradation directly by means of environmental policies. We have examined the impact of a range of environmental policies on soil erosion and compared their efficacy not merely in terms of environmental impacts, but also in terms of trade-offs as measured by changes in employment and aggregate real income. Such trade-offs, as well as other intersectoral implications of trade or environmental policies, can only be fully captured in a general equilibrium framework.

The general equilibrium approach used here overcomes many of the weaknesses of previous approaches; nevertheless, our analysis is also subject to important limitations. To maintain the focus on the broad policy reform issues, we have abstracted from some major institutional aspects affecting land degradation, notably insecure or ill-defined property rights (land tenure) and imperfect capital markets. These problems, significant even in partial equilibrium analysis, are magnified in general equilibrium; in practice it is extremely difficult to incorporate them adequately in economy-wide modelling approaches. But this difficulty in no way minimizes their importance for policy.

Despite the limitations imposed by both data and methodological constraints, some policy conclusions can be drawn with considerable confidence. Our results indicate that trade liberalization and institutional reforms are likely to be environment-friendly rather than, as often conjectured, environmentally harmful. The analysis helps to address the challenge of formulating a set of specific environmental policies and institutional reforms that can complement the mildly pro-environment impact of trade reforms. Some combinations of tax and subsidy policies can be helpful; in addition, public investment to promote productivity growth in the tea industry is itself likely to pay an environmental dividend. But clearly, large reductions in erosion require that economically attractive technologies are developed and brought to the attention of agricultural producers. In the Sri Lanka context, perhaps the most important message that comes through is that there are no serious environmental grounds for opposing trade liberalization. However, environmental problems, such as land degradation, are serious economic problems that should be addressed with targeted policies.

NOTES

1. This chapter is based on the products of a collaborative research project on land degradation in the hilly regions of Sri Lanka conducted in collaboration with the Ministry of Public Administration, Home Affairs, Plantation Industries and Parliamentary Affairs of Sri Lanka (MPA/HA/PI/PA), with the financial support of the Australian Centre for International Agricultural Research (ACIAR) conducted by a team that comprised the authors, Professor Anthony Chisholm, Dr Jay Bandara, Dr Anura Ekanayake and several other economists and leading scientists. A detailed description of the project, including a full list of the team members and the scientific papers that underpinned the economic models and specific policy recommendations presented to the government, is given in Chisholm, Ekanayake and Jayasuriya (1999).
2. The zones are defined by the following criteria: rainfall (75 per cent expectancy): dry zone, less than 900 mm per annum; intermediate zone, 900–1,400 mm; wet zone, over 1,400 mm. Elevation: low-country: 0–300 m; mid-country: 300–1,000 m; up-country, more than 1,000 m.
3. The Mahaweli is the longest and most important river in the country. The Upper Mahaweli catchment area provides water for 56 per cent of hydro power and 22 per cent of rice (paddy) production.
4. Government of Sri Lanka (1987).
5. For many years, a sliding scale of taxes ensured that even the benefits of world price increases were captured by the government (see Athukorala and Jayasuriya 1994). The burden of direct export taxes has been considerably reduced in recent years.
6. This is a particularly quaint use of the term 'non-traditional', as historical records indicate that Sri Lanka has been exporting spices for at least two millennia.
7. The structure of protection in Sri Lanka is reviewed by Edwards (1993). Many resources, land in particular, are largely specific to agriculture, making the relative incentive structure within agriculture the main determinant of resource movements.
8. See Athukorala and Jayasuriya (1994) for details of the 1977–78 reforms, and Dunham and Kalegama (1997) for the post-1989 reforms.
9. Chisholm *et al.* (1999) reproduce an indicative map of land degradation.
10. See Wijeratne (1999) and Samarasinghe (1999) for a discussion of the impact on hydropower and the road network in Sri Lanka.
11. Technical papers that provided the basis for economic modelling are in Chisholm *et al.* (1999).
12. Seedling tea refers to the older vintage of tea cultivars that were propagated by seed.
13. Samaratunga (1996) presents a detailed discussion of the methodological issues involved in valuing on-site and off-site soil losses.
14. Bandusena (1995) presents an estimate for off-site losses associated with one of the reservoirs in the Mahaweli irrigation system.

15. These broadly follow the classification of agro-ecological regions by the Land and Water Use Division, Department of Agriculture.
16. Deforestation produced by encroachment, however, does remain an issue of some concern in parts of the country. As discussed later, the model results can be interpreted to shed light on the likely direction of change.
17. However, the administrative costs of implementing such a policy (ignored here) are likely to be quite high in a developing country context.
18. Hartman *et al.* (1997) indicate this for a sample of feed mills in Asia.
19. See, in particular, Jayasuriya (1998) and Samaratunga (1996).
20. A separate study used survey techniques to explore farmers' perceptions of the environmental costs of tea cultivation (Ananda *et al.* 2001).

8.   Environmental effects of investment and trade policy reform during Thailand's economic 'miracle'

8.1   THAILAND'S ECONOMIC BOOM AND AGRICULTURAL BUST

In the middle and late 1980s, a remarkable combination of domestic and international factors came together to 'make a miracle' in Thailand: an acceleration of real economic growth from about 6 per cent per year in 1976–85 to above 8 per cent in 1986–95. At its peak in 1988–90, growth averaged 12 per cent per year. This growth was associated with policy and institutional changes that led to a major surge in both domestic and foreign investment. Low wages, reductions in trade barriers and conservative economic management resulting in low inflation and a stable exchange rate made the Thai economy an ideal host for foreign investment. From late in the 1980s, financial liberalization (the opening of capital markets) encouraged further foreign direct investment (FDI) as well as foreign borrowing, thus adding further fuel to the ongoing investment boom. From 1980 Thailand, along with Malaysia and subsequently China, pulled clear of the other 'second-generation' Asian industrializing countries in terms of gross fixed capital formation and FDI (Table 3.2). Political instability notwithstanding, and despite doubts about the robustness of its financial institutions, Thailand had become a model developing economy, winning a place in the group of eight 'high-performing Asian economies' that the World Bank in 1993 dubbed the East Asian Miracle.

The gains from the boom were not uniformly shared among sectors. Agriculture, historically the mainstay of the Thai economy, the primary employer and major source of export earnings, captured only a tiny fragment of the investment boom and, as the most labour-intensive sector, found itself increasingly unable to compete with the rising wages offered in non-agricultural and urban sectors (Figure 8.1). After 1989, as close to three million workers out of a total agricultural labour force of about 20 million walked off the land (Figure 8.2), planted area began to decline (Figure 8.3) and agricultural output growth rates decelerated (Table 8.1).

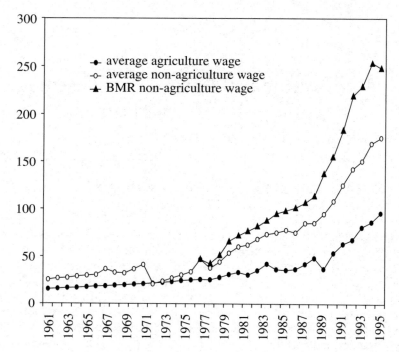

Note: BMR = Bangkok Metropolitan Region.

Source: Coxhead and Jiraporn (1999)

Figure 8.1   Thailand: agricultural and non-agricultural wage, 1961–95 (baht/day)

The transfer of resources from agriculture was such that the *relative* decline of the sector, an inevitable and generally welcome trend in a growing economy, almost became an absolute contraction.

In this chapter we first examine the implications of Thailand's boom, and of some of the trade pricing policy reforms that preceded and accompanied it, for the allocation of productive resources between sectors and within agriculture. We then trace the implications of the structural and price effects of these changes through to the valuation and use of resources in upland agriculture and other sectors. The analyses, using both economet-ric models and AGE simulations, are conducted using aggregate data; nevertheless, as we show, they are revealing of the ways in which the boom and associated economic changes altered incentives for agricultural land

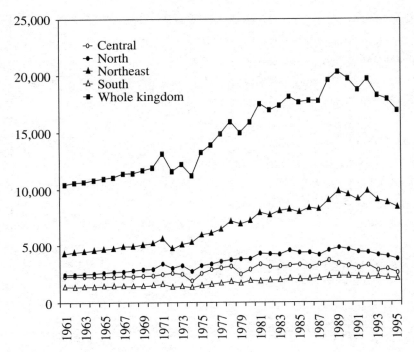

Source: Coxhead and Jiraporn (1999)

*Figure 8.2   Thailand: agricultural labour by region, 1961–95
('000 workers)*

use in uplands and at the cultivated frontier, and produced significant compositional changes within the manufacturing sector.

8.2   EXPLAINING AGRICULTURAL DECLINE AND CHANGES IN LAND AREA

As is well known, economic growth reduces the relative profitability of agriculture through several mechanisms. Of these, the most important are changes in relative prices (Stolper–Samuelson effects), and unequal rates of factor endowment growth, which cause factors to migrate to sectors where their relative productivity is higher (Rybczinski effects). Previous studies have shown that both of these intersectoral effects are important components of the relative decline of Thai agriculture over the period 1960–85

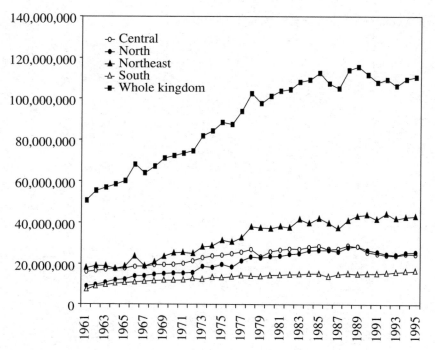

Source: Coxhead and Jiraporn (1999)

Figure 8.3   Thailand: agriculture planted area by region, 1961–95 (rai)

(Martin and Warr 1994; Siamwalla 1996). Rising prices for non-traded goods (produced mainly in non-agricultural sectors) and growth of non-agricultural capital have apparently been the main engines of structural change in the Thai economy. Both rising prices and non-agricultural investment increase labour productivity outside the farm sector. Wage pressures and declining relative agricultural prices squeeze farm profits and discourage investment, and this reduces the agricultural growth rate relative to rates in the rest of the economy.

Relative prices themselves are subject to significant policy influence. In the case of Thailand, agricultural policies historically discriminated against rice (paddy), the largest agricultural industry and a major source of export revenue. Less directly, agriculture was subjected to indirect taxation through the relative price effects of tariffs and other industrial promotion policies (Siamwalla and Setboonsarng 1990). Econometric analysis taking account of the effects of policies separately from those of 'secular' changes

Table 8.1 *Aggregate and agricultural output growth rates, Thailand (% per year)*

Period	GDP	Agriculture	Difference	Agricultural growth as % of GDP growth
1965–80	7.2	4.6	2.6	64
1980–90	7.6	4.0	3.6	53
1990–94	8.2	3.1	5.1	38

Source: World Bank, *World Development Report*, various years

in relative prices (due, for example, to terms of trade shocks) has identified the price effect of policy reforms as the most important single 'driver' of agriculture's relative decline (Punyasavatsut and Coxhead 2000).

The studies just reviewed contribute to our understanding of broad sectoral shifts under the assumption that total factor stocks grow exogenously. They are inadequate, therefore, to explain such phenomena as the expansion of agricultural land area. We quantify this for the Thai case in the following econometric analysis.[1]

We begin by asking what factors explain agricultural factor demand at the level of the sector. The conventional approach is to model the sector as a price-taker and to derive optimal output and factor demands in terms of exogenous prices, fixed factor endowments and technology. However, Thai agriculture cannot be said to be a price-taker in the labour market, since more than half of the labour force is recorded as being employed in that sector. While the total agricultural labour force is by no means fixed even in the short run, the agricultural wage is endogenous to agricultural labour demand. Therefore, we must simultaneously explain agricultural wage formation. As we shall shortly see, accounting for endogenous wage formation pays an additional dividend, since we are then able to capture the intersectoral determinants of changes in agricultural factor demand. In particular, since land and labour are complementary inputs in agriculture, we expect to find that some part of the explanation for the observed land area decline is to be found in trends in intersectoral labour markets.

The model explains agricultural land and labour demand in terms of product prices, prices of other variable inputs, fixed input quantities, technical progress and wages. Wages in turn are explained by reference to the intersectoral labour market, as follows. First, agricultural labour demand is determined by the agricultural wage (WA)[2] and the price of fertilizer (PF), both expressed in terms of agricultural prices (PA); the quantities of non-labour factors including land (NA), irrigation (IR) and agricultural machinery (KA); and a measure of technological progress (T):

$$LA = LA(WA/PA^-, PF/PA^-, NA^+, IR^+, KA^-, T), \qquad (8.1)$$

where superscripts indicate the signs of the partial derivatives as predicted by theory. *Ceteris paribus*, we expect labour demand to decline with a rise in wages or fertilizer prices (fertilizer is usually complementary to agricultural labour). We expect that an increase in physical land or effective land (through irrigation) will increase labour demand. We expect that mechanization (an increase in non-land agricultural capital) will reduce labour demand.

While the total land endowment may be regarded as fixed in the short run, planted area may fluctuate from year to year. In our model the demand for land, measured as the area planted in each period, is determined by agricultural prices, a measure of labour availability or wages, the price of fertilizer, the quantities of other inputs (irrigation, labour, agricultural machinery), and technology:

$$NA = NA(PA^+, WA/PA^-, PF/PA^+, IR^-, KA^+, T). \qquad (8.2)$$

Equations (8.1) and (8.2) are interdependent since endogenous variables appear on their right-hand sides. There are two additional complications. First, some or all equations may be under-identified, depending on the exact combination of exogenous variables included and excluded from each. Second, due to the large share of agriculture in total employment, the agricultural wage is also not invariant with respect to changes in agriculture, another potential source of simultaneity bias. We resolve these problems, and capture economic links between agricultural and non-agricultural development, by explaining the agricultural wage by reference to the intersectoral labour market.

The Thai labour market exhibits a high degree of intersectoral mobility at the margin, and the agricultural wage has tracked the non-agricultural wage fairly closely over time. We expect that agricultural wages (WA) and non-agricultural wages (WN) are related, but that the correspondence is not exact due to transactions costs and adjustment lags, that is, $WA = WA(WA_{-1}, WN)$. We then explain WN by constructing an inverse non-agricultural labour demand function in terms of non-agricultural prices (PN), the aggregate capital stock (KN), labour supply (LF), and a time trend (T) capturing technical progress:

$$WN = WN(PN^+, KN^+, LF^-, T).$$

If a linear combination of these variables is correlated with the non-agricultural wage, then we can explain the agricultural wage by (8.3):

$$WA = WA(WA_{-1}, WN) = WA(WA_{-1}{}^+, PN^+, KN^+, T, LF^-), \quad (8.3)$$

in which the current value of WA depends on contemporaneous and lagged values of exogenous variables determining the non-agricultural wage.[3]

The simultaneous solution of (8.1), (8.2) and (8.3) resolves the identification problem, and captures the main intersectoral linkages through product and labour markets. By substitution, it is readily seen that the reduced form of the system is a pair of agricultural factor demand equations in which the explanatory variables are all exogenous, at least in the short to medium term. They are prices (PA, PN), fixed factor stocks (KA, KN, IR) and technological progress (T).

Estimation of this system uses a time series of Thai regional data that spans the years 1961–95, and four regions as well as the Bangkok metropolitan area (for full details, see Coxhead and Jiraporn 1999). We include regional dummy variables and a set of categorical variables accounting for the aggregation of crops with different characteristics into univariate measures of agricultural output and factor demand. We include FT, the ratio of field crop to tree crop area, in the labour demand equation to capture differences in the labour intensity of crops. We include IN, the value of production of land-intensive crops divided by that of land-saving crops, in the land demand functions to capture variation in the land intensity of crops. Defining all continuous variables except the time trend in logarithms (denoted by a prime, for example $LA' = \ln(LA)$), the system to be estimated, excluding regional dummies, is:

$$LA' = a_1 + b_1(WA' - PA') + c_1(PF' - PA') + d_1 NA' + e_1 IR' + f_1 KA'$$
$$+ g_1 FT' + h_1 T + \varepsilon_1 \qquad (8.4)$$

$$NA' = a_2 + b_2 PA' + c_2(PF' - PA') + d_2(WA' - PA') + e_2 IR' + f_2 KA'$$
$$+ g_2 IN' + h_2 T + \varepsilon_2 \qquad (8.5)$$

$$WA' = a_3 + b_3 PN' + c_3 KN' + d_3 LF' + e_3 WA'_{-1} + h_3 T + \varepsilon_3. \qquad (8.6)$$

In these expressions, lower-case letters (such as a_1) are coefficients to be estimated. Three-stage least-squares (3SLS) provides estimators that are both consistent and asymptotically efficient for a system of equations of this type (Greene 1993). We use SHAZAM (White 1993) for this purpose. The results (Table 8.2) indicate that most of the estimates are highly significant and of the predicted sign.

Table 8.2   3SLS estimates of labour and land demand and agricultural wages

Variable	Abbreviation	Labour demand (LA)	Land demand (NA)	Agric. wage (WA)
Agricultural land	NA	0.8179 (0.0745)[a]	—	—
Agricultural wage/ agricultural price	WA	−0.4874 (0.0876)[a]	−0.1580 (0.0684)[b]	—
— lagged	WA_{t-1}	—	—	0.00007 (0.00008)
Agricultural price	PA	—	0.1288 (0.0644)[b]	—
Non-agricultural price	PN	—	—	1.2781 (0.1046)[a]
Fert. price/agricultural price	PF	0.1825 (0.0462)[a]	0.1198 (0.0481)[b]	—
Irrigation	IR	0.1854 (0.0232)[a]	−0.0399 (0.0174)[b]	—
Agricultural machinery	KA	−0.1620 (0.0221)[a]	0.2112 (0.0150)[a]	—
Non-agricultural capital	KN	—	—	0.4181 (0.0859)[a]
Field crops/tree crops	FT	−0.0015 (0.0006)[b]	—	—
Land intensity	IN	—	0.4166 (0.0265)[a]	—
Labour force	LF	—	—	−1.8428 (0.2115)[a]
Time	T	0.0314 (0.0042)[a]	−0.0104 (0.0046)[b]	0.0170 (0.0108)
N/d.f.		140/127	140/129	140/131
Adj. R^2		0.9624	0.9697	0.9511

Notes:
1. Standard errors are in parentheses. Superscripts [a], [b], and [c] denote significance at 1%, 5% and 10% respectively.
2. All variables except T are measured in logs. For units and descriptors, see text and Coxhead and Jiraporn (1999).
3. R^2 is indicative only (not bounded in [0,1]). Coefficient estimates for regional dummy variables and 1974 dummy are excluded from this table.

Source: Coxhead and Jiraporn (1999)

As expected, labour demand is positively associated with land area and negatively with the agricultural wage and the stock of agricultural machinery. Consistent with expectations, an increase in the fertilizer price contributes to increased labour demand. The complementarity of fertilizer use with labour arises because most fertilizer is used in irrigated rice production, where applying fertilizer results in substantial increases in plant growth and yield. The coefficient of the time trend suggests that, over the entire period, technical progress in agriculture has been labour using at a rate of approximately 3 per cent per year.

The estimated parameters of the land demand function also conform to expectations, and all are significant at conventional levels. Higher agricultural prices are associated with increased land demand, as are increases in the quantities of complementary inputs (agricultural capital) and the price of a substitute (fertilizer). Higher agricultural wages reduce land demand. An increase in irrigated area represents a positive land supply 'shock' that causes planted area to expand, but by less than a proportional amount: indicating that, as irrigated area expands, demand for non-irrigated land contracts. On average, technical progress in agriculture has been land saving over the period covered by the data, at a rate of about 1 per cent per year.

All estimates of the agricultural wage equation (8.6) were also of the predicted sign. Surprisingly, the dynamic component of the model had no impact, with the estimated coefficient of WA_{-1} being just smaller than its standard error and very small in magnitude. By contrast, the contemporaneous determinants of non-agricultural wages, PN, KN and LF, were all found to exert strong effects on WA. The coefficient of non-agricultural productivity growth was not significant.

To aid interpretation of these results, Table 8.3 shows elasticities of the reduced form equations. The results confirm that in spite of significant agricultural investments, for example in irrigation, the evolution of agricultural factor demand is largely driven by non-agricultural phenomena – specifically, non-agricultural prices and investment. These raise agricultural wages and this in turn drives agricultural resource allocation decisions. These estimates help quantify the Rybczinski effect of non-agricultural growth.

The econometric result provides strongly intuitive explanations both for the decline of agricultural land area and labour use, as well as for the increase in agricultural wages. With massive outflow of labour from the sector, a considerable amount of agricultural land was also taken out of production.

Table 8.3　Estimated elasticities of agricultural labour and land demand

With respect to:	Elasticity of:	
	Labour demand	Land demand
Land use	0.82	—
Labour use	—	—
Agricultural wage	−0.62	−0.16
Agricultural prices	0.44	0.17
Non-agricultural prices	−0.79	−0.20
Fertilizer price	0.28	0.12
Irrigated area	0.15	−0.04
Agricultural machinery	0.01	0.21
Non-agricultural investment	−0.26	−0.07
Labour supply	1.14	0.29
Time trend	0.01	−0.01

Source:　3SLS estimates reported in Coxhead and Jiraporn (1998)

8.3　LAND RETIREMENT DURING THE BOOM: A CLOSER LOOK

The overall decline of agricultural land area can also be seen in provincial data, and these yield some revealing insights. Regionally, the decline in planted area has occurred in the central and northern regions, areas with a high proportion of upland and mountainous terrain. However, land use change has not been uniformly distributed at the provincial level. A brief analysis of provincial data from Northern Thailand enables a somewhat more detailed picture of the pattern of land retirement.

Inspection of the aggregate Northern Thailand planted area data (Figure 8.3) suggests that a structural break occurred in 1988, after which agricultural area, having increased steadily for nearly three decades, began to decline. We can test the hypothesis of a structural break in the series by fitting a spline function, in which dummy variables are used to permit a curve fitted to the data to take a new slope and intercept after 1988. Define a time trend t, a dummy variable (D89) taking the value 0 for 1961–88 and 1 thereafter, and their product, tD89. The spline function yields the following estimates:

$$\text{Planted area} = 8.91 \quad +0.70{*}t \quad +33.35{*}\text{D89} \quad -1.21{*}t\text{D89}$$
$$(0.348)^a \quad (0.021)^a \quad (5.436)^a \quad (0.1705)^a$$

(Adj. $R^2 = 0.98$; figures in parentheses are standard errors; superscript [a] indicates significance at 1%; units = million rai.)

The estimates strongly support the hypothesis of a structural break in the regional data, with planted area increasing by 700,000 rai/yr until 1988, but declining by 510,000 rai/yr from 1989 – an average annual decline of about 2.5 per cent.

If all provinces faced uniform conditions, we would expect similar results from the same spline function separately to the provincial data. Some provinces exhibit strong downturns after 1989; others, however, show no change in the trend (for details of provincial estimates, see Coxhead with Jiraporn 1998). What factors explain divergent land area responses? *A priori*, we expect to find that much of the variation is due to differences in agricultural land quality and productivity, labour mobility, and infrastructure-related costs such as marketing expenses. As the opportunity cost of resources that are complementary with land rises, less productive land will tend to be removed from production. Other things equal, higher labour mobility should be associated with more rapid reductions in planted area. Better infrastructure, such as roads, should be associated with lower transactions costs and thus with agricultural productivity, since roads extend the reach of the market into agricultural areas and thus facilitate specialization. On the other hand, better infrastructure should also permit mobility and may be a proxy for other development indicators, and may thus be associated with more rapid agricultural decline.

We test these propositions using provincial data for Northern Thailand. The percentage change in planted area between 1989 and 1995 is expressed as a function of variables hypothesized to capture the foregoing explanations. These are: irrigation expenditures per agricultural labourer (IRR, a proxy for land quality); forested area as a percentage of total area in 1988 (FOR, a proxy for highland/upland area); average education levels (ED, a proxy for labour mobility); and the intensity of roads per unit area (RD, a measure of infrastructural development).[4] We hypothesize that agricultural area growth is positively associated with land productivity and negatively with forested area and labour mobility; infrastructural development may have ambiguous results, as just suggested. The results of a linear regression on the provincial data were as follows:

$$\Delta P8995 = 51.99 + 0.146*IRR - 0.272*FOR - 17.313*ED - 0.07*RD$$
$$(20.92)^b \quad (0.043)^a \qquad (0.122)^b \qquad (5.502)^a \qquad (0.156)$$

(Adj. $R^2 = 0.4708$; $N = 16$; figures in parentheses are standard errors; superscripts [a] and [b] indicate significance at 1% and 5% respectively.)

Although the sample is small and the variables imperfectly measured, these results support the first three hypotheses; as anticipated, the test of the fourth hypothesis is inconclusive.[5] Land quality is positively associated with the change in planted area. Forested area, which we interpret as indicating the importance of upland and highland agriculture in the provincial land base, shows a negative association. Labour mobility also has a negative association. The clear implication is that land retirement will be more likely to occur in areas, especially upland and highlands, where land is of relatively poor quality, and where farmers and their children are more capable of moving to other jobs.

From the perspective of environmental management, the results suggest that the highland areas most 'at risk' of degradation in Northern Thailand are those that are agronomically suited to high-value crops but which have farm labour forces that are older or relatively poorly educated (the two are likely to be highly correlated). Within such areas, the environmental risks may be lowered when the high-value crops planted are fruit trees or other relatively soil-conserving perennials, or increased when planted with vegetables or other short-season, highly land-degrading and erosive crops such as corn. Consideration of these emerging land use patterns in the context of trends in the Thai labour market will help sharpen the focus of environmental policy debates on upland and highland land use.[6]

The foregoing analysis suggests that capital accumulation in non-agricultural sectors explains much of the decline in total planted area observed during the boom period, with the labour market providing the conduit through which intersectoral differences in profitability were resolved. Long-term non-agricultural growth, whatever its environmental effects in other sectors, appears to have conferred environmental benefits in upland and highland areas by raising the returns to labour beyond the point at which it is profitable to cultivate land at the arable margin.

8.4　EFFECTS OF TRADE POLICY REFORMS: AN AGE APPROACH

The PARA Model of the Thai Economy

Along with capital accumulation, the Thai economy during the 1980s and early 1990s was also marked by dramatic policy reforms, notably a reduction in protective tariffs for manufacturing industry. The econometric analysis by Punyasavatsut and Coxhead (2000) indicates that trade policy reforms exert a very large influence over the rate of decline of agriculture as a whole in the Thai economy. That analysis, however, sheds no light on incentives to use agricultural land for particular purposes, information that is clearly of value to any environmental assessment. As we have argued in earlier chapters, the intersectoral effects of trade policies are best analysed in a general equilibrium context. In this section we explore the results of an AGE study of Thai trade liberalization, tracing its effects on variables that indicate likely changes (or incentives for change) in the use of environmental and natural resource assets.

We use the results of a simulation experiment with the PARA model of the Thai economy, the basic structure of which is described in Kanok and Warr (1995). PARA is a Johansen-type AGE model with the basic structure conforming to that described in summary fashion in Chapter 5. It contains 60 producer goods and services, including 20 agricultural products. The model embeds a flexible system to account for primary factor demands by industry, with the parameters of such systems estimated econometrically from time-series data.

The model contains four types of intersectorally mobile primary factors as well as one factor that is specific to each sector. The four mobile factors are skilled and unskilled labour, and mobile agricultural and non-agricultural capital. Unskilled labour is mobile across all sectors, while skilled labour is used only in non-agriculture. Non-agricultural capital can be reallocated among non-agricultural sectors. Agricultural capital (that is, land) is fixed in quantity, but can be reallocated among industries within the sector. The assumption that the quantity of land planted does not change is consistent with the other assumptions on factor endowments in the model, even if not with longer-run Thai realities, as seen in earlier sections of this chapter. However, the returns to land are endogenous; in simulations with the model, therefore, changes in the return to land are indicative of changing incentives to expand or contract the agricultural area by crop as well as in total. This information, used together with the model's predictions of changes in the production of each type of agricultural good, makes possible a range of statements about the effects of trade liberalization on incentives for agricultural intensification and expansion in the Thai context.

The model is neoclassical in structure, imposing constant returns to scale, competitive markets and flexible prices across all production, consumption and trade activities. The Thai economy is treated as a small economy in world markets with the exception of rice and cassava, for which export demand elasticities take values of –2.5 and –5.0 respectively. The model closure is also neoclassical. Domestic prices and all quantities produced and consumed are all endogenous. Household savings are fixed in real terms, and real investment and real government spending are also fixed. This ensures that the full effect of any simulated change in the economy will lead to changes in the real consumption of households (for further details of the model and closure, see Kanok and Warr 1995). Finally, the model database embeds a variety of distortions in the form of taxes and subsidies, of which tariffs are just one category. Since any exogenous change in a tax or tariff must leave the government budget in balance, trade liberalization (that is, a reduction in tariffs) is compensated by an endogenous increase in the income tax. With the supply of labour held fixed, this income tax is a non-distortionary tax on households.

Simulation Results: Tariff Reduction

We use the PARA model to simulate the effects of a 25 per cent across-the-board tariff reduction. The major macroeconomic effects of this counter-factual change are summarized in Table 8.4; sectoral results are shown in Table 8.5, and results pertaining to incentives for agricultural expansion and intensification in Table 8.6.

The tariff reduction leaves real GDP practically unchanged (Table 8.4). Nominal wages for both skilled and unskilled labour rise, as does the return to intersectorally mobile capital used in the manufacturing and services sectors. The return to agricultural capital falls. The real consumption expenditure of households also falls slightly, a result that is somewhat unexpected given that the policy experiment involves the revenue-neutral replacement of a highly distortionary tax by one that is non-distortionary. On the other hand, this is not entirely surprising. If tariffs were the only distortion, liberalization would unambiguously increase household welfare as reflected in real consumption. But of course no such prediction can be made when many other distortionary taxes remain.

Among industry sectors, the tariff reform reduces the producer prices and output of a wide range of manufacturing activities (Table 8.5). Exportable manufacturing sectors (such as spinning and weaving, textiles and leather products) all expand. The same pattern can be seen among agricultural industries (Table 8.6), with the most highly protected sectors (soybean, sorghum, tobacco and vegetables) all contracting, while exportable sectors, notably plantation crops such as oil palm, coconut, rubber and sericulture, expand. Returns to all specific factors in the contracting sectors fall. Rice and maize both contract also, shedding mobile factors such as labour and capital, and showing slight declines in the returns to specific factors. Thus all traditional upland and highland agricultural sectors – rice, maize, soybean, and vegetables and fruit contract, and returns to land in each fall. This is a very strong indication that – for upland farmers, trade liberalization has reduced incentives to produce the field crops that occupy the greatest share of area and which, as annual or short-season crops, also

Table 8.4 Macroeconomic effects of a 25 per cent tariff reduction (% change)

Description	% change
Overall economy	
Gross domestic product	
Nominal (local currency)	−0.25
Real	−0.01
Consumer price index	−0.20
GDP deflator	−0.25
Wage (nominal)	
Skilled labour	0.21
Unskilled labour	0.18
Return to mobile capital (nominal)	
Non-agriculture	0.18
Agriculture	−0.07
External accounts	
Export revenue (foreign currency)	0.17
Import bill (foreign currency)	0.23
Government budget	
Nominal revenue (baht)	0.42
Expenditure	
Nominal (baht)	0.57
Real	0.49
Budget deficit (in levels, foreign currency)	0.00
Households	
Consumption	
Nominal (baht)	−0.38
Real	−0.19

Source: PARA model simulations

contribute the greatest share of agricultural land degradation and soil erosion. The reasons are not hard to find, and confirm the econometric predictions reported earlier in the chapter: trade liberalization raises wages across the board and thus reduces profitability in all labour-intensive sectors. Further, labour-intensive sectors that formerly received protection shrink more, as they experience not only higher labour costs but also a decline in output prices.

Comparing the trade liberalization result with that of non-agricultural capital accumulation (section 8.2) reveals an interesting parallel. During Thailand's investment boom, a very large share of new investment was directed to labour-intensive manufacturing sectors such as garments (listed

Table 8.5   *Sectoral effects of a 25 per cent tariff reduction: manufacturing and services (% change)*

Sector	Domestic production	Producer price	Sector	Domestic production	Producer price
Food processing	0.47	−0.01	Basic metals	−0.32	−0.32
Rice milling	−0.04	0.03	Metal products	−0.15	−0.26
Sugar refining	−0.01	0.00	Agric. machinery	−0.02	−0.57
Animal feeds	0.10	−0.16	Other machinery	−0.08	−0.40
Beverages	−0.23	−0.20	Elect. machinery	−0.05	−0.39
Cigarettes	−0.54	−0.60	Motor vehicles	−0.11	−1.60
Spinning	0.56	−0.02	Motor veh. repair	−0.06	−1.05
Textiles	0.64	−0.02	Other manufg	0.00	−0.11
Leather	0.63	−0.01	Construction	0.00	−0.10
Wood & paper	−0.15	−0.19	Elect., gas & water	0.07	0.09
Printing	−0.06	−0.25	Transport serv.	−0.03	0.00
Chemicals	−0.19	−0.28	Trade	−0.18	0.02
Fertilizer	0.43	−0.19	Banking	0.02	0.15
Petroleum prod.	0.01	−0.06	Public admin.	0.00	0.20
Rubber & plastic	0.29	−0.01	Other services	−0.07	0.05
Cement	−0.08	−0.02	Other sectors	0.00	−0.14

Source: PARA model simulations

as 'textiles' in the PARA model results). This growth raised labour productivity and, through migration, contributed to a decline in the agricultural labour force and land use. Trade liberalization, as the PARA simulations show, had very similar results: within manufacturing, it was the labour-intensive industries that gained, while more highly protected sectors contracted. However, since the protected sectors are capital-intensive, their contraction did not by itself release enough labour to fuel the expansion of labour-intensive manufacturing. Accordingly, labour was once again pulled out of agriculture. Within that sector, it was the relatively labour-intensive sectors (especially rice and maize) that contracted most, while the less labour-intensive crops expanded. With rural labour leaving marginal areas first, both the investment boom and trade liberalization appear to have had pro-environment effects in large areas of the uplands and highlands.[7] Both these results are consistent with predictions made in Chapter 4 for the stylized 'tuk-tuk' economy producing labour-intensive exportable manufactures and in the uplands, mainly tradable food.

Finally, we can use the AHTI data on emissions (Figure 5.1) to assess the likely effects of trade liberalization on changes in industrial pollution. The

Table 8.6 Effects of a 10 per cent tariff reduction on agriculture and natural resources (% change)

Sector	Domestic production	Producer price	Labour use	Variable capital use	Return to land/ specific factor
Paddy	−0.04	0.00	−0.07	−0.19	−0.30
Maize	−0.01	0.03	−0.09	−0.07	−0.14
Cassava	0.10	0.22	0.10	0.05	1.01
Soybean	−0.04	−0.01	−0.09	−0.15	−0.44
Sugar	−0.01	−0.01	−0.02	−0.07	−0.20
Kenaf	0.55	1.23	0.55	0.61	7.39
Cotton	0.06	0.28	0.06	0.06	2.58
Vegetables & fruit	−0.09	−0.10	−0.09	−0.24	−1.28
Coconut	0.23	0.32	0.23	0.46	1.06
Oil palm	0.46	0.34	0.46	0.96	1.93
Coffee	−0.06	0.00	−0.07	−0.26	−0.67
Tobacco	−0.51	−0.49	−0.54	−0.97	−4.95
Rubber	0.25	0.98	0.27	0.32	5.82
Sorghum	−0.13	−0.07	−0.51	−0.59	−0.61
Other crops	−0.11	−0.11	−0.11	−0.32	−1.34
Cattle	0.26	1.21	0.27	0.43	9.68
Pigs	−0.08	−0.13	−0.09	−0.25	−2.26
Other livestock	0.07	0.21	0.06	0.00	1.09
Poultry	−0.07	−0.04	−0.10	−36.68	0.05
Silkworms	0.54	0.70	0.78	2.67	1.27
Agric. services	0.00	0.06	0.00	0.01	0.19
Forestry	−0.07	0.04	−0.10	−1.12	0.05
Ocean fishery	0.29	0.14	0.41	0.88	0.60
Inland fishery	0.10	0.17	0.18	1.94	0.41
Mining	0.00	0.05	0.00	0.00	0.18
Meat products	−0.08	−0.02	−0.09	−1.37	0.08

Source: PARA model simulations

story is a mixed one. Generally 'clean', labour-intensive industries, including food processing and the manufacture of garments, expand; at the same time, some other expanding industries, including fertilizer, rubber and plastic products, and leather and tannery products, are among the most emissions-intensive manufacturing industries. Empirical experience supports these model predictions; the rapid growth of tanneries, for example, has been a source of growing environmental problems in the Bangkok hinterland over the past decade.

Overall, the environmental implications of Thailand's trade liberalization are mixed. Contractions in the largest and most pollution-intensive industries – a composition effect of the reform – are offset by expansions in others which may be relatively less emissions-intensive but which expand enough to increase absolute levels of emissions. At the same time, the stimulus to labour-intensive manufacturing industries also significantly reduces pressures on upland and highland agricultural soils, forests and watersheds. As in the previous case studies, trade policy is not a panacea for environmental damage. The simulation results not only indicate the need for supplementary environmental policies, but also provide guidance as to which industries should be most closely monitored, and indeed targeted for industry-specific environmental policies, in a liberalized trade policy regime. The advantage of the AGE approach is that these predictions take account not merely of the direct impacts of tariff reductions, but also of their indirect effects operating through factor markets and the markets for intermediate inputs. Finally, in an economy in which the vast majority of manufacturing enterprises are located in or around the capital city, the sectoral distribution of expanding and contracting industries also provides strong clues as to the spatial distribution of changes in environmental stresses.

8.5 CONCLUSIONS

The spectacular growth of the Thai economy from the mid-1980s through to the onset of the Asian crisis in 1997 was driven by a boom in domestic and foreign investment. The tremendous vote of confidence in the economy that these flows represented was itself fuelled by an increasingly favourable overall investment climate due to economic policy reforms including trade liberalization. Rapid growth created scale effects that have placed environmental and natural resources under tremendous stress, while the composition effects of both the investment boom and trade policy reform are mixed. Both appear to have been generally favourable for the conservation of upper-watershed and forest resources, by raising labour wages and making it more costly to engage in labour-intensive farming practices at the arable margin. These environmental gains in rural areas have been offset, to an extent, by increased demands on resources and environmental services in urban and industrial areas.

NOTES

1. The following quantitative analysis draws heavily on Coxhead and Jiraporn (1999).
2. Variables without time subscripts are current values. Only lagged values are subscripted, for example, WA_{-1} is the agricultural wage in the previous period.
3. A more complete model of the labour market would include the possible effects of wages on the supply of labour through changes in the labour force participation rate.
4. Data were obtained from Siamwalla *et al.* (1987, table 3), and from Office of Agricultural Economics, (1991).
5. The equation was re-estimated using an additional 15 observations from the provinces of Northeast Thailand. Parameter estimates and significance levels were essentially unchanged.
6. Of course, the provincial data are too highly aggregated to reveal details of what kind of land is being added to or removed from the planted area base in any year. To understand the relationship between aggregate economic growth and changes in upland or highland land use, it is necessary to go to the farm or village level, where not merely land use but a range of other data pertaining to local agronomic, cultural and economic conditions can be brought into the analysis.
7. There are exceptions, of course, especially in areas where rising domestic demand for horticultural crops such as cabbage has resulted in wholesale conversion of hillsides to intensive vegetable gardening. These pockets of land (mainly in Northern Thailand) present their own environmental problems associated with water demand, pesticide emissions and soil erosion. It is notable that these crops (especially cabbage and potato) have also continued to receive high levels of trade protection in an era of generally declining tariffs (Coxhead 1997; WTO 1999b).

9. Conclusion

The broad objective of this book has been to contribute to a deeper understanding of the links between economic activities and environmental outcomes in developing countries experiencing the multifaceted impact of globalization and policy reforms. Such an understanding is essential to the formulation of economy-wide policies to promote better patterns of natural resource use and sustain environmental quality in developing countries.

Our particular emphasis has been on developing economies of Asia confronting serious environmental challenges. These have been caused not only by air and water pollution in urban areas but also by changes in patterns of land use that have had major effects on levels of resource degradation and overall environmental outcomes. Land degradation and deforestation in major watersheds are issues of overriding concern, and different types of land use and associated agricultural techniques have markedly different environmental effects. We have been guided in our analytical approach by the recognition that policies to address environmental goals must form an integral part of a country's strategy for achieving major development goals, such as rapid economic growth, distributional equity, poverty alleviation and macroeconomic stability. Optimal development policies must establish a politically sustainable balance among economic, social and environmental goals. Hence, we have adopted an economy-wide framework to capture the general equilibrium repercussions of exogenous changes and policy measures on key variables of policy interest, presenting both low-dimensional analytical models that encompass the most important country-specific characteristics as special cases, and richer, more fleshed out, empirical AGE models of three Asian economies (the Philippines, Sri Lanka and Thailand). Our broad analytical framework, used in conjunction with these models, enabled us to explore the consequences of empirically important exogenous shocks and policy scenarios both qualitatively and quantitatively. Although our empirical policy focus has been on 'composition effects' of land use changes that alter environmental outcomes within the agricultural and forestry sectors, the models are sufficiently general and flexible to be used to analyse other key environmental issues facing developing economies undergoing structural changes in the course of economic growth.

Our models are based explicitly on an open economy framework, one that recognizes the role of international economic links and the interdependence of environmental and other economic variables. This area has spawned a large and important literature, the key contributions and insights of which were reviewed in Chapter 2. In the light of that review, we extended the two-sector general equilibrium analysis of the impact of trade liberalization on industrial emissions to derive analytical insights into the associated welfare effects, and demonstrated how that framework can illuminate the environmental effects of economic growth resulting from different types of endowment and policy changes and technological improvements. In one example, we explored the specific circumstances in which opening up an economy to foreign capital inflows may generate either positive or negative environmental effects. Building on this two-sector model, we proceeded to develop a 'core' analytical model as presented in Chapter 4. It incorporates several major structural and institutional features of national economies that interact with each other and bear critically on resource use decisions. Of these, three features have been central to our model specification.

First, we recognize that in developing countries geography can often create market segmentation in goods and factor markets, thereby influencing land use patterns. Hence the models were given an explicit spatial – 'regional' – dimension, with some degree of factor specificity distinguishing each region within the national economy. Second, we recognize a key institutional feature of developing countries that impacts on natural resource use, particularly in the geographically remote regions at the cultivated land frontier: the absence of well-defined and enforced property rights over forests. Third, we recognize a key empirical fact about almost all developing countries with significant agricultural sectors: that domestic food supply and demand influence domestic food prices. A 'small country' model which assumes changes in domestic food prices to be determined entirely by changes in world food prices cannot be used to analyse the critical importance of domestic food supplies (often impacted on by various types of food policies) and associated resource use decisions for environmental outcomes. Our model allows domestic food prices to vary in response to domestic demand and supply changes. Though each of these features has been presented separately in previous analytical models, to our knowledge they have not until now been brought together in a single integrated model. In turn, this richer model specification allows us to go beyond the strong but rather simplistic conclusions reached in previous writings about the environmental implications of globalization and major policy reforms such as trade and investment liberalization.

Analysis using this model makes it clear that overall economic and environmental outcomes depend on the interaction of the structural features of an economy with its policy regime. In Chapter 3, we described four representative types of economies – the 'jeepney' economy, the 'tuk-tuk' economy, the 'becak' economy and the 'proton' economy – each differing in key structural and policy features. The policy regimes represented by these economic types include the two major development strategies (ISI and EOI) that have dominated modern economic policy making in almost all Asian developing countries. They also incorporate specific structural features of such economies (the relative factor intensities of agricultural industries in the uplands, for instance, or whether manufacturing output is mainly import competing or for export). Environmental implications of major policy changes, such as trade liberalization, are shown to depend critically on these structural features.

The shift from ISI to EOI is a major ongoing policy reform in most developing countries. Many environmentalists hold this policy shift responsible for increased environmental stress. However, our analysis suggests that freer trade and greater integration with the global economy may *in some circumstances* have a pro-environment effect, at least in terms of deforestation and land degradation. For example, trade liberalization tends to increase deforestation in some situations – such as in the 'jeepney' economy, where manufacturing is essentially a protected import-competing activity while upland agriculture is dominated by relatively more labour-intensive food production. In contrast, in the 'proton' economy, which exports manufactures and imports food (with a protected domestic food sector), trade liberalization may well have exactly the opposite effect. Similar differences emerge in analyses of other policy reforms, such as food security policies or investment liberalization. Thus, the models developed here enable us to present more nuanced analytical conclusions, bring out the role of key structural features, and avoiding blanket generalizations about the environmental outcomes of policy changes.

In case studies of the Philippines, Sri Lanka and Thailand, we proceeded to explore our theoretical insights further. We used a range of analytical tools, including richer, more fully specified applied general equilibrium models that both simplified (in some respects) and expanded (in other respects) our core model. Experiments were conducted with the AGE models to derive the analytical and policy implications of different kinds of shocks and their impacts on environmental and other key economic variables. In particular, we analysed some important policy shifts and related developments – such as those associated with 'globalization', national food security policies, and the effects of R & D and interventions in agriculture – whose impact on deforestation and land degradation has been contentious, in Asia and elsewhere in the developing world. The results of these policy experiments were interpreted using insights from the analytical models so as to shed light on the economic mechanisms through which environmental outcomes were generated.

Analysis of the Philippines' environmental problems using our framework suggested that past development strategies had directly and indirectly impacted on, and aggravated, environmental and natural resource depletion rates, in some cases quite severely. The ISI policies that dominated Philippine economic policy making from the early 1950s not only constrained economic growth; by perpetuating rural poverty, they encouraged population transfers from the agricultural hinterland to crowded cities and to ecologically fragile uplands alike. By distorting agricultural incentives they encouraged cultivation of more soil-erosive crops in uplands. In combination with the abuse of state power that allowed favoured groups to disregard regulatory controls on deforestation and on industrial emissions and effluents, these policy-induced distortions generated very poor environmental outcomes. An AGE model of the Philippines was used to explore the likely implications of the partial dismantling of trade protection and liberalization of domestic markets that began in the early 1990s. Again, the results were consistent with insights from the analytical models: liberalization not only tends to improve overall export performance, and confer both growth and equity benefits, but even the environmental impacts may be positive. Indeed, there are some indications that land degradation and deforestation, and the intensity (if not the volume) of industrial emissions, may be lower under a more liberal trade regime because of changes in the composition of the industrial sector that favour cleaner industries. But free trade is not a panacea; reform must be complemented by other policy measures if it is to significantly alleviate environmental damages.

The AGE model for the Philippines was also used to address the environmental impact of the Green Revolution, an issue with both historical and current policy interest, and of particular relevance to decisions on the national and international allocation of agricultural research funds. In contrast to the view that the Green Revolution diverted resources away from upland agricultural improvements, thereby further impoverishing already poor upland farmers and aggravating environmental degradation, our empirical results supported an almost diametrically opposed conclusion: the Green Revolution in the lowlands, by reducing national food prices, significantly reduced incentives for deforestation and land degradation in the uplands. Indeed, the analysis suggests that but for the salutary impact of the Green Revolution, land degradation and deforestation may have been much worse in many parts of Asia.

In the case of Sri Lanka, past policies conferring high levels of protection on import-competing manufactures and heavy export taxes on agriculture had aggravated the effects of long secular declines in the world prices

of export tree crops such as tea and rubber. In some of the most environmentally sensitive areas, land use had shifted away from less soil-erosive tree
crops to highly erosive crops such as potatoes (that gained high protection
due to the efforts of a small but politically powerful lobby), resulting in
rapid land degradation and silting of river beds and reservoirs. The models
were calibrated with environmental data drawn from a large multidisciplin-
ary research project that traced and measured the impact of land use
changes on the on-site and off-site productivity of crops, on reservoir
capacity and reductions in irrigation water supply, and on the efficiency of
hydropower generation. The results confirmed the insight from previous
analytical models that trade liberalization and institutional reforms can be
environment-friendly rather than (as often conjectured) necessarily environmentally harmful. On the other hand, trade policy reforms were again
shown to yield only relatively minor environmental benefits in terms of
reduced levels of land degradation; significant reductions in the latter
require specific policies directly targeting land degradation and the availability of economically attractive conservation technologies. The results of
the modelling exercise were used to formulate and evaluate policy packages
– such as particular tax-cum-subsidy combinations – for their impact on
key environmental and economic variables.

The case study of Thailand enabled us to study the environmental outcomes associated with economic growth in a context where trade and
investment liberalization were accompanied by a boom in foreign and
domestic investment. In line with the analysis in Chapter 2, the overall environmental outcomes were influenced by major scale effects associated
with rapid growth that placed environmental and natural resources under
tremendous stress, as well as composition effects resulting from both the
investment boom and trade policy reforms. Though the composition effects
of both the investment boom and trade reforms appear to have been generally favourable for the conservation of upper-watershed and forest
resources, these were offset, to an extent, by increased demands on
resources and environmental services in urban and industrial areas. Labour
market changes that made it more costly to engage in labour-intensive
farming practices at the arable margin turned out to be the primary mechanism through which pro-conservation effects were generated.

In the Thai AGE analysis, all traditional upland and highland agricultural sectors – rice, maize, soybean, and vegetables and fruit – contract, and
land returns to each diminish. Thus, trade liberalization reduces incentives
to produce the field crops that occupy the greatest share of land area and
which, as annual or short-season crops, also contribute the greatest share
of agricultural land degradation and soil erosion. The reasons are not hard
to find and are consistent with the econometric predictions: trade liberal-

ization raises wages across the board, and thus reduces profitability in all labour-intensive sectors. However, the overall environmental implications of Thailand's trade liberalization appear to be mixed once the impact on industrial emissions is also taken into account. Contractions in the largest and most pollution-intensive industries – a composition effect of the reform – are offset by expansions in others which may be less emissions-intensive but whose growth increases the absolute level of emissions. At the same time, the stimulus to labour-intensive manufacturing industries also alleviates pressures on upland and highland agricultural soils, forests and watersheds through labour absorption effects. As in the cases of the Philippines and Sri Lanka, it is seen that trade policy is not a panacea for environmental damage.

While these case studies demonstrate the relevance and value of our approach, some important limitations should be noted. Our deliberate choice of a 'macro' view of development, growth and environmental degradation meant operating at a level of abstraction that necessarily ignores some of the complexities of real-world decision making. Further, to focus on the medium-term equilibria of economies, we chose not to address important aspects of dynamic adjustments to various shocks, even though the objects of our analysis are obviously not static phenomena but dynamic processes evolving and unfolding over time. Because our analytical approach focuses on underlying *economic* forces, it has the obvious disadvantage that the socio-cultural, political and other factors that shape power relationships in societies and influence both environmental and distributional outcomes are not captured. We do not underestimate the value or importance of alternative research and analytical approaches. But we do believe that our approach, despite its limitations, has compensating advantages that have been demonstrated in the significant new insights and useful policy guidelines generated by the analytical and empirical models presented in this volume. We see our contribution as complementary to insights emerging from other approaches, and hope that it will be found useful by researchers and policy makers grappling with the daunting challenge of achieving rapid and equitable economic development while maintaining environmental quality.

References

Abler, David G., Adrian G. Rodriguez and James S. Shortle (1999), 'Trade liberalization and the environment in Costa Rica', *Environment and Development Economics*, 4(3), 357–73.

Alavalapati, Janaki R.R., W. White, P. Jagger and A. Wellstead (1996), 'Effect of land use restrictions on the economy of Alberta: a general equilibrium analysis', *Canadian Journal of Regional Science*, 19(3), 349–65.

Alexandratos, Nikos (1995), *World Agriculture: Towards 2010. An FAO Study*, Chichester: John Wiley for the FAO.

Aminuddin, B.Y., W.T. Chow and T.T. Ng (1991), 'Resources and problems associated with sustainable development of upland areas in Malaysia', in Graeme Blair and Rod Lefroy (eds) *Technologies for Sustainable Agriculture on Marginal Uplands in Malaysia*, Canberra: Australian Centre for International Agricultural Research.

Ananda, J., G. Herath and A. Chisholm (2001), 'Determination of yield and erosion damage functions using subjectively elicited data: application to smallholder tea in Sri Lanka', *Australian Journal of Agricultural and Resource Economics*, 45(2), 275–89.

Anderson, J.R. and J. Thampapillai (1990), 'Soil conservation in developing countries: project and policy intervention', Agriculture and Rural Development Department, Policy and Research Series, Paper no. 8, Washington, DC: World Bank.

Anderson, Kym (1992), 'The standard welfare economics of policies affecting trade and the environment', in K. Anderson and R. Blackhurst (eds) *The Greening of World Trade Issues*, Ann Arbor: University of Michigan Press, pp. 23–48.

Anderson, Kym and Richard Blackhurst (1992), *The Greening of World Trade Issues*, Ann Arbor, MI: University of Michigan Press.

Anderson, Kym and Anna Strutt (2000), 'Will trade liberalization harm the environment? The case of Indonesia to 2020', *Environmental and Resource Economics*, 17(3), November, 203–32.

Andreoni, J. and A. Levinson (1998), 'The simple analytics of the environmental Kuznets curve', NBER Working Paper no. W6739, Cambridge, MA: National Bureau for Economic and Social Research.

Angelson, Arild and David Kaimowitz (1998), *Economic Models of*

Tropical Deforestation: A Review, Bogor, Indonesia: Centre for International Forestry Research.

Antweiler, Werner, Brian R. Copeland and M. Scott Taylor (2001), 'Is free trade good for the environment?', *American Economic Review*, 91(4), 877–908.

Asian Development Bank (ADB) (1990), 'Sri Lanka', in *Economic Policies for Sustainable Development*, Manila: ADB, pp. 209–29.

Asian Development Bank (ADB) (1997), *Emerging Asia: Changes and Challenges*, Manila: ADB.

Athukorala, Premachandra (2001), *Crises and Recovery in Malaysia: The Role of Capital Controls*, Cheltenham, UK and Northampton, MA, USA: Edward Elgar.

Athukorala, Premachandra and Sisira Jayasuriya (1994), *Macroeconomic Policies, Crises and Growth in Sri Lanka 1969–90*, Washington, DC: World Bank.

Australian Centre for International Agricultural Research (ACIAR) (1993), *Optimal Land Use in Sri Lanka with Particular Application to Land Degradation and the Planning Industries*, Project Number 9212, Canberra: ACIAR.

Babiker, Mustafa H. (2001), 'The CO_2 abatement game: costs, incentives, and the enforceability of a sub-global coalition', *Journal of Economic Dynamics and Control*, 25(1–2), 1–34.

Baldwin, R.E. (1975), *Foreign Trade Regimes and Economic Development: The Philippines*, New York: Columbia University Press.

Balisacan, A. (1992), 'Parameter estimates of consumer demand systems in the Philippines', Quezon City: Policy and Planning Division, Philippine Department of Agriculture, Workshop on the APEX CGE Model of the Philippine Economy, Paper E.

Bandara, J.S. (1989), 'A multisectoral general equilibrium model of the Sri Lankan economy with applications to the analysis of the effects of external shocks', unpublished PhD thesis, La Trobe University, Melbourne.

Bandara, J.S. and Ian Coxhead (1999), 'Can trade liberalization have environmental benefits in developing countries? A Sri Lankan case study', *Journal of Policy Modeling*, 21(3), 349–74.

Bandara, S.J., A. Chisholm, A. Ekanayake and S. Jayasuriya (1995), 'Environmental cost of land degradation in Sri Lanka: tax/subsidy options', *Environmental Modelling and Software*, 16, 497–508.

Bandara, S.J. and I. Coxhead, in collaboration with A.H. Chisholm, A. Ekanayake and S. Jayasuriya (1995), 'Economic reforms and the environment in Sri Lanka', Agricultural Economics Discussion Paper 27/95, La Trobe University, Melbourne.

Bandarathilake, H.M. (1999), 'Optimal land use in the hill country of Sri

Lanka, land degradation and forestry', in A. Chisholm, A. Ekanayake and S. Jayasuriya (eds) *Economic Policy Reforms and the Environment: Land Degradation in Sri Lanka*, Colombo: ACIAR and MPA/HA/PI/PA, pp. 202–67.

Bandusena, W.M. (1995), 'An economic assessment of off-site impacts of soil erosion: a case study of Sri Lanka', paper presented at the Environmental Economics and Policy Workshop, International Environment Program, Harvard Institute for International Development, Harvard University, Cambridge, MA.

Barbier, E.B. (1998), *The Economics of Environment and Development: Selected Essays,* Cheltenham, UK and Northampton, MA, USA: Edward Elgar.

Barbier, E.B. and J.T. Bishop (1995), 'Economic values and incentives affecting soil and water conservation in developing countries', *Journal of Soil and Water Conservation*, 50(2), 133–7.

Barker, R. and R.W. Herdt, with Beth Rose (1985), *The Rice Economy of Asia*, Washington, DC: Resources for the Future.

Baumol, William J. and Wallace E. Oates (1988), *The Theory of Environmental Policy*, 2nd edn, Cambridge: Cambridge University Press.

Bautista, Romeo, M. (1985), 'Effects of trade and exchange rate policies on export production incentives in Philippine agriculture', *Philippine Economic Journal*, 24(2/3), 87–115.

Bautista, R.M. and A. Valdes (1993), *The Bias Against Agriculture: Trade and Macroeconomic Policies in Developing Countries*, San Francisco: International Center for Economic Growth.

Bautista, R.M., J. Power and Associates (1979), *Industrial Promotion Policies in the Philippines*, Manila: Philippine Institute for Development Studies.

Bee, O.J. (1987), 'Depletion of forest reserves in the Philippines', *Field Report Series No. 18*, Singapore: Institute of Southeast Asian Studies.

Bergman, Lars (1995), 'General equilibrium costs and benefits of environmental policies', in Gianna Boerro and Aubrey Silberston (eds) *Environmental Economics: Proceedings of a Conference Held by the Confederation of European Economic Associations at Oxford, 1993*. Confederation of European Economic Associations Conference Volumes. New York: St. Martin's Press; London: Macmillan Press, pp. 3–16.

Binswanger, Hans P. (1991), 'Brazilian policies that encourage deforestation in the Amazon', *World Development*, 19(7), July, 821–9.

Blaikie, P.M. (1985), *The Political Economy of Soil Erosion in Developing Countries*, London and New York: Longman.

Blaikie, P.M. and H. Brookfield (1987), *Land Degradation and Society*, London and New York: Methuen.

Bovenberg, L. and R. de Mooij (1994), 'Environmental levies and distortionary taxation', *American Economic Review*, 86(4), 1085–9.

Bovenberg, L. and L. Goulder (1996), 'Optimal environmental policies in the presence of other taxes: general equilibrium analyses', *American Economic Review*, 986(4), 985–1000.

Brander, James A. and M. Scott Taylor (1997), 'International trade and open-access renewable resources: the small open economy case', *Canadian Journal of Economics*, 30(3), 526–52.

Brander, James A. and M. Scott Taylor (1998), 'The simple economics of Easter Island: A Ricardo–Malthus model of renewable resource use', *American Economic Review*, 88(1), March, 119–38.

Brandon, C. and R. Ramankutty (1992), 'Toward an environmental strategy for Asia', Washington, DC: World Bank Discussion Paper no. 224.

Bromley, D.W. (1991), *Environment and Economy: Property Rights and Public Policy*, Oxford, UK and Cambridge, USA: Blackwell.

Burniaux, Jean-Marc, Giuseppe Nicoletti and Joaquim Oliveira-Martins (1992), 'A global model for quantifying the costs of policies to curb CO_2 emissions', *OECD Economic Studies*, (19), 49–92.

Burt, O.R. (1981), 'Farm level economics of soil conservation in the Palouse area of the Northwest', *American Journal of Agricultural Economics*, 63(1), February, 83–92.

Carraro, Carlo and Domenico Siniscalco (1996), *Environmental Fiscal Reform and Unemployment*, Dordrecht and Boston, MA: Kluwer Academic.

Cassman, K.G. and P.L. Pingali (1995), 'Intensification of irrigated rice systems: learning from the past to meet future challenges', *Geo-Journal*, 35, 299–305.

Centre for International Economics (CIE) (1992), 'The composition and level of effective taxes for exporting and import competing production in Sri Lanka', draft report prepared for Sri Lanka Export Development Board, Centre for International Economics, Canberra, Australia.

Chenery, H.B. and T.N. Srinivasan (eds) (1988), *Handbook of Development Economics*, vols 1 and 2, Amsterdam: North-Holland.

Chisholm, A.H. (1992), 'Australian agriculture: a sustainability story', *Australian Journal of Agricultural Economics*, 36(1), 1–29.

Chisholm, A.H. and R.G. Dumsday (1987), *Land Degradation: Problems and Policies*, Cambridge: Cambridge University Press.

Chisholm, A., A. Ekanayake and S. Jayasuriya (eds) (1999), *Economic Policy Reforms and the Environment: Land Degradation in Sri Lanka*, Colombo: Australian Centre for International Agricultural Research and Ministry of Public Administration, Home Affairs, Plantation Industries and Parliamentary Affairs of Sri Lanka.

Chomitz, Kenneth M. and Kanta Kumari (1998), 'The domestic benefits of tropical forests: a critical review', *World Bank Research Observer*, 13(1), 13–35.

Clarete, R.L. and P.G. Warr (1992), 'The theoretical structure of the APEX model of the Philippine economy', Workshop on the APEX CGE Model of the Philippine Economy, Philippine Department of Agriculture and Philippine Economic Society, Makati, July (mimeo).

Clarke, H.R. (1992), 'The supply of non-degraded agricultural land', *Australian Journal of Agricultural Economics*, 36(1), April, 31–56.

Clark, R. (1994), 'Economic valuation of soil erosion and conservation measures: a case study of the Perawella Area in the Upper Mahaweli Catchment', Technical Report no. 20, Forest/Land Use Mapping Project, Environment and Forest Conservation Division, Mahaweli Authority, Polgolla, Sri Lanka.

Coase, R.H. (1960), 'The problem of social cost', *Journal of Law and Economics*, 3, 1–44.

Coomaraswamy, A., A. Ekanayake, A.H. Chisholm and S. Jayasuriya (1999), 'Effect of land degradation on tea productivity', in A. Chisholm, A. Ekanayake and S. Jayasuriya (eds) *Economic Policy Reforms and the Environment: Land Degradation in Sri Lanka*, Colombo: ACIAR and MPA/HA/PI/PA, pp. 299–313.

Copeland, Brian R. (1994), 'International trade and the environment: policy reform in a polluted small open economy', *Journal of Environmental Economics and Management*, 26(1), 44–65.

Copeland, Brian R. and M. Scott Taylor (1994), 'North–South trade and the global environment', *Quarterly Journal of Economics*, 109(3), 755–87.

Corden, W. Max (1971), *The Theory of Protection*, Oxford: Clarendon Press.

Corden, W. Max (1997), *Trade Policy and Economic Welfare*, 2nd edn, Oxford: Clarendon Press.

Coxhead, Ian (1992), 'Environment-specific rates and biases of technical change in agriculture', *American Journal of Agricultural Economics*, 74(3), 592–604.

Coxhead, Ian (1994), 'The welfare and distributional consequences of land degradation: an analytical framework', paper presented at the Annual Meeting of the American Agricultural Economics Association, San Diego, CA, 7–10 August.

Coxhead, Ian (1997), 'Induced innovation and land degradation in developing countries', *Australian Journal of Agricultural and Resource Economics*, 41(3), 305–32.

Coxhead, Ian (2000), 'The consequences of Philippine food self-sufficiency policies for economic welfare and agricultural land degradation', *World Development*, 28(1), 111–28.

Coxhead, Ian and Sisira Jayasuriya (1986), 'Labour-shedding with falling real wages in the Philippines', *Asian Survey*, XXVI(10), 1056–66.

Coxhead, Ian and Sisira Jayasuriya (1994), 'Technical change in agriculture and the rate of land degradation in developing countries: a general equilibrium analysis', *Land Economics*, 70(1), 20–37.

Coxhead, Ian and Sisira Jayasuriya (1995), 'Trade and tax policies and the environment in developing countries', *American Journal of Agricultural Economics*, 77 (August), 631–44.

Coxhead, Ian and Sisira Jayasuriya (2002), 'Economic growth, development policy and the environment in the Philippines', in H. Hill and A. Balisacan (eds) *The Philippine Economy: Development, Policies, and Challenges*, New York: Oxford University Press, and Quezon City, Philippines: Ateneo de Manila University Press (in press).

Coxhead, Ian with Jiraporn Plangpraphan (1998), 'Thailand's economic boom and agricultural bust: some economic questions and policy puzzles', University of Wisconsin, Department of Agricultural and Applied Economics, Staff Paper Series no. 419, September.

Coxhead, Ian and Jiraporn Plangpraphan (1999), 'Economic boom, financial bust, and the decline of Thai agriculture: was growth in the 1990s too fast?', *Chulalongkorn Journal of Economics*, 11(1), 76–96.

Coxhead, Ian and Gerald Shively (1998), 'Some economic and environmental implications of technical progress in Philippine corn agriculture: an economy-wide perspective', *Journal of Agricultural Economics and Development*, XXVI(1/2), July, 60–90.

Coxhead, Ian and Peter G. Warr (1995), 'Does technical progress in agriculture alleviate poverty? A Philippine case study', *Australian Journal of Agricultural Economics*, 39(1), 25–54.

Coxhead, Ian, Agnes C. Rola and Kwansoo Kim (2001), 'How do national markets and price policies affect land use at the forest margin? Evidence from the Philippines', *Land Economics*, 77(2), 250–67.

Coxhead, Ian, Gerald E. Shively and Xiaobing Shuai (2002), 'Development policies, resource constraints, and agricultural expansion on the Philippine land frontier', *Environment and Development Economics* 7, pp. 341–63.

Cropper, M. and C. Griffiths (1994), 'The interaction of population growth and environmental quality', *American Economic Review*, 84(2), 250–4.

Cropper, Maureen and Wallace E. Oates (1992), 'Environmental economics: a survey', *Journal of Economic Literature*, 30(2), 675–740.

Cruz, M. Concepcion (2000), 'Population pressure, poverty and deforestation: Philippines case study', Washington, DC: World Bank (mimeo).

Cruz, M.C. and R. Repetto (1992), *The Environmental Effects of Stabilization and Structural Adjustment Programs: The Philippines Case*, Washington, DC: World Resources Institute.

Cruz, W. and H. Francisco (1993), 'Poverty, population pressure and deforestation in the Philippines', paper presented at a workshop on 'Economy-wide Policies and the Environment', World Bank, Washington, DC, 14–15 Dec.

Cruz, W., H. Francisco and Z. Tapawan-Conway (1988), *The On-site and Downstream Costs of Soil Erosion*, Manila: Philippine Institute for Development Studies, PIDS Working Paper no. 88–11.

Dasgupta, P. and K. Mäler (1995), 'Poverty, institutions and the natural resource base', in J. Behrman and T.N. Srinivasan (eds) *Handbook of Development Economics*, vol. 3A, Amsterdam: North-Holland, pp. 2371–408.

David, Cristina C. and Jikun Huang (1996), 'Political economy of rice price protection in Asia', *Economic Development and Cultural Change*, 44(3), 463–83.

David, Cristina C. and Keijiro Otsuka (eds) (1994), *Modern Rice Technology and Income Distribution in Asia*, Boulder, CO and London: Lynne Rienner; Los Baños, Philippines: International Rice Research Institute.

David, Wilfrido P. (1988), 'Soil and water conservation planning: policy issues and recommendations', *Journal of Philippine Development*, 15(1), 47–84.

Deacon, Robert (1995), 'Assessing the relationship between government policy and deforestation', *Journal of Environmental Economics and Management*, 28(1), 1–18.

Dean, Judith (1999), 'Does trade liberalization harm the environment? A new test', manuscript, School of Advanced International Studies, Johns Hopkins University.

Deardorff, A. (1999), 'Patterns of trade and growth across cones', Ann Arbor, MI: University of Michigan School of Public Policy, Research Seminar in International Economics, Discussion Paper no. 443.

Department of Census and Statistics (1993), *Statistical Abstract*, Colombo, Sri Lanka: Department of Census and Statistics.

Deutsch, W.D., A.L. Busby, J.L. Orprecio, J.P. Bago-Labis and E.Y. Cequiña (2001), 'Community-based water quality monitoring: from data collection to sustainable management of water resources', in I. Coxhead and G. Buenavista (eds) *Seeking Sustainability: Challenges of Agricultural Development and Environmental Management in a Philippine Watershed*, Los Baños, Philippines: PCARRD, pp. 138–60.

Dixit, Avinash and Victor Norman (1980), *Theory of International Trade*, Cambridge: Cambridge University Press.

Dixon, P.B. and B.R. Parmenter (1994), 'Computable general equilibrium modelling', Preliminary Working Paper no. IP-65, Melbourne: Centre of Policy Studies and the Impact Project, Monash University, July.

Dixon, Peter, B.R. Parmenter, J. Sutton and D.P. Vincent (1982), *ORANI: A Multisectoral Model of the Australian Economy*, Amsterdam: North-Holland.

Dixon, Peter B., Brian R. Parmenter, Alan A. Powell and Peter J. Wilcoxen (1992), *Notes and Problems in Applied General Equilibrium Analysis*, Amsterdam: North-Holland.

Dollar, David (1992), 'Outward oriented developing economies really do grow more rapidly: evidence from 95 LDCs, 1976–85', *Economic Development and Cultural Change*, 40(3), 523–44.

Doolette, John B. and William B. Magrath (eds) (1990), *Watershed Development in Asia: Strategies and Technologies*, Washington, DC: World Bank.

Dornbusch, Rudiger (1974), 'Tariffs and non-traded goods', *Journal of International Economics*, 7, 177–85.

Dunham, David and Saman Kalegama (1997), 'Does leadership matter in the economic reform process? Liberalization and governance in Sri Lanka, 1989–93', *World Development*, 25(2), 179–90.

Edwards, C. (1993), *A Report on Protectionism and Trade Policy in Manufacturing and Agriculture in Sri Lanka*, prepared for submission to the World Bank and the Presidential Tariff Commission, Colombo: Institute of Policy Studies of Sri Lanka.

Ethier, Wilfred E. (1982), 'Higher-dimensional issues in trade theory', in R.W. Jones and P.B. Kenen (eds) *Handbook of International Economics*, vol. 1, Amsterdam: North-Holland, pp. 131–84.

Food and Agriculture Organization of the United Nations (FAO) (2000), *Land Resource Potential and Constraints at Regional and Country Levels*, Rome: FAO, World Soil Resources Report no. 90.

Food and Agriculture Organization of the United Nations (FAO) (2001), *FAO Statistical Databases*, http://apps.fao.org/, accessed 2 May 2001.

Fossati, Amedeo (1996), *Economic Modelling Under the Applied General Equilibrium Approach*, Aldershot, Hants., and Brookfield, VT: Avebury.

Fredriksson, Per G. (1999), 'Trade, global policy and the environment', in Per G. Fredriksson (ed.) *Trade, Global Policy and the Environment*, Washington, DC: World Bank, pp. 1–12.

Fujisaka, S., P. Sajise and R. del Castillo (eds) (1986), *Man, Agriculture and the Tropical Forest: Change and Development in the Philippine Uplands*, Bangkok: Winrock International.

Fujita, M., P. Krugman and A.J. Venables (1999), *The Spatial Economy: Cities, Regions and International Trade*, Cambridge, MA: MIT Press.

Fullerton, D. and G. Metcalf (1997), 'Environmental taxes and the double dividend: did you really expect something for nothing?', NBER Working Paper no. 6199, Cambridge, MA: National Bureau for Economic Research.

Gamage, H. (1999), 'Land use in the hill country of Sri Lanka', in A. Chisholm, A. Ekanayake and S. Jayasuriya (eds) *Economic Policy Reforms and the Environment: Land Degradation in Sri Lanka*, Colombo: ACIAR and MPA/HA/PI/PA, pp. 16–77.

Garrod, G.D. and K.G. Willis (1999), *Economic Valuation of the Environment: Methods and Case Studies*, Cheltenham, UK: Edward Elgar.

Gérard, Françoise and François Ruf (2001), *Agriculture in Crisis: People, Commodities and Natural Resources in Indonesia, 1996–2000*, Montpellier, France: CIRAD, and Richmond, UK: Curzon.

Gersovitz, Mark R. (1989), 'Transportation, state marketing, and the taxation of the agricultural hinterland', *Journal of Political Economy*, 97(5), October, 1113–37.

Goulder, Lawrence H. (1995), 'Environmental taxation and the "double dividend": a reader's guide', *International Tax and Public Finance*, 2(2), 157–83.

Goulder, Lawrence H., Ian W.H. Parry, Roberton C. Williams III and Dallas Burtraw (1998), 'The cost-effectiveness of alternative instruments for environmental protection in a second-best setting', NBER Working Paper no. 6464, Cambridge, MA: National Bureau for Economic Research.

Greene, William H. (1993), *Econometric Analysis* (3rd edn), Englewood Cliffs, NJ: Prentice-Hall.

Griffen, R.C. and D.W. Bromley (1982), 'Agricultural run-off as non-point externality', *American Journal of Agricultural Economics*, 64(3), 547–55.

Grossman, G. and A.B. Krueger (1993), 'The environmental impacts of a North American free trade agreement', in P. Garber (ed.) *The U.S.–Mexico Free Trade Agreement*, Cambridge, MA: MIT Press, pp. 13–56.

Grossman, G. and A.B. Krueger (1995), 'International trade and the environment', *Quarterly Journal of Economics*, 110(2), 353–77.

Harrison, W. Jill and K.R. Pearson (1996), 'Computing solutions for large general equilibrium models using GEMPACK', *Computational Economics*, 9(2), 83–127.

Hartman, R.S., M. Huq and D. Wheeler (1997), 'Why paper mills clean up: determinants of pollution abatement in developing countries', World Bank: Policy Research Department Working Paper no. 1710, http://www.worldbank.org/nipr/work_paper/1710/index.htm, accessed February 2002.

Hayami, Yujiro and Masao Kikuchi (2001), *A Rice Village Saga: Three Decades of Green Revolution in a Philippine Village*, Lanham: Barnes and Noble; Los Baños, Philippines: International Rice Research Institute.

Hefner, R.W. (1990), *The Political Economy of Mountain Java: An Interpretive History*, Berkeley, CA: University of California Press.

Hettige, H., P. Martin, M. Singh and D. Wheeler (1995), 'IPPS: the Industrial Pollution Projection System', *Policy Research Department Working Paper*, Washington, DC: World Bank.

Hyde, William F., Gregory S. Amacher and William Magrath (1996), 'Deforestation and forest land use: theory, evidence, and policy implications', *World Bank Research Observer*, 11(2), August, 223–48.

Intal, Ponciano S. and John H. Power (1990), *Trade, Exchange Rate, and Agricultural Pricing Policies: The Philippines*, Washington, DC: World Bank.

International Rice Research Institute (IRRI) (1991), *World Rice Statistics 1990*, Los Baños, Philippines: IRRI.

International Rice Research Institute (IRRI) (2001), *Rice Facts*, http://www.cgiar.org/irri/Facts.htm, accessed 2 May 2001.

IRRI (International Rice Research Institute) (1978), *Consequences of the New Rice Technology*, Los Baños, Philippines: International Rice Research Institute.

Jayasuriya, Rohan (1998), 'Technological change and scarcity of soil in the tea sector of Sri Lanka', Unpublished PhD thesis, La Trobe University, Melbourne, Australia.

Jayasuriya, Sisira (2001), 'Agriculture and deforestation in tropical Asia: an analytical framework', in A. Angelsen and D. Kaimovitz (eds) *Agricultural Technologies and Tropical Deforestation*, Wallingford: CABI International, pp. 317–34.

Jayasuriya, S. and R.T. Shand (1986), 'Technical change and labour absorption in Asian agriculture: some emerging trends', *World Development*, 14(3), 415–28.

Jewell, N. and C.A. Legg (1994), 'A remote sensing GIS data base for forest management and monitoring in Sri Lanka', in Simon T.D Turner and Roger White (eds) *Geographical Information Systems for Natural Resource Management Systems in South East Asia*, Environment and Forest Conservation Division, Mahaweli Authority, Sri Lanka.

Jha, Raghbendra and John Whalley (1999), 'The environmental regime in developing countries', NBER Working Paper no. 7305, Cambridge, MA: National Bureau for Economic Research.

Jones, R.W. (1965), 'The structure of simple general equilibrium models', *Journal of Political Economy*, 73, 557–72.

Jones, Ronald W. (1971), 'A three-factor model in theory, trade and history', in J.N. Bhagwati, R.W. Jones, R.A. Mundell and J. Vanek (eds) *Trade, Balance of Payments, and Growth: Essays in Honor of Charles P. Kindleberger*, Amsterdam: North-Holland, pp. 3–21.

Jorgenson, Dale W. (1998), *Growth*, vol. 2, *Energy, the Environment, and Economic Growth*, Cambridge and London: MIT Press.

Keyfitz, Nathan (1965), 'Indonesian population and the European industrial revolution', *Asian Survey*, 5(10), 503–14.

Kanok, Khatikarn and Peter G. Warr (1995), 'Protection, regional agriculture and income distribution in Thailand', *Chulalongkorn Journal of Economics*, 7(2), 151–73.

Kikuchi, M. and Y. Hayami (1983), 'New rice technology, intrarural migration, and institutional innovation in the Philippines', *Population and Development Review*, 9(2), 247–57.

King, Benjamin (1981), *What is a SAM? A Layman's Guide to Social Accounting Matrices*, World Bank Staff Working Papers no. 463, Washington, DC: World Bank.

Kneese, A.V. and J.L. Sweeney (eds) (1985), *Handbook of Natural Resource and Energy Economics*, Vols 1 and 2, Amsterdam: North-Holland.

Krishnarajah, P. (1985), 'Soil erosion control measures for tea land in Sri Lanka', *Sri Lanka Journal of Tea Science*, 54(1), 91–100.

Krueger, Anne O., Maurice Schiff and Alberto Valdés (1988), 'Agricultural incentives in developing countries: measuring the effect of sectoral and economy-wide policies', *World Bank Economic Review*, 2(3), 255–71.

Krueger, Anne O., Maurice Schiff and Alberto Valdés (1991), *The Political Economy of Agricultural Pricing Policy*, Baltimore, MD: Johns Hopkins University Press for the World Bank.

Kummer, David (1992), *Deforestation in the Post-war Philippines*, Chicago: University of Chicago Press.

Lamberte, M.B., G.M. Llanto and A.C. Orbeta, Jr (1992), 'Micro impacts of macro adjustment policies (MIMAP): phase II integrative report', Philippine Institute of Development Studies Working Paper no. 92–13, Manila.

Land Commission (1987), *Report of the Land Commission*, Columbo: Government of Sri Lanka.

Lantican, F.A. and L.J. Unnevehr (1987), 'Rice pricing and marketing policy', in UPLB Agricultural Policy Working Group, *Policy Issues in the Philippine Rice Economy and Agricultural Trade*, College, Laguna: University of the Philippines at Los Baños, Centre for Policy and Development Studies, pp. 31–72.

Leamer, Edward E. (1987), 'Paths of development in the three-factor, *n*-good general equilibrium model', *Journal of Political Economy*, 95(5), 961–99.

Levine, Ross and David Renelt (1992), 'A sensitivity analysis of cross-country growth regressions', *American Economic Review*, 82(4), 942–63.

Levinson, Arik (1997), 'A note on environmental federalism: interpreting some contradictory results', *Journal of Environmental Economics and Management*, 33(3), 359–66.

Lewis, Martin W. (1992), *Wagering the Land: Ritual, Capital, and Environmental Degradation in the Cordillera of Northern Luzon, 1900–1986*, Berkeley, CA: University of California Press.

Lin, Justin Yifu and Fan Zhang (1998), 'The effects of China's rural policies on the sustainability of agriculture in China', paper prepared for the 11th Biannual Workshop on Economy and Environment in Southeast Asia, Singapore, 10–13 November 1998, at www.eepsea.org/publications/ special/ACF348.html, accessed December 2001.

Lindert, Peter H. (1999), 'The bad earth? China's soils and agricultural development since the 1930s', *Economic Development and Cultural Change*, 47(4), 701–36.

Lindert, Peter H. (2000), *Shifting Ground: The Changing Agricultural Soils of China and Indonesia*, Cambridge and London: MIT Press.

Lipton, M. with Richard Longhurst (1989), *New Seeds and Poor People*, London: Unwin Hyman.

Lopez, Ramon and Mario Niklitschek (1991), 'Dual economic growth in poor tropical areas', *Journal of Development Economics*, 36(2), 189–211.

Lutz, E. (1994), *Natural Resources Accounting*, Washington, DC: World Bank.

McConnell, K.E. (1983), 'An economic model of soil conservation', *American Journal of Agricultural Economics*, 65(1), February, 83–9.

Malayang, Ben S. (1993), 'Laguna Lake Basin: cauldron of opportunities and conflicts. A review of the institutional and policy structures of the Laguna Lake Basin', in Peter Sly (ed.) *Laguna Lake Basin, Philippines: Problems and Opportunities*, Los Baños, Philippines: University of the Philippines, and Dalhousie University, Canada: Environment and Resource Management Program.

Manthritilleke, H.M. (1999a), 'Land use changes and soil erosion: a hydrological perspective', in A. Chisholm, A. Ekanayake and S. Jayasuriya (eds) *Economic Policy Reforms and the Environment: Land Degradation in Sri Lanka*, Colombo: ACIAR and MPA/HA/PI/PA, pp. 414–35.

Manthritilleke, H.M. (1999b), 'Hydrological impact of land use changes', in A. Chisholm, A. Ekanayake and S. Jayasuriya (eds) *Economic Policy Reforms and the Environment: Land Degradation in Sri Lanka*, Colombo: ACIAR and MPA/HA/PI/PA, pp. 370–88.

Martin, Will (2001), 'Trade policies, developing countries and globalization', background paper for World Bank, *Globalization, Growth and Poverty: Building an Inclusive World Economy*, New York and Washington, DC: Oxford University Press and the World Bank.

Martin, Will and Peter G. Warr (1994), 'Determinants of agriculture's relative decline: Thailand', *Agricultural Economics*, 11, 219–35.

Matthews, Emily (2001), 'Understanding the FRA 2000', *Forest Briefing No. 1*, World Resources Institute, March, www.wri.org/pdf/fra2000.pdf.

Medalla, E.M., G.R. Tecson, R.M. Bautista and J.H. Power (1985), *Philippine Trade and Industrial Policies: Catching Up With Asia's Tigers*, Manila: Philippine Institute for Development Studies.

Mendoza, Meyra S. and Mark W. Rosegrant (1995), *Pricing Behavior in Philippine Corn Markets: Implications for Market Efficiency*, Washington, DC: International Food Policy Research Institute, Research Report 101.

Metrick, Andrew and Martin L. Weitzman (1998), 'Conflicts and choices in biodiversity preservation', *Journal of Economic Perspectives*, 12(3), Summer, 21–34.

Midmore, D., T.M. Nissen and D.D. Poudel (2001), 'Making a living out of agriculture: some reflections on vegetable production systems in the Manupali watershed', in I. Coxhead and G. Buenavista (eds) *Seeking Sustainability: Challenges of Agricultural Development and Environmental Management in a Philippine Watershed*, Los Baños, Philippines: PCARRD, pp. 94–111.

Ministry of Plantation Industries (1994), *Plantation Sector Statistical Pocket Book*, Colombo, Sri Lanka: Ministry of Plantation Industries.

Molnar, Augusta (1990), 'Land tenure issues in watershed development', in John B. Doolette and William B. Magrath (eds) *Watershed Development in Asia: Strategies and Technologies*, Washington, DC: World Bank, pp. 131–58.

Munasinghe, M. and W. Cruz (1995), *Economy-wide Policies and the Environment: Lessons from Experience*, Washington, DC: World Bank, Environment Department Paper no.10.

NRAP (Natural Resources Accounting Project) (1991), *The Philippine Natural Resources Accounting Project*, Quezon City: NRAP (mimeo).

NSCB (National Statistical and Coordination Board) (1995), *Philippine Statistical Yearbook 1995*, Manila: NSCB.

National Statistics Office [of the Philippines] (1981), *Census of Agriculture 1980*, Manila: NSO.

Neary, J.P. and K.W.S. Roberts (1980), 'The theory of household behavior under rationing', *European Economic Review*, 13(1), 25–42.

Newbery, D. and J. Stiglitz (1981), *The Theory of Commodity Price Stabilization*, Oxford: Clarendon Press.

Oates, Wallace E. and Robert Schwab (1988), 'Economic competition among jurisdictions: efficiency enhancing or distortion inducing?', *Journal of Public Economics*, 35(3), 333–54.

Office of Agricultural Economics (1991), *Agricultural Statistics of Thailand, Crop Year 1990–91*, Bangkok: Ministry of Agriculture.

Paderanga, C. (1986), 'A review of land settlement policies in the

Philippines, 1900–1975', *School of Economics Discussion Paper No. 8613*, Manila: University of the Philippines.

Pagulayan, A.C. Jr (1998), 'Philippines', in Asian Productivity Organization (ed.) *Agricultural Price Policy in Asia and the Pacific*, Tokyo: Asian Productivity Organization, pp. 265–78.

Panayotou, Theodore (1993), *Green Markets: The Economics of Sustainable Development*, San Francisco, CA: ICS Press.

Papageorgiou, D., M. Michaely and A.M. Choski (eds) (1991), *Liberalizing Foreign Trade*, Oxford, UK, and Cambridge, MA: Basil Blackwell.

Pearson, A. and M. Munasinghe (1995), 'Natural resource management and economy wide policies in Costa Rica: a computable general equilibrium (CGE) modeling approach', *World Bank Economic Review*, 9(2), May, 259–86.

Persson, Torsten and Guido Tabellini (1994), 'Is inequality harmful for growth?', *American Economic Review*, 84(3), 600–21.

Philippine Department of Agriculture (1990), *Philippine Agricultural Development Plan 1991–1995*, Manila: Philippine Department of Agriculture.

Pimentel, D., C. Harvey, P. Resosudarmo, K. Sinclair, D. Kurz, M. Mcnair, S. Crist, L. Shpritz, L. Fitton, R. Saffouri and R. Blair (1995), 'Environmental and economic costs of soil erosion and conservation benefits', *Science*, 267, 1117–23.

Pingali, P. (1997), 'Agriculture–environment interactions in the Southeast Asian humid tropics', in S. Vosti and T. Reardon (eds) *Sustainability, Growth and Poverty Alleviation: A Policy and Agroecological Perspective*, Baltimore, MD: Johns Hopkins University Press for the International Food Policy Research Institute, pp. 208–28.

Punyasavatsut, Chaiyuth and Ian Coxhead (2000), 'Structural change and the relative decline of agriculture: a decomposition analysis for Thailand', University of Wisconsin and Thammasat University, (mimeo).

Repetto, Robert (1989), 'Economic incentives for sustainable production', in Gunter Schramm and Jeremy J. Warford (eds) *Environmental Management and Economic Development*, Washington, DC: World Bank.

Repetto, Robert and Malcolm Gillis (1988), *Public Policy and the Misuse of Forest Resources*, Cambridge: Cambridge University Press.

Repetto, Robert, William Magrath, Michael Wells, Christie Beer and Fabrizio Rossini (1989), *Wasting Assets: Natural Resources in the National Income Accounts*, Washington, DC: World Resources Institute.

Republic of the Philippines (1998), *The Philippine National Development Plan: Directions for the 21st Century*, Manila: Republic of the Philippines.

Ribaudo, M.O. (1989), *Water Quality Benefits from the Conservation Reserve Program*, US Department of Agriculture, Economic Research Service, Agricultural Economics Report no. 606.

Roche, Frederick (1988), 'Java's critical uplands: is sustainable development possible?', *Food Research Institute Studies*, XXI (1), 1–43.

Rodrik, D. (1995), 'Trade and industrial policy reform', in Jere Behrman and T.N. Srinivasan (eds) *Handbook of Development Economics*, vol. 111B, Amsterdam: North-Holland.

Rola, A.C. and I. Coxhead (2002), 'Does non-farm job growth encourage or retard soil conservation in Philippine uplands?', *Philippine Journal of Development*, in press.

Rola, Agnes C. and Prabhu L. Pingali (1993), *Pesticides, Rice Productivity and Farmers' Health: An Economic Assessment*, Los Baños, Philippines: International Rice Research Institute and Washington, DC: World Resources Institute.

Rudel, Thomas K. (2001), 'Did a green revolution restore the forests of the American South?', in A. Angelsen and D. Kaimowitz (eds) *Agricultural Technologies and Tropical Deforestation*, Wallingford, Oxon: CAB International, pp. 53–68.

Salas, R. (1987), *The World of Rafael Salas: Service and Management in the Global Village*, Manila: Solar Publishing Corporation.

Samarappuli, I.N., A. Ekanayake, I. Samarappuli and N. Yogaratnam (1999), 'Modelling the effect of land degradation on yield of rubber', in A. Chisholm, A. Ekanayake and S. Jayasuriya (eds) *Economic Policy Reforms and the Environment: Land Degradation in Sri Lanka*, Colombo: ACIAR and MPA/HA/PI/PA, pp. 314–34.

Samarasinghe, S.N.R. de A. (1999), 'Land degradation: impact on road systems', in A. Chisholm, A. Ekanayake and S. Jayasuriya (eds) *Economic Policy Reforms and the Environment: Land Degradation in Sri Lanka*, Colombo: ACIAR and MPA/HA/PI/PA, pp. 345–69.

Samaratunga, P.A. (1996), 'Optimal replacement of long-lived crops grown on erosive soils with an application to the tea sector of Sri Lanka', Occasional Paper no. 24, School of Agriculture, La Trobe University, Melbourne.

Sandmo, Agnar (2000), *The Public Economics of the Environment*, Oxford: Oxford University Press.

Schiff, Maurice and Alberto Valdés (1991), *The Political Economy of Agricultural Pricing Policy*, vol. 4: *A Synthesis of the Economics in Developing Countries*, Baltimore, MD: Johns Hopkins University Press for the World Bank.

Schweithelm, J. and D. Glover (1999), 'Causes and impacts of the fires', in D. Glover and T. Jessup (eds) *Indonesia's Fires and Haze: The Cost of*

Catastrophe, Singapore: Institute for Southeast Asian Studies, and Canada: International Development Research Center, pp. 1–13.

Selden, T. and D. Song (1994), 'Neoclassical growth, the J-curve for abatement, and the inverted U curve for pollution', *Journal of Environmental Economics and Management*, 27(2), 162–8.

Shafik, Nemat (1994), 'Economic development and environmental quality: an econometric analysis', *Oxford Economic Papers*, 46(4), 757–73.

Shafik, Nemat and S. Bhandyopadhyay (1992), *Economic Growth and Environmental Quality: Time Series and Cross-Country Evidence*, World Bank Policy Research Working Paper no. WPS 904, Washington, DC: World Bank.

Shah, J. and T. Nagpal (eds) (1997), *Urban Air Quality Management in Asia: Metro Manila Report, World Bank Technical Paper No. 380*, Washington, DC: World Bank.

Shively, Gerald E. (1997), 'Impact of contour hedgerows on upland maize yields in the Philippines', *Agroforestry Systems*, 39(1), 59–71.

Shively, Gerald E. (1998), 'Economic policies and the environment: the case of tree planting on low-income farms in the Philippines', *Environment and Development Economics*, 3(1), 83–104.

Shively, Gerald E. (1999), 'Risks and returns from soil conservation: evidence from low-income farms in the Philippines', *Agricultural Economics*, 21(1), 53–67.

Shively, Gerald E. (2000), 'Conducting economic policy analysis at a landscape scale: an optimization-simulation approach with examples from the agricultural economy of a Philippine watershed', manuscript, Purdue University, at http://www.agecon.purdue.edu/staff/shively/manupali, accessed March 2002.

Shoven, J. and J. Whalley (1984), 'Applied general equilibrium models of taxation and international trade: an introduction and survey', *Journal of Economic Literature*, XXII, September, 1007–51.

Siamwalla, Ammar (1996), 'Thai agriculture: from engine of growth to sunset status', *TDRI Quarterly Review*, 11(4), 3–10.

Siamwalla, Ammar and Suthad Setboonsarng (1989), *Trade, Exchange Rates and Agricultural Pricing Policies in Thailand*, Washington, DC: World Bank.

Siamwalla, Ammar and Suthad Setboonsarng (1990), *Trade, Exchange Rates and Agricultural Pricing Policies in Thailand*, Washington, DC: World Bank, World Bank Comparative Studies: The Political Economy of Agricultural Pricing Policy.

Siamwalla, Ammar, Direk Patmasiriwat and Suthad Setboonsarng (1987), *Productivity and Competitiveness in Thai Agriculture*, Bangkok: Thailand Development Research Institute, 1987 TDRI Year-end Conference.

Silvapulle, Param and Sisira Jayasuriya (1994), 'Testing for Philippines rice market integration: a multiple cointegration approach', *Journal of Agricultural Economics*, 45(3), September, 369–80.

Simpson, R. David, Roger A. Sedjo and John W. Reid (1996), 'Valuing biodiversity for use in pharmaceutical research', *Journal of Political Economy*, 104, 163–85.

Somaratne, W.G. (1998), 'Policy reforms and the environment: a general equilibrium analysis of land degradation in Sri Lanka', Unpublished PhD thesis, La Trobe University.

Sri Lanka, Government of (1987), *Report of the Land Commission*, Sessional Paper no. 111-1990, Colombo.

Sri Lanka, Government of (1995), *Policy Statement by Her Excellency Chandrika Bandaranaike Kumaratunga, President of the Democratic Socialist Republic of Sri Lanka*, Colombo.

Stern, D.I., M.S. Common and E.B. Barbier (1996), 'Economic growth and environmental degradation: the environmental Kuznets curve and sustainable development', *World Development*, 24(7), 1151–60.

Stocking, M.A. (1992), 'Soil erosion in the upper Mahaweli catchment, Sri Lanka', Environment and Forestry Division, Mahaweli Authority of Sri Lanka, Colombo.

Strutt, Anna and Kym Anderson (2000), 'Will trade liberalization harm the environment? The case of Indonesia to 2020', *Environmental and Resource Economics*, 17(3), 203–32.

TDRI (Thailand Development Research Institute) (1994), *Assessment of Sustainable Highland Agricultural Systems*, Bangkok: Thailand Development Research Institute.

Timmer, C. Peter (1986), *Getting Prices Right: The Scope and Limits of Agricultural Price Policies*, Ithaca, New York: Cornell University Press.

Timmer, C. Peter (1988), 'The agricultural transformation', in H.B. Chenery and T.N. Srinivasan (eds) *Handbook of Development Economics Vol. I*, Amsterdam: North-Holland, pp. 275–332.

Townsend, Blair and Ravi Ratnayake (2000), *Trade Liberalisation and the Environment: A Computable General Equilibrium Analysis*, Singapore and River Edge, NJ; World Scientific Publishing Co.

Tropical Science Centre and World Resources Institute (1991), *Accounts Overdue: Natural Resource Depreciation in Costa Rica*, Washington, DC: World Resources Institute.

Ulph, Alistair M. (1999), 'International trade and the environment: a survey of recent economic analysis', in A.M. Ulph, *Trade and the Environment: Selected Essays of Alistair M. Ulph*, Cheltenham, UK and Northampton, MA, USA: Edward Elgar, pp. 3–42.

United Nations (1999), *The State of the World Population 1999*, at http://www.unfpa.org/swp/1999/thestate.htm, accessed 1 May 2000.

Varian, Hal R. (1992), *Microeconomic Analysis*, 3rd edition, New York: Norton.

Vennemo, Harkkon (1997), 'A dynamic applied general equilibrium model with environmental feedbacks', *Economic Modelling*, 14(1), 99–154.

Vincent, Jeffrey R., Rozali Mohammed Ali and Associates (1997), *Environment and Development in a Resource-rich Economy: Malaysia Under the New Economic Policy*, Cambridge, MA: Harvard Institute for International Development, and Kuala Lumpur: Institute of Strategic and International Studies.

Vousden, Neil (1990), *The Economics of Trade Protection*, New York: Cambridge University Press.

Warford, J.J. (1989), 'Environmental policy and economic policy in developing countries', in Gunter Schramm and Jeremy Warford (eds) *Environmental Management and Economic Development*, Washington, DC: World Bank, pp. 7–22.

Warr, P.G. and Ian Coxhead (1993), 'The distributional impact of technical change in Philippine agriculture: a general equilibrium analysis', *Food Research Institute Studies*, XXII(3), 253–74.

White, Kenneth (1993), *SHAZAM, Version 7*, Vancouver: Department of Economics, University of British Columbia.

Wiersum, K.F. (ed.) (1984), *Strategies and Designs for Afforestation, Reforestation and Tree Planting*, Proceedings of an international symposium on the occasion of 100 years of forestry education and research in the Netherlands, Wageningen, 19–23 September 1983, Wageningen: Pudoc.

Wijeratne, D.G.D.C. (1999), 'Land degradation: impacts on hydropower', in A. Chisholm, A. Ekanayake and S. Jayasuriya (eds) *Economic Policy Reforms and the Environment: Land Degradation in Sri Lanka*, Colombo: ACIAR and MPA/HA/PI/PA, pp. 335–44.

Williams, Jeffrey C. and Brian D. Wright (1991), *Storage and Commodity Markets*, Cambridge, UK and New York: Cambridge University Press.

Woodland, A. (1982), *International Trade and Resource Allocation*, Amsterdam: North-Holland.

World Bank (1989), *Philippines Natural Resource Management Study*, Washington, DC: World Bank.

World Bank (1990), *Indonesia: Sustainable Development of Forests, Land, and Water*, Washington, DC: World Bank.

World Bank (1992), *The Philippines: Public Sector Resource Mobilization and Expenditure Management*, Washington, DC: World Bank, Country Economic Report no. 10056-PH.

World Bank (1993), *The East Asian Miracle*, Washington, DC: Oxford University Press for the World Bank.

World Bank (2000a), *World Development Indicators 2000*, Washington, DC: World Bank.

World Bank (2000b), *Greening Industry: New Roles for Communities, Markets and Governments*, Washington, DC: World Bank.

World Bank (2001a), *Thailand: Environmental Monitor*, http://www.worldbank.or.th/environment/index.html, accessed April 2002.

World Bank (2001b), *Globalization, Growth and Poverty: Building an Inclusive World Economy*, New York and Washington, DC: Oxford University Press and World Bank.

World Bank (various years), *World Development Report*, Washington, DC: Oxford University Press for the World Bank.

World Commission on Environment and Development (WCED) (1987), *Our Common Future*, Oxford and New York: Oxford University Press.

World Resources Institute (WRI) (1989), *Wasting Assets: Natural Resources in the National Income Accounts*, Washington, DC: WRI.

World Resources Institute (WRI) (2000), *World Resources 1998–99*, Washington, DC: WRI.

World Trade Organization (WTO) (1999a), *Philippines: Trade Policy Review*, www.wto.org, accessed December 2001.

World Trade Organization (WTO) (1999b), *Thailand: Trade Policy Review*, www.wto.org, accessed December 2001.

Zhang, Zhong Xiang (1998), *The Economics of Energy Policy in China: Implications for Global Climate Change*, Cheltenham, UK and Northampton, MA, USA: Edward Elgar.

Index